SOCIALISM
SINCE MARX

ROBERT KILROY-SILK

TAPLINGER PUBLISHING COMPANY
NEW YORK

First published in the United States in 1972 by
TAPLINGER PUBLISHING CO., INC.
New York, New York

Library of Congress Catalog Card Number: 72-2817

ISBN 0-8008-7242-8

JAN

CONTENTS

Contents

Contents

PREFACE

In the preparation of this book I have received invaluable help from Jean Blondel. To him my thanks are due.

The author, however, denies responsibility for any shortcomings that the book may have. These should be attributed to Adam Smith's 'divine Providence' which, as he told us, works in mysterious ways.

It is customary for authors in a preface to thank their wives and their families for their practical help, their forbearance and their sympathy. I, too, have received all of these. But this book was written in spite of the distractions posed by the presence of my wife, nine dogs, two cats and two boisterous children.

Robert Kilroy-Silk

INTRODUCTION

Beginning his book *The Socialist Tradition* Alexander Gray wrote:

> One question barks for an answer on the threshold of our journey; but Prudence and Cowardice (a combination of potent masters) unite in suggesting that the question should meantime be avoided. What, it may at the outset reasonably be asked, are we to understand by socialism?[1]

But instead of answering the question, he chose to discuss the doctrines of those men who were generally accepted as being 'the great socialists'.

Prudence and Cowardice are not always good masters. A spirit of adventure is important too. Yet we must not let a spirit of adventure degenerate into reckless abandon. Thus, whilst such a precise thing as a definition of socialism will not be offered here, an attempt will be made to isolate some of the common themes in socialist theory.

First, it should be said that socialism is used in a variety of different ways. As R. H. Tawney once wrote, 'Like other summary designations of complex political forces, socialism is a word the connotation of which varies, not only from generation to generation, but from decade to decade.'[2] There is not, nor can there be, a definitive meaning of socialism. There have been, and still are, numerous schools of socialist thought, many of which are in conflict with each other and none of which has a better right to the title of socialist than any other. Words, as David Caute has written in a related context, 'are inherently democratic and incapable of complete expropriation'.[3]

1. Alexander Gray, *The Socialist Tradition from Moses to Lenin*, 1948, p. 1.
2. Quoted in C. A. R. Crosland, *The Future of Socialism*, p. 80.
3. David Caute, *The Left in Europe*, London, 1966, p. 11.

Here is a sample, picked more or less at random from the vast literature that is available to the avid searcher after definitions, of what is offered. Proudhon tells us that socialism is 'every aspiration towards the amelioration of society', Bradlaugh confidently asserts that 'socialism denies individual private property, and affirms that society organized as the state should own all wealth, direct all labour and compel the equal distribution of all produce'. Janet and Laveleye place a similar emphasis on the role of the state. The former writes that 'we call socialism every doctrine which teaches that the state has a right to correct the inequality of wealth which exists among men, and to legally establish the balance by taking from those who have too much in order to give to those who have not enough'. The latter asserts that 'every socialistic doctrine aims at introducing greater equality in social conditions; and ... at realizing those reforms by the law of the State'.

We need go no further. Our search for what some used to call a 'meaningful' definition looks like being as fruitful an exercise as Michael Foot seeking votes from members of the Monday Club. If we accepted Proudhon's definition, then anyone with anything of a social conscience would be a socialist and we could include Shaftesbury and even Bismarck. Bradlaugh goes too far in asserting that no private property should exist and begs the question of what is an equal distribution 'of all produce'. Is it an absolute equality in terms of work, needs or other criteria? Janet and Laveleye would appear to be satisfied by the introduction of a progressive income tax.

Perhaps it would be better if we could inhabit the cosy world of Herbert Morrison and defiantly state that 'socialism is what the Labour Government does' and leave to others the task of definition. But then we are pandering to Prudence and Cowardice. At least we can isolate some common themes of socialist theory. Socialism is, first of all, a protest against the material and cultural poverty inflicted by capitalism on the mass of people. It expresses a concern for the social welfare of the oppressed, the unfortunate and the disadvantaged. It affirms the values of equality, a classless society, freedom and democracy. It rejects the capitalist system and its competitive ethos as being inefficient in its use of resources, for inculcating a selfish, grasping ethic and for making labour into a commodity. Above all, it is a critique of liberalism and the social and economic order it rationalizes and supports. Instead it affirms the need for a cooperative society based on production for social use. To achieve this, socialists are not content with a mere tinkering with the existing social, economic and political system. They want a new system, whether by reform or revolution, in which productive wealth is owned and controlled by the community and used for communal ends.

Most socialists profess adherence to these ideas, though their emphasis differs. Most are agreed on the evils of capitalism, but some want to change it by reformist means while others insist that only revolution will suffice. Some argue that the factors of production should be owned by the state, others that only control is necessary. There is disagreement, too, on the role of the state in a socialist society. Some, like the Fabians, give the state an important role to perform, while the Marxists want to use the state to smash the state, and the anarchists want to smash everything that smacks of authority. There is also disagreement on what is considered to be an equitable distribution of income in a socialist society.

Perhaps, after all, it might be best to say that socialism is what those who call themselves socialists say it is. This suffers from vagueness but it does at least have the merit of recognizing that ideas are dynamic, that they change as they pass into new hands and confront new circumstances. Indeed, socialism would be a rather peculiar doctrine if it could be placed within one all-encompassing definition applicable to all socialists at all times. Certainly, it would be much less exciting and interesting than it now is.

Many of the ideas and sentiments to be found in contemporary socialist theories can also be found in Greek philosophy, Christianity and the *Utopia* of Sir Thomas

More. Those who wish to establish socialism's pedigree, and make it a distinguished one at that, do in fact engage in this kind of exercise. Yet neither the Old nor the New Testament urged a reconstruction of the social order and even Plato's so-called communist system was one of common consumption, not common ownership.

Socialism as a word is relatively new. The ideas it expressed grew out of the French Revolution with its ideals of freedom, the dignity of work and labour, fraternity, the equality of men and, perhaps most important, the emphasis on the power of reason to construct political institutions and society according to man's will. No less important to the development of socialist ideas was the industrial revolution. The revolution in France might have prepared the ideological groundwork for the emergence of a socialist doctrine, but it was the industrial revolution in Britain which, with its factories, prepared the conditions for the growth of a working class and a critique of capitalism. Hence, two countries and two strands of thought stemming from different circumstances combined, in the early part of the nineteenth century, to form a socialist doctrine. The word was in fact used by the Owenite movement in Britain, though it soon gained a wide currency in France among the followers of Henri de Saint-Simon and Charles Fourier.

Often referred to as the founder of British socialism, Robert Owen represents one of the best combinations of theory and practice. A successful businessman, he repudiated the system that had made possible his success and, whilst admiring the material benefits of the industrial revolution, condemned the social consequences.

As a manufacturer Owen was struck by the diligent attention paid to the maintenance of machines and the general disregard for the workpeople. He appealed to manufacturers, if only out of self-interest, to have more regard for their workers and to pay them better wages and provide more congenial working conditions. Had he stopped at this, Owen would have been no more than a shrewd factory reformer, a precursor of Elton Mayo. As it was, he went much further and advocated the construction of a completely new social order.

At the basis of Owen's philosophy was his belief that a man's character was made for him and not by him. The notion that a man could form his own character he described as 'a fundamental error of the highest possible magnitude'. The capitalist system with its emphasis on competition had created avaricious and selfish characters, it perverted human nature and was responsible for the unemployment, poverty and vice with which society was afflicted. And as he believed that human nature was plastic and could be moulded by environment and education, so he believed that a new type of character could be created by, and was dependent upon, the creation of a new type of society.

Owen put his belief into practice first at New Lanark, where he became a model employer concerned with all aspects of the workers' welfare, and then in his cooperative communities. Though first set up to provide work for the unemployed, they soon became for him the means of abolishing capitalism. The communities he proposed were to be self-supporting cooperatives – agricultural and industrial settlements accommodating approximately eight hundred persons governed by an elected committee. Owen wanted them to be financed by the state, but he failed to obtain financial help and set up his own. Though all of Owen's communities failed, his ideas had a profound influence on the working-class movement that developed in the 1830s.

Though there were communist secret societies aiming at insurrection in France in the 1840s, French socialism was dominated by men with ideas similar to those of Robert Owen; men, that is to say, who wanted social reform, preferably by legislation rather than revolution or a coup d'état, and who had great faith in the power of reason. Chief amongst these were Saint-Simon and Fourier.

Saint-Simon drew up a number of plans and blue-prints for a centrally planned industrial society directed and controlled by industrial magnates. Wanting 'the exploitation of the globe by association', he sought to replace the feudal remnants of French society by industrialists working for the common good. He advocated the abolition of privilege, whilst advocating the creation of a more powerfully privileged governing class, and asserted that society should be organized to the advantage of the largest class with the aim of ameliorating its moral and physical existence. Yet it was his followers, particularly the eccentric Bazard and Enfantin, who drew the socialist implications from his theories. These criticized the exploitation of man by man, advocating the abolition of inheritance, the nationalization of the factors of production and the creation of a scientific autocracy – a social hierarchy dependent upon merit with reward according to work. They were also more concerned with the collective regulation of industry than collective ownership of property.

While Saint-Simon and his followers emphasized centralization, Fourier, an even more eccentric figure, criticized capitalism for its anarchy, waste and immorality and stressed the value of local and individual freedom. In his vision of the new society the commune, or phalange as he called it, occupied the central position. This was to consist of four hundred families working together in a self-contained and self-sufficient community. All officials would be elected, and men would work in groups and could divide their time as they saw fit among a number of different tasks. Distribution would be according to need but with extra rewards for extra work, capital or talent. Fourier imagined that the communes, starting in a small way, would develop exchange relations with other communes specializing in other products and eventually federate to form a world-wide system of cooperation.

All of these men were autocratic and paternalistic. They knew what was best for society and the working man; they did not have to trouble themselves by asking. With supreme arrogance they tried to shape the world and human nature according to their own ideas. Without exception they failed.

Yet whilst their utopian dreams and communities crumbled, their ideas did not. Strange and eccentric they no doubt were, but they were also important in providing the raw material which many used to build a new socialist theory. In their criticisms of capitalism and their proposals for a new society were ideas that came to form the basis of socialist theory as it developed in the nineteenth century. At least they made socialism a subject for debate and helped to spread its ideas to a wide audience.

But whilst they are properly recorded as the founders of socialism, most of their schemes and adherents were admitted failures by the 1840s. It is to Karl Marx that we must look for the beginning of a logical and coherent socialist theory which provided the intellectual backcloth for the emerging working-class movement.

Hence Part One begins with an outline of his theory and the alternative theory proffered by the anarchists. The growth and revision of Marxist ideas in Germany and the rest of Europe is then traced and an account of the reformist socialist movements provided. The section ends with a discussion of the challenge to socialist orthodoxy posed by the anarchists, anarcho-syndicalists and Lenin.

In Part Two the emphasis is still upon Europe. The development of socialism in Russia under Stalin and Khrushchev is discussed, and the revisionist stirrings in Eastern Europe in the early 1950s outlined. And to see what the main opponents of communism were up to, the last chapter charts the activities of the social democratic parties.

Part Three shows how the idea of socialism spread from its base in Europe to China, Asia, Cuba, and Africa. Finally, we return to the 'old world', to Europe, to look at the developments in communism, democratic socialism and the rise of a so-called New Left.

PART ONE

I

KARL MARX AND THE BEGINNING OF MODERN SOCIALISM

No account of modern socialism is complete unless it contains a summary, however brief, of the main ideas of Karl Marx, for socialism after Marx is inseparably linked with his doctrines. Indeed, modern socialism begins with Marx. An interpretation of post-Marxian socialism as either a reaffirmation of Marx, a reinterpretation of Marx, a revision of Marx or a reaction to Marx would not be too much of an exaggeration. At least it is necessary constantly to refer to his ideas when discussing European social democracy, anarchism and communism, as well as when discussing the contemporary socialist movements in what has come to be known as the Third World, and the New Left and student movements in the West. It is therefore necessary to indicate the main lines of his theory, and especially those aspects that assume importance in the programmes, policies and controversies of subsequent socialist movements.

First, a few words about his life. Marx was born in Trier in 1818, of Jewish parents. In 1842 he joined the staff of the *Rheinische Zeitung*, a Cologne liberal–radical paper, and soon became its editor. After the suppression of the paper in 1843, he left to study socialism in Paris, where he met Proudhon, whose doctrine he later attacked in the *Poverty of Philosophy* (1847), and Bakunin, with whom he later fought for control of the First International. It was in Paris, too, that he renewed and deepened his friendship with Engels, a friendship that lasted the lifetime of Marx and provided him with moral, material and intellectual support. Expelled from Paris at the bidding of the Prussian government in 1845, he left with Engels for Brussels where they made contact with other political exiles and engaged in

3

agitation and propaganda in the Communist League. Marx took no part in the revolutions of 1848. Instead he watched their progress from London where in 1883 he died, as Sidney Hook puts it, from the effects of eating dust for so many years in the British Museum.[1]

Marx was not only the major political thinker of the nineteenth century but was also the first to develop a systematic and coherent theory of social revolution. In the words of Isaiah Berlin, his theory is 'the most formidable, sustained and elaborate indictment ever delivered against an entire social order, against its rulers, its supporters, its ideologists, its willing slaves, against all whose lives are bound up with its survival'.[2] Yet Marx was not only one of the most penetrating of writers; he was also one of the most obscure and is certainly the most difficult to find in any complete and systematic form. Much of what he wrote was in the form of polemics directed to the circumstances of his time and the ideas of his contemporaries and, in fact, large parts of his theory were developed in response to the criticisms and ideas of his adversaries. For this reason it is necessary to go to different texts for different aspects of his theory: to the *Communist Manifesto* (1848) for the most condensed statement of the doom of capitalism; to the Preface to *The Critique of Political Economy* (1859) for the most complete, if in itself incomplete, formulation of the doctrine of historical materialism; to the three volumes of *Capital* (1867, 1885, 1894) for his theory of value, surplus value and the analysis of the workings of capitalism; to Engels's *Origin of the Family, Private Property and the State* (1884) for an exposition of their theory of the state; to the *Address to the Communist League* (1850) and the *Eighteenth Brumaire of Louis Bonaparte* (1852) for the tactical principles of revolution: and to the *Critique of the Gotha Programme* (1891) for the few remarks on the dictatorship of the proletariat.

1. Sidney Hook, *Towards the Understanding of Karl Marx*, London, 1933, p. 20.
2. Isaiah Berlin, *Karl Marx: His Life and Environment*, p. 21.

Probably the best general summary of Marxism, however, is to be found in Engels's *Anti Duhring* (1877), to which Marx contributed and of which he allegedly approved.[3]

In view of the variety of his interests and the encyclopaedic scope of his work, it is not surprising that there is no one Marx. There are Marx the agitator, the propagandist, the philosopher of history, the economist, the economic historian, the sociologist and the political scientist, as well as the moralist and the humanist of his earlier writings. Marx, of course, was fortunate in living in an age when the boundaries of separate disciplines existed to be broken down and synthesized, not jealously protected as the sovereign preserve of the initiated. In his attempt to encompass all knowledge within his theoretical framework he was the complete Victorian man, the greatest system-builder in an age of systems. Nor is it surprising that, faced with the interpretations and distortions of his ideas during his lifetime, and often by his friends, he should have exclaimed, 'Je ne suis pas un marxiste.' What he would have said today we leave to those who like to speculate about such things.

Any interpretation of Marx's work must necessarily be partial, if not arbitrary. But if we like our theory simple then the 'work of Marx taken as a whole is a savage sustained indictment of one alleged injustice: that the profit, the comfort, the luxury of one man is paid for by the loss, the misery, the denial of another'.[4] It is, moreover, an indictment that has sustained many a revolutionary, been used by them to justify a multiplicity of often conflicting policies, and given rise, in a very real sense, to the division of the contemporary world into opposed ideological systems.

A number of intellectual debts were owed by Marx. He was a disciple of Hegel in his twenties, and it was from him that he obtained the notion of the dialectic, of change and development resulting from a conflict of opposites, and the

3. A useful guide to the literature on Marxism is John Lachs, *Marxist Philosophy, A Bibliographical Guide*, Oxford, 1968.
4. C. Wright Mills, *The Marxists*, London, 1963, p. 35.

notion of the self-creation of man. But whereas Hegel viewed this as a result of forces external to man, for Marx it was a social development based on the increasing mastery of man over nature. Ludwig Feuerbach, author of the *Critique of the Hegelian Philosophy* (1839), supplied the materialism and Saint-Simon some, at least, of the historiography. From his study of French socialism Marx probably derived the theory of class war, though he substituted a war between employers and employed for that between rich and poor. His critique of English political economy, and in particular the work of Ricardo, led to the formulation of the theory of value, while the English socialists Thompson, Hodgskin and Bray were probably instrumental in the development of the theory of surplus value. English Chartism and trade unionism were important in indicating the value of working-class political and industrial action as a means towards the evolution of class and revolutionary consciousness, while the Paris Commune provided both an object lesson in the techniques of revolution and an insight into the likely functioning of the dictatorship of the proletariat. The fact that Marx obtained his materials from many sources does not, as John Plamenatz observes, 'impugn the originality of Marx'.[5] The way he put them together, and the use to which they were put, were distinctively his own. With the help of Engels, he summed up the accumulated knowledge of centuries and endowed it with a distinct revolutionary orientation.

Friedrich Engels, the 'Grand Lama of the Regents Park Road', as H. M. Hyndman called him,[6] frequently tends to be forgotten in discussions of Marxism, or at best becomes only a shadow hovering in the background. In fact he was a writer of some repute before he met Marx and had already come to the conclusion that the conflict between the bourgeoisie and the proletariat was the clue to the future. He

5. John Plamenatz, *German Marxism and Russian Communism*, p. xvii.
6. Quoted in Henry Pelling, *Origins of the Labour Party*, p. 20.

was part author of the *Communist Manifesto*, but probably his best-known work other than those on military strategy, and one which influenced Marx, is the *Conditions of the Working Class in England* (1845). Engels provided Marx with the economic illustrations for his theories and introduced him to the works of Ricardo, Hodgskin and Thompson as well as to the leaders of the English trade unions. It was Engels too who pointed out to Marx the significance of Chartism and trades unionism in England, and of England in the development of capitalism. And it fell to Engels to defend and reinterpret Marxism after Marx's death. That in doing so he almost emasculated historical materialism and watered down the revolutionary content of Marxism is something that Marx might have reproached him for. Certainly it lent plausibility to those social democrats who, while casting off a great deal of the intellectual baggage of Marxism, still claimed to be Marxists.[7] Less theoretical but more practical than Marx, he was more relaxed with people and adept at organization and gave tactical guidance to the emerging European socialist movement in the 1880s and 1890s. Without him Marx, as Harold Laski wrote, would still have been 'a great social philosopher of the Left: with him it became possible for Marx to combine superb intellectual achievement with immense practical influence'.[8]

Marx claimed to be the founder of 'scientific socialism'. By this he meant that it dealt with matter. For Marx it was an axiom that the material world is reality. Socialism was not a pious, utopian dream but was based on the potentialities and possibilities of the present; it had a scientific basis in historical materialism, even though Marx had become a socialist before he developed his sociological theory of history, and was deduced from his analysis of the capitalist mode of production. He ridiculed what he called the utopian socialists, like Fourier, Robert Owen and Saint-Simon, even though the latter had a philosophy of history

7. See Chapter 3.
8. H. J. Laski, Introduction to *Communist Manifesto: Socialist Landmark*, London, 1948, p. 14.

7

almost, if not equally, as intellectually respectable as that of Marx. In the *Communist Manifesto* he reproached the utopians for a lack of knowledge of the proletariat (just as he had been criticized by Andreas Gottschalk for having only a 'scientific doctrinaire interest' in them), and for appealing to the whole of society rather than a class. They were criticized further for appealing to absolute truths like freedom, equality, fraternity and justice (though Marx was to do the same in his Address to the International Working-men's Association), for constructing an ideal society in their dreams and then seeking, as Owen and Fourier had done, a benevolent capitalist to launch it. The utopians attempted to reconcile class antagonisms and thus deaden the class struggle through a 'fanatical and superstitious belief in the miraculous effects of their social science'.

Marx, on the other hand, analysed capitalism in depth and claimed to have discovered the laws governing the development of society. These, he claimed, showed socialism to be a necessary and inevitable product of history. For the dreams and aspirations of the utopians, Marx substituted the underlying laws of history. But Marx did more than this. His doctrines do not merely describe the processes of history, the workings of capitalism, the phenomena of class society and class struggle but, in the words of Sidney Hook, that most sympathetic interpreter of Marxism, they are 'offered as instruments in waging that struggle, as guides to a mode of action which he believed would for ever eliminate class struggle from social life'.[9]

(a) Dialectical and Historical Materialism

Marx, as I have indicated, took over the Hegelian notion of change and progress resulting from the conflict of opposites. To Hegel history was a process in which reality, by means of the dialectic, progressively unfolds itself, and reveals more

9. Sidney Hook, op. cit., p. 18.

of its true nature in later periods. The existing state (thesis) gives rise to its opposite (antithesis) which overcomes and transforms the thesis to form a new and higher synthesis. This, in turn, becomes a new thesis so that the whole process starts again. History therefore becomes intelligible as a gradual progress towards the realization of reality. Hegel and the Idealists, however, saw history as change resulting from the unfolding of the *Idea* working upon matter. They argued that men were fashioned by their laws, art, literature and religion. All events and institutions were no more than the manifestations of the rational Idea. Marx, under the influence of Feuerbach, and yet retaining the dialectic, reversed the relationship so that history became the development of social institutions and relationships, ideas their manifestation. Ideas were derivative of matter, not the other way round as Hegel had thought. The evolution of history is thus the evolution not of ideas but of matter; hence the term dialectical materialism and Marx's claim to have put Hegel the right way up. And for Marx the most important, but by no means exclusive, factor in the development of history and ideas was the economic structure of society. Men make their own laws, art, literature and religion to correspond to their particular society. In the words of what has become a famous aphorism, 'It is not the consciousness of men that determines their being, but, on the contrary, their social being that determines their consciousness.' Thus, 'Man makes religion, religion does not make man.'

More important than dialectical materialism is historical materialism, 'the heart of Marxism', the application of the former to human social relations though the connection is purely formal. It is an attempt not to describe the specific circumstances under which certain social phenomena will occur as to describe the general character of all social evolution, the process, or progress, of human society. As Engels claimed, 'Just as Darwin discovered the law of evolution in organic nature, so Marx discovered the law of evolution in human history.'

Marx argues that the economic basis of society, the

substructure, is the fundamental conditioning factor of the general characteristic of a society and its culture. The economic basis of society includes the forces of production – natural resources, physical equipment, skills and science – and the relations of production – the institution of private property and the consequent class relations between those who do and do not own property. It is the relations of production that determine the character of the superstructure of a society, its laws, religion, culture and politics, and which themselves reflect the interests of the dominant class. In the words of Marx, in the Preface to *The Critique of Political Economy*:

In the social production which men carry out they enter into definite relations that are indispensable and independent of their will; these relations of production correspond to a definite stage of development of their material forces of production. The sum total of these relations of production constitutes the economic structure of society – the real foundation on which rises a legal and political superstructure and to which definite forms of social consciousness correspond.

All the elements of the superstructure have been devised, perhaps unconsciously, to keep society together, to maintain the present class structure, to deflect the exploited from the class struggle, to obscure it from and make it more palatable to them. The superstructure is then a secret weapon in the class struggle, the fountain of false consciousness. Such a doctrine denies the validity of any absolute moral code but rather affirms that all values are socially conditioned and, more important, are the weapons of the dominant class. Hence the amoralism of Marx and his communist followers.

A certain class structure and a certain stage of technological development then presuppose each other and social relationships that do not correspond to the mode of production will not for long be maintained, even by force or law. In every society, however, changes take place in the material forces of production so that at a certain point they come into conflict with the relations of production. From 'forms of the development of the forces of production the relations of production become their fetters', and there begins a period of social revolution leading to the transformation of the superstructure. In the words of Alfred Meyer, the economic basis of society is 'the central variable to which all other variables are functionally related'.[10] Marx did, however, add that the superstructure changes at a different and slower pace to that of technological and social change. It lags behind and acts as a brake on the progress of society because of the inertia of institutions or the recalcitrant actions of those who have a vested interest in the old social relations. Thus, as Meyer puts it, the concept of lag 'is an implicit admission that the economic substructure does not directly determine the superstructure as cause determines effect'.[11] Whether or not Marx was an economic determinist we can safely leave to others, and their interpretations of Engels's final remarks on the subject, in a letter to Joseph Bloch, where he speaks of interaction between the substructure and superstructure. The key to this important subject would seem to lie in the definition of 'determinism'.

In reviewing history Marx distinguished five economic modes of production: Asiatic, ancient, feudal, capitalist and, in the future, socialist. In each of these historical epochs the development of the forces of production gave economic power to the class seeking to control society, and which found expression in a class struggle between the ruling class and the class increasing its economic power through its mastery and control of the new forces of production. Though it may have been unaware of its class interests and fought under the banner of religion or liberty, the class standing to gain by a modification of the relations of production became revolutionary, developed a revolutionary ideology and organized itself as a political force with the objective of achieving an expansion of the forces of production. Thus, in the words of the *Communist Manifesto*, 'the history of all hitherto existing societies is the history of

10. Alfred G. Meyer, *Marxism: The Unity of Theory and Practice*, p. 22.
11. ibid., p. 63.

the class struggle'. The class struggle is the agency of historical change and history a series of contradictions and their resolution in class struggle, with each new society establishing new classes and new forms of oppression and exploitation. Thus, as Engels wrote, 'the bourgeoisie shattered the feudal system, and, on its ruins established the bourgeois social order, the realm of free competition, freedom of movement, equal rights for commodity owners and all the other bourgeois glories.'

(b) Capitalism

The capitalist system of production is characterized by a struggle between the class that derives its livelihood from ownership of the factors of production – the capitalists – and the class dependent for its existence on the sale of its labour power – the proletariat. Between these two classes there is an irreconcilable conflict of interest arising from the exploitation of the latter by the former.

Marx attempts to explain the nature of the exploitation and the cause of conflict with his theories of value and surplus value. These are intricate and unsuccessful. Whilst to Engels the theory of surplus value is the core of socialism, to Max Beer, the historian of socialism, it is more of a social slogan than an economic truth. To Joan Robinson, a contemporary economist, it provides no more than the incantation for the Marxist political theory. What Marx argues, put simply, is that the worker sells his labour power as a commodity on the open market and so sells his entire capacity to create wealth. In return, he is paid in wages only that amount which is necessary to produce and maintain a requisite supply of that particular type of labour. The difference between what he is paid and what he produces is appropriated by the capitalist as surplus value and distributed in the form of profit, interest and rent. Or, as Adam Smith had put it, 'the value which the workers add to their materials resolves itself into two parts of which one pays their wages and the other is the profit of their employer.' Although, according to Marx, the wages of the workers may rise, due to their increased expectations of a minimum standard of living or trade union action, there will always be a difference between what they receive and what they produce. It is this fact of exploitation that eventually leads to revolution.

Professor Tawney was right when he wrote that we did not need the theory of surplus value to tell us that the worker produced more than he received in wages. The existence of profit, interest and economic rent tells us that. The theory of surplus value does, however, provide a pseudo-scientific justification for the demands for revolution and the overthrow of capitalism. It is worth saving, as Sidney Hook points out, if the struggle against capitalism is worth the fight. Every struggle to wrest surplus value from the control of the propertied classes is a struggle to put it to social use and if a myth aids the struggle, then so much the better, it might be said, for the myth.

Marx did not condemn capitalism because of exploitation; rather he regarded it as perfectly just in terms of the norms of capitalism, and these are the only ones that are relevant. The capitalist has purchased the labour power for a day and the surplus value it produces is rightfully his. Marx did however condemn capitalism and no one who has read the vivid descriptions of conditions in a capitalist society to be found in the pages of *Capital* can doubt that, for all his claims to be scientifically detached, Marx had a profound and intense hatred of the system. He condemned it not so much for the unjust distribution of wealth but for dehumanizing man through the division of labour. He condemned capitalism for making the worker a 'cripple' in forcing him to become highly specialized and so impeding his full development and self-realization. His moral evaluation of capitalism is based upon a conception of a golden age of primitive communism, itself based upon the work of Lewis Morgan. This society, so Marx believed, was characterized by liberty and equality and the absence of division of labour. Production was communal and social in a well-integrated and harmonious society without exploiters or classes. Nevertheless, primitive communistic man was at the mercy of nature and the growth of the forces of production have been progressive in establishing man's mastery over nature. At the same time, their growth has been evil and inhuman in causing the alienation of men from their environment and themselves, and which has reached a peak in bourgeois society. The means of production have become the masters of man, with man being adjusted to the needs of production rather than vice versa. The division of labour also alienates man from his tools, in that another class owns and controls the means of production, and from the product of his labour. Marx wanted the abolition of all inequalities, an extension of liberty and the destruction of 'all relationships in which man is humbled, enslaved, abandoned, despised'. This radical humanism is, as Meyer points out, 'a direct continuation of the Christian-Humanist-Democratic tradition in our civilization. Marx, with his humanist critique of civilization, is a direct heir of Jan Hus, Thomas Moore, Thomas Paine and Jean-Jacques Rousseau.'[12]

But to return to the theory of surplus value and the functioning of capitalism; it is from the theory of surplus value that Marx deduced those laws governing the working of capitalism which led to those of his predictions that have been most assailed, by Marxists and non-Marxists alike. First is the law of capital accumulation. Competition forces capitalists to employ increasing amounts of labour-saving machinery in order to increase productivity and surplus value by decreasing that portion of the working day or week in which the worker produces for himself (what Marx called socially necessary labour time). The introduction of machinery, however, leads to an increase in production and a decrease in the labour force, and hence purchasing power, with the result that gluts, crises and a fall in profits occur. The purchasing power of the workers is necessarily less than the value of their product so that there exists a surplus of

12. ibid., p. 51.

14

production which has to be disposed of by the opening of new markets; hence the colonist drive of capitalist economies. The law of the concentration of capital follows directly the operation of the first law. The fall in profits leads to the disappearance of small businesses and the middle classes, and the emergence of monopolies and cartels and a polarization of classes. Finally, there is the law of increasing misery. The increasing introduction of machinery and concentration of capital leads to the development of what Marx called a reserve army of labour, subject to misery, oppression, slavery, degradation and exploitation. In fact, one of the characteristic features of capitalism in crisis is high profits and high unemployment.

The immanent crises of capitalism can be overcome for a time by overseas expansion but the development of a world-wide capitalist system brings world-wide economic crises. And as the crises become more frequent and severe, so the final crisis and the victory of the proletariat draws nearer. Even an increase in the absolute standard of living of the proletariat cannot eliminate the possibility of crisis since it does not eliminate the inherent tendency of capitalism towards overproduction. Indeed, crises can only be eliminated by the elimination of capitalism and this required the overthrow of the capitalist state.

(c) The State, Revolution and Dictatorship of the Proletariat

For some political philosophers, like Hobbes, the state creates civil society. For Marx, like Locke, the state is created by civil society. But unlike both Hobbes and Locke, Marx did not concern himself with the legitimacy of the state, for it had none. For Marx the state was not the nightwatchman or benevolent overseer of orthodox liberal theory nor the expression of the common good of society but a class organ representing the interests and reflecting the ideas of the ruling class while creating and cultivating the myth that it is above classes. As Engels wrote in the *Origin of the Family*:

The state of antiquity was above all the state of the slave owners for the purpose of holding down the slaves, as the feudal state was the organ of the nobility for holding down the peasant serfs and bondsmen, and the modern representative state is an instrument of exploitation of wage labour by capital.

Standing for the power of the dominant class, it has as its objective the preservation of the *status quo* which it performs by punishing those who threaten the existing system of class and property relations. It is the guardian of private property, and behind its laws is the privilege of a minority, not the ideals of justice. In the capitalist system, and in the words of Marx, the state is the 'executive committee of the bourgeoisie', political power 'merely the organised power of one class for oppressing another'. The liberal-democratic state is a hidden dictatorship of the bourgeoisie and its system of representative government the mere opportunity of 'deciding once in three or six years which member of the ruling class was to misrepresent the people in parliament'. Yet both Marx and Engels did at times conceive of the state as being independent of classes and society as, for example, they considered France to be at the time of Louis Bonaparte.

Nevertheless, this was a minor aberration in the course of historical developments. Most states were class states. The task of the proletariat is then the destruction of the capitalist state and with it its forms of oppression and exploitation. But before this is possible, not only must capitalism be in the process of break-up but the proletariat must have become aware of itself as a class. Capitalism has already created the proletariat as a class in itself. The bourgeoisie, as the *Communist Manifesto* puts it, produces its 'own grave-diggers. Its fall and the victory of the proletariat are alike inevitable.' From being a class in itself, the proletariat must become a class for itself, aware of its true interests and its role in society and history.

It is only when the proletariat rids itself of false consciousness, becomes aware of the causes of its own existence and animated by ideals that this suggests, that it becomes class conscious, and class consciousness develops into revolutionary consciousness only under the leadership of a revolutionary political organization. Thus the function of those who would lead the revolution, the 'advanced section' as Marx called them, is to develop class antagonisms into revolutionary consciousness, to make explicit in the programme of the political party of the working class what is implied in the daily economic struggles of the proletariat. With the workers organized as a permanent revolutionary opposition to the capitalist state, every sporadic strike, riot and demonstration must be turned into the long and difficult campaign for the overthrow of capitalism. Marx enjoined the revolutionaries to support all revolutionary movements, make the question of private property the central issue and insist upon the international solidarity of the workers even though their national organizations may have different degrees of revolutionary consciousness. In this context it should be noted that although Marx and Engels quarrelled with almost every leader of the working classes in Europe, and often over fundamentals, they never attempted to found their own party but worked with English liberals just as they did with Italian patriots. It should also be noted that whilst they believed the political party of the working class should play an important role in preparing the workers for, and organizing, the revolution, they never envisaged it as being their master. The support of the majority was for them a necessary condition for the success of the revolution.

They were not, however, prepared to sanction the activities of those socialists who put their faith in democracy as a means to the emancipation of the exploited. Marx, as Engels said of him at Highgate cemetery, was 'before all else a revolutionist' and revolution, as Robert Tucker observes, was the 'master-theme of Marx's thought'.[13] The social democrats

13. Robert C. Tucker, *The Marxian Revolutionary Idea*, p. 5.

were criticized for appealing to the 'people' when it was a class they should have been leading, for assuming that the state could be used in the interests of the workers when it was, in fact, a class organ, for calling for a 'fair distribution of the proceeds of labour' when it was the mode of production that had to be abolished, for retarding the development of a revolutionary consciousness by their acceptance of social legislation and compromises with the bourgeoisie, and for getting themselves embroiled in making a success of capitalism.

Marx anticipated that the proletarian revolution would be the greatest social upheaval in history and entail the use of force, though he excepted England and North America from the latter. In fact he believed that it would be the ruling classes that would be the initiators of violence. Faced with the rise of legal socialism and, in a democracy, the increasing threat to them of the introduction of socialist legislation, they would act to defend the system of property by force and, in so doing, break the Constitution. The cost of the revolution in terms of bloodshed might be high, but the cost of poverty, unemployment, misery, moral degradation and war, immanent in capitalism, were greater. The choice, if indeed it was a choice, was between the sufferings inflicted by capitalism and a new era in history, the communist society.

However, this takes time to accomplish, at least a generation, and the ground must be prepared by the dictatorship of the proletariat. Now the apparatus of state power will be in the hands of the workers and, as such, it is no more than the opposite of the dictatorship of the bourgeoisie. Yet, whereas the bourgeoisie sought to establish the primacy of their own conditions of appropriation, the proletariat has as its mission the destruction of the entire legal superstructure created for the protection of private property. Whereas all previous class movements were minorities aiming to achieve privilege for themselves, the proletariat is the majority aiming to abolish all privilege, to destroy the capitalist mode of production and eliminate the division of labour and classes. Instead of being the subject of reform as in the schemes of the utopians and social democrats, the worker is both the instigator and beneficiary of revolution.

Though he was to write in 1881 that 'the [Paris] Commune was merely the rising of a town under exceptional conditions; the majority of the Commune was in no sense socialist, nor could it be. With a small amount of commonsense, they could have reached a compromise with Versailles', he nevertheless drew upon it for the brief remarks he made on the dictatorship of the proletariat. It would, he believed, be a government of producers elected by universal suffrage with binding instructions and subject to recall. Legislative and executive functions would be united and there would be an expansion of democracy through the increased participation of the workers in economic and political life.

More utopian and anarchistic was Marx's vision of the future communist society. It would be a classless society, what Bertrand Russell called a state of 'Byzantine immobility'. As the state is the instrument of a class, the introduction of a classless society means the end of the state. The state 'withers away', and 'the government of men gives way to the administration of things'. The bourgeoisie had trained the proletariat in modern industry and rationalized and concentrated production processes to the extent that they could now be centrally planned, thus making the entrepreneur redundant. Moreover, specialization was now unnecessary so that the division of labour, and with it alienated man, could be a thing of the past. And man became universal man,

to do one thing today and another tomorrow, to hunt in the morning, fish in the afternoon, rear cattle in the evening, criticise after dinner, just as I have a mind, without ever becoming hunter, fisherman, shepherd or critic.

Marx had an optimistic view of the future of man in which he tames nature and provides an abundance of the means of life, produced for use not profit, and so enabling him to pursue artistic and cultural activities. 'For Marx,' as Robert Tucker writes, 'history is the growth-process of humanity from primitive beginnings to complete maturity and self-realisation in future communism.'[14] A society in 'which the free development of each will be the condition of the free development of all', where labour is not only a means of life but life's prime want, and whose motto is: 'From each according to his ability, to each according to his needs.' With a vision such as this, it is not surprising that Marx could say: 'The proletarians have nothing to lose but their chains. They have a world to win.' What is ironical is that 'a doctrine of liberation and freedom' has given rise to two of the most despotic and bureaucratic of states.

Bernstein adequately deals with the economic predictions of Marx.[15] It is appropriate now for some brief remarks on other aspects of his doctrine. Whether or not Marx was an economic determinist there can be little doubt that he emphasizes the importance of the economic basis of society in structuring the rest of society. Yet neither he nor Engels clearly stated the exact relationship between the economic basis and the superstructure. As Arthur Koestler vividly put it, 'Marxist society has a basement – production and an attic – intellectual production; only the stairs and lifts are missing.'[16] Nor, indeed, is the distinction between them clear-cut. Again, he simply asserted that contradictions appear within capitalism and that the relations of production become 'fetters' upon the forces of production. He did not produce evidence to support this. He also overestimated the role of capitalism in the modernization of backward countries. In some areas politics, and particularly revolutionary politics, has been the driving force behind modernization, as in Russia for example, and also the Middle East, Africa and China. And in the context of these coun-

14. ibid., p. 9.
15. See Chapter 3.
16. Arthur Koestler, *The Yogi and the Commissar*, New York, 1945, p. 70; London, 1965.

tries, Marx had no consistent theory of nationalism and little to say about the peasants.

His vision of the future communist society is strangely utopian in seeing industrial society as being one that does not need specialists. Modern experience not only does not bear this out but indicates that society has become more complex and, far from diminishing the number of specialized functions, has increased them. Furthermore, Marx is a typical Victorian in taking progress for granted and in assuming that vast changes in human nature could take place with the birth of his new society. In this, Marxism, as Lunacharsky put it, is 'the fifth great religion formulated by Jewry'.[17] The introduction of the division of labour represents man's fall from grace, and its abolition his salvation.

Nor is Marx's view of the proletariat less utopian. He assumes that the proletariat could be freed from the bondage of false consciousness by inspired intellectuals, whereas in fact the evidence suggests that they want to remain in the political and economic system and get the best that they can out of it. The evils of the present society might be great, but the evils of an unknown future might be greater still. Again, it is difficult to see the existence of a real class interest among the working classes. If proof is needed, then the history of the last hundred years would suffice, especially the fate of the Second International. There would seem to be more divisions within the working class than between it and the bourgeoisie, as any history of trade unionism would show. Of course the Marxist would retort that this indicated no more than that the workers are still bound by false consciousness and have not become a class for themselves – the most convenient and frequently used excuse for the lack of militancy of the working classes. Yet the frequent exhortations of the Marxist to the workers to unite is something of an acceptance that the brotherhood they so glibly talk of

17. Quoted by Bohdan Bociurkiw in *Lenin: The Man, the Theorist, the Leader: A Reappraisal*, ed. Leonard Schapiro and Peter Reddaway, p. 122.

is a myth. As Norman Mailer wrote in *The Armies of the Night*, the 'working class is loyal to friends, not ideas'.

But 'Marx was never less of a realist than when he imagined the working class, after they had become the politically organized majority in capitalist society, having to use force to take control of the state.'[18] There has not yet been a revolution that has been made by an organized majority, as we shall see in subsequent chapters. Once the majority have become politically organized, they become integrated into the political system and have as much, if not more, of a vested interest in maintaining the system as any other class, as was exhibited best of all by the behaviour of the German social democrats. That they need to use force is a mistaken idea based on a false view of the transformations that could take place within capitalist systems and the manner in which economic conflicts could be, and have been, institutionalized. That they would, in fact, be induced to use force belongs to the realm of fantasy. This does not mean to say, however, that the social democratic representatives of the workers have not often been effete. It does not mean to say that they have always attempted to press demands that could be legitimately pressed and met, or that they have not often seemed to care more for the maintenance of the system of capitalism as they found it than the interests of the workers.

18. John Plamenatz, op. cit., p. 175.

2

THE ANARCHIST CHALLENGE
TO MARXISM

In spite of the fact that the volume of his written work might indicate otherwise, Marx did not spend all of his adult life reading and writing in the British Museum. He engaged in political and industrial action in many countries and was, throughout his life, in contact with the leaders of the working classes. He helped to form the Communist League out of the remnants of the League of the Just and the Workers' Educational Society, and which included people like Bauer, Engels, Joseph Moll and Karl Schapper. Throughout the 1850s, as Cole points out, he tried to encourage Ernest Jones to revive Chartism, but without success.[1] Hardly a socialist leader in the 1870s and early 1880s failed to visit Marx for ideological instruction and organizational advice, and most of those who did not visit him did at least engage in correspondence.

But Marx's influence in the emerging socialist movement of the 1870s and early 80s was largely at second hand. He relied upon faithful disciples to carry his message and though most were faithful to what they thought Marx meant they were often at variance with his doctrine, as we shall see when we come to discuss the development of German Marxism in Chapter 3.

Marx's main contribution in a direct way to working-class organization and agitation was in the International Workingmen's Association, the First International, founded in London in 1864. Here, for the first time, Marx found a world stage from which to publicize his doctrine. And it

1. G. D. H. Cole, *History of Socialist Thought*, Vol. I, p. 255.

was within this organization that he encountered the first major challenge to his ideas and leadership; first from the followers of Proudhon and then from the anarchist leader Bakunin.

(a) The First International

The International was founded as a joint British and French trade union venture to secure international cooperation in strikes, but it soon developed a predominantly political character. Marx was responsible for drawing up the Inaugural Address and Statutes of the Association. Convinced of the need for organization by the failure of the revolutions of 1848, it was the intention of Marx to use the International to build up the industrial and political strength of the workers and develop their revolutionary consciousness. He had, however, to tread carefully, as the International was composed of a mixed bunch of individual members, including liberal English trade unionists and Italian and Spanish anarchists. Thus, although his Address contrasted the rapid growth in income and wealth in the developed economies with the poverty of the workers, and asserted that the workers could only achieve their emancipation by political means, it also hailed the great victory of the British working class in obtaining the Ten Hours Act of 1847 and welcomed the establishment of cooperatives. Similarly, the demand for the socialization of the factors of production was omitted for fear of alienating the English liberals and French Proudhonists. The latter were followers of Pierre-Joseph Proudhon, the first man willingly to call himself an anarchist in his celebrated book *What is Property?* (1840). They envisaged the world of the future as a great federation of communes and workers' cooperatives on a pattern of individual and small group producers. To this end they advocated the creation of a People's Credit Bank to advance capital to small groups in order that all could and would own property, and obtain the full product of their labour. Until 1868 the main internal dispute in the International was between the followers and supporters of Proudhon and the rest over the question of collective ownership. After the defeat of the Proudhonists, the dispute between Marx and Bakunin, who complained, among other things, that Marx was 'ruining the workers by making theorists of them', dominated the International until its virtual break-up in 1872, when Marx had its general council moved to New York.

(b) Bakunin versus Marx

Called by Marx 'A Mahomet without a Koran', Bakunin is credited with being the founder of modern anarchism. He was, as George Woodcock has written, 'monumentally eccentric, a rebel who in almost every act seemed to express the most forceful aspects of anarchy'.[2] A romantic and energetic figure, always fleeing from authority and always in pursuit of plots and uprisings, he was more a man of action than a theorist and left relatively little in the way of complete expositions of his doctrine. As E. H. Carr commented in his biography of Bakunin, there 'are few men whose life and thought have exerted such immense influence on the world as Michael Bakunin, and yet who have left such an inadequate and confused account of their views'. Even the numerous plots and uprisings in which he claimed to have been involved were more apparent than real and those that were real were unsuccessful. As Professor Venturi notes, 'Bakunin succeeded in making a revolutionary mentality rather than a revolutionary organization.'[3] Nevertheless, it was a revolutionary mentality of great influence and one that is still to be found among the fringe groups of the contemporary New Left.

Proudhon had, of course, preceded Bakunin in the

2. George Woodcock, *Anarchism*, p. 134.
3. Franco Venturi, *Roots of Revolution*, Vol. II, p. 699.

advocacy of cooperative anarchism. Bakunin differed however from Proudhon in viewing the collectivity as the basic unit of social and economic organization and from Kropotkin, a later anarchist, in affirming the principle of 'from each according to his means, to each according to his deeds' rather than the communist principle of distribution. He was at one with them both in attacking the coercive power of the state and in arguing that whereas society was natural to man, the state was an artificial instrument created for the exercise of power over others. Nor was the church any better. He attacked it for encouraging the idea of hierarchy and superiority and for enslaving men to authority. To Bakunin it was no more than an instrument of the state charged with the task of preserving and sanctifying order and inequality.

Like the more orthodox socialists, Bakunin constantly attacked the evils of private property and competition. Instead he advocated the abolition of inheritance so that reward would equal productive effort. Labour was the slave of, and was exploited by, capital and property. But this was only one aspect of authority that he disliked so intensely. As he saw it, the main task of the revolutionary was the destruction of all authority and its subsidiary satraps like private property, the police, army and church.

Yet in spite of his anti-authoritarian philosophy Bakunin was authoritarian and despotic as a person. He demanded absolute submission from his followers in 1870 and talked of the need for an 'invisible dictator' to guide the revolution. Marx had already discerned Bakunin's dictatorial tendencies. He had written to Engels in 1869 that 'this Russian wants to become the dictator of the European workers' movement'.

Bakunin had a great urge to destroy. But, as he pointed out, the 'desire for destruction is at the same time a creative desire'. He said in 1867 he wanted the destruction of the present states

in order that on the ruins of these forced unions organised from above by right of authority and conquest, there may arise free unions organised from below by the free federations of communes into provinces, of provinces into nations, and of nations into the United States of Europe.

These new states would not, however, resemble those in existence at the moment. No centralized states would be admitted and states would be allowed to secede, as would the communes within states.

Bakunin believed that men were naturally endowed with sociability and cooperativeness. 'The optimism and the faith in human nature, which was inherent in the romantic creed, was in the marrow of his bones. Bakunin believed as passionately as Rousseau in the innocence of an untrammelled and unperverted human nature.'[4] Bakunin anticipated that with the destruction of all authority individuals would spontaneously form cooperative primary social groups which would establish a cooperative society with final power resting with the local commune. Other than this brief outline of principles he was not particularly concerned about the details of the organization of the future anarchist society. It was obviously too difficult a task for Bakunin and, in any case, was one that was properly left to the individuals concerned. The immediate task was the destruction of the existing states. Once this had been achieved men could safely be left alone to establish their new social order and solve the problems of 'reconstruction' as they arose.

The revolution that would destroy the existing order, and which he believed would be a regenerative and purifying activity, was not conceived of by Bakunin as a general European uprising, so much as localized disturbances leading to general insurrection. Under the influence of Blanqui he rejected the idea that socialism could be achieved peacefully; under the direct influence of Nechaev he advocated the use of terror; under the influence of Weitling he believed that the *Lumpenproletariat* would be the most likely source of revolution. To Bakunin they were socialists without knowing it, just as Marx and Lenin viewed the

4. E. H. Carr, *The Romantic Exiles*, p. 258.

proletariat and Mao the peasants. They lacked only the leadership that would canalize their natural revolutionary instincts. Moreover, Bakunin was preoccupied with the fate of the Slavs living under the autocratic rule of Russia, Austria and Turkey. He anticipated nationalist revolutions starting with the Slavs leading to a general European social revolution and his *Appeal to the Slavs* called for the destruction of the Austrian Empire and the creation of a Slav federation.

Marx, of course, was something of an anarchist in his vision of the future communist society. He regarded freedom as the supreme human value and believed its realization to be impossible within the confines of the state. The anarchists, however, wanted to abolish the state immediately whilst Marx wanted to create a new workers' state to abolish the state. As Engels wrote to Theodor Cuno in 1872, that to Bakunin:

> The state is the chief evil, it is above all the state which must be done away with and then capitalism will go to hell of itself. We, on the contrary say: do away with capital, the appropriation of the whole means of production in the hands of the few, and the state will fall away of itself.

Whilst Marx and the anarchists regarded the state as evil, they differed in that whereas the anarchists saw the state as the primary cause of evil, Marx saw it in the division of labour in society and from which the state derived. For Marx capitalism had to be destroyed first, the destruction of the state would follow.

Marx and Bakunin differed on a number of important issues which was reflected in their disputes over the policy to be adopted by the First International. Marx stressed the importance of organizing the workers and of the objective conditions for revolution being ripe, while Bakunin believed in spontaneity. Marx wanted a centrally controlled movement; Bakunin saw this as an obstacle to local initiative and wanted, instead, the local movement to have complete freedom to shape its own policy. In addition, he asserted that if the revolutionary movement was authoritarian, as Marx wanted, then the new society would also be authoritarian. He was, theoretically, just as much opposed to the revolutionaries who were the 'future dictators' as he was against the existing order. Marx believed the revolution would start among the best organized and educated workers in the economically advanced countries. Bakunin looked hopefully to the slum-dwellers of the backward countries, and particularly the Russian peasants, to set a revolutionary example to the proletariat of the West. For Bakunin, the dictatorship of the proletariat was a state as evil and unnecessary as any other, and he had no time for Marx's policy of working with the bourgeoisie and the radical movements.

The first public clash between the two came at the Basle Congress of the First International in 1869, though Marx fought by proxy. Bakunin demanded that the International endorse his policy for the abolition of inheritance which he viewed as the first step towards social and economic equality. Marx and his supporters regarded it as an irrelevance, even though Marx had advocated its abolition in the *Communist Manifesto*. To Marx it was an irrelevance that would both alienate the middle classes before their value to the proletariat had been exhausted and deflect the working class from the goal of the destruction of capitalism to that of immediate social reform. Although Marx was prepared to accept higher death duties as a compromise, the outcome of the debate was a victory for Bakunin.

As a result, Marx prepared for, and attended, the next Congress in The Hague in 1872, when the conflict between the two came to a head. Though many subjects were discussed, the Congress became a contest between the 'centralizers' or 'authoritarian communists' led by Marx and Engels, and the 'autonomists' or 'free collectivists' led by Bakunin, though on this occasion Bakunin fought by proxy, the Swiss James Guillaume being his spokesman. The result, this time, was a decisive majority for political action as opposed to anarchism. And to ensure that the International did not again become influenced or dominated by the anarchists, Marx had its general council moved to the United States where it soon expired.

Yet Bakunin had adherents in many countries, especially in Italy, Spain, Switzerland and France. They continued to propagate his ideas, along with those of Proudhon and later Kropotkin, long after his death in 1876. In Spain, the dissemination of Bakunin's ideas by Giuseppe Fanelli soon attracted the artisans, especially in Barcelona and Madrid. Anarchist ideas, and with them the idea of revolution, were kept alive in Spain long after they had expired elsewhere. Fermin Salvochea founded an anarchist journal in 1886 and organized demonstrations in the 1890s, which was itself a period of bombings, assassinations and insurrections.

In Italy, as in Spain, the ideas of Proudhon had at first been best received, but in the 1870s Carlo Cafiero, Errico Malatesta and Carmelo Palladino built up the anarchist movement under Bakuninist auspices, though the planned uprising in Bologna in 1874 proved abortive. 'All told, Bakunin's disciples remained true to the legacy of their master. Ruin and disaster followed them wherever they went, and the working class had to suffer the consequences.'[5]

Anarchism, as James Joll has rightly pointed out, is a creed of all or nothing. It has, therefore, been less influential in countries when there was hope of concessions from the existing system. It has been most successful, in terms of gathering followers at least, in the less economically and politically advanced countries. In this Bakunin has been vindicated in looking to the backward countries and their workers.

(c) The Demise of the International

In the United States the International helped in the large unemployed demonstrations in Chicago and New York and supported the 1873 miners' strike. Victoria Woodhull, the

5. George Lichtheim, *A Short History of Socialism*, p. 213.

leader of one American section, attempted to launch a separate United States Movement on a platform which included women's rights and free love, but was suspended by London. The International was finished off so far as participation in American affairs was concerned by a General Council resolution of 1874 forbidding its members from belonging to any political party organized by the propertied classes and it finally expired in Philadelphia in 1876.

Besides the dispute with Bakunin, the Paris Commune helped to destroy the First International. It led to the destruction of the working class of Paris which had been the mainstay of the International, and Marx's defence of the Commune, in *The Civil War in France* (1871), led to the defection of the more respectable elements. The most significant of these were the English trade unionists, who were, in any case, more inclined towards liberalism, reconciled to the *status quo* and embroiled in their own domestic affairs, especially the enactment of trade union legislation. They were never revolutionaries and what is surprising is that they ever belonged to the International with its foreigners and socialist overtones. Even if they had not deserted the International when they did, it is unlikely that they would have stayed had it become more Marxist.

Thus the First International was an effective force in working-class politics for a mere eight years. Even during these years it was not the driving force in developing trade unionism and political unity that Marx had hoped for. Though developments in Italy and Spain took place in its name, they were under the influence of Bakuninist anarchism rather than Marxian socialism. Nevertheless, though working-class movements in each country went their own ways, the International did give help in strikes by organizing collections and helping to prevent the importation of strike-breakers. But its real importance was in providing an organ for the expression and distribution on an international level of some of the ideas of Marx and Bakunin and in indicating the possibilities of united international working-class industrial and political action.

The demise of the International left Marx and Engels without any significant following outside Germany, where the party of Bebel and Liebknecht had maintained close links with both Marx and the International. Yet even in Germany developments in socialist theory were not entirely to the satisfaction of Marx.

3

THE GERMAN SOCIAL DEMOCRATIC
PARTY TO 1914

Although the end of the First International was the end, for
the time being, of the international socialist movement, it
by no means signalled the end of socialism or Marxian
socialism. Indeed, socialism of one kind or another, experienced a revival and spread to most European countries. In
the 1880s parties professing some form of Marxist socialism
were established in several countries. Jules Guesde had
established the Parti Ouvrier in France by 1882, H. M.
Hyndman established the Social Democratic Federation in
Britain in 1884, and Caesar de Paepe the Parti Socialiste
Belge in Belgium in 1879, while the Socialist Labour Party
had been formed as early as 1877 in the United States. Besides these, Pablo Iglesias helped form the Spanish Social
Democratic Party in 1879, a Danish party was formed the
same year, the Norwegian Social Democratic Party in 1887,
Austrian and Swiss parties in 1888, Swedish in 1889 and
an Italian Labour Party in 1892.

Yet whilst most professed adherence to the Marxist gospel,
the parts they emphasized and the interpretations they
followed were as different as the personalities of the leaders
of the international socialist movement. Nor did Marxian
socialism have things all its own way. Besides its anti-
socialist opponents, it had socialist rivals both on the right
and the left.

By far the most important and influential of the Marxist
political parties was the German Social Democratic Party,
founded at Gotha in 1875. It was the first to adopt the
philosophy of Marx and was generally accepted as the leading Marxist and socialist party. It was the first socialist party
to be organized on a national scale and also, in spite of

33

severe repression, the first to gain electoral victories. Out of a total of 438,231 votes cast for socialist candidates throughout the world in 1878, 437,158 were cast in Germany. The party was the largest, best organized and most revolutionary, in its theoretical aspects at least, of the emerging European socialist parties. It dominated the Second International and became the model which most other parties tried to copy.

The German Social Democratic Party was formed by an amalgamation of two formerly opposed socialist parties: the Universal German Workingmen's Association, and the Social Democratic Workingmen's Party. The former was virtually the creation of Ferdinand Lassalle, the 'miraculous child' as von Humbolt described him, the latter that of Wilhelm Liebknecht and August Bebel. For years there was more bitterness between the parties than between either and the government, an endemic feature of socialist movements. The Lassallians were reformist, the Eisenachers (as the party of Liebknecht and Bebel was called) were revolutionary. The Lassallians wanted universal suffrage so that the workers could gain control of the state. This would then be used to build producer cooperatives. Whereas Lassalle viewed the state as having the function of helping the 'development of the human race towards freedom' and was prepared to work for immediate reforms, and indeed courted Bismarck for this purpose, the Eisenachers viewed the state, with Marx, as an instrument of class oppression and were more concerned to create revolutionary consciousness so that the state could be destroyed. The Lassallians wanted an independent all-German working-class party and favoured cooperation with the aristocracy against the bourgeoisie. The Eisenachers followed a policy of being independent allies of the bourgeois Progressives in the struggle against aristocratic rule. The Lassallians supported Bismarck on the question of German unification while the Eisenachers opposed anything that strengthened Prussian influence, as they viewed Prussia as the epitome of autocratic and militarist rule. It should, perhaps, be noted that the support of the Lassallians lay mainly in the North whilst that of the Eisenachers was to be found in the South, though this, of course, was not the only, or even the most important, determinant of their respective attitudes. Again, the Lassallians were nationalist, the Eisenachers internationalist. The latter abstained on the vote for war credits for the war against France, opposed the annexation of Alsace-Lorraine, and advocated an honourable peace. The former voted for the credits and supported the war.

Yet in spite of these predominantly tactical differences, it is difficult to assess, from a superficial reading of their programmes, which was redder than the other. Marx and Engels favoured and encouraged the party of Liebknecht and Bebel, and poured scorn on that of Lassalle. Moreover, it was the personal animosity that existed between the leaders of the rival parties that kept them apart in the early 1870s. The unification of Germany under Prussian leadership in 1871 and the end of the Franco-German war eliminated two major sources of conflict and the fact that the two parties polled roughly the same number of votes in Reichstag elections and often spoiled each other's candidates' chances in the run-off elections led to demands for fusion. This was finally accomplished in 1875 when the Socialist Working-men's Party of Germany was formed. As one would expect, unification was made possible by a compromise. The most important demands of both parties were written into the programme of the new party.

The Gotha Programme asserted that 'Labour is the source of all wealth and culture, and since useful labour is possible only in and through society, the entire proceeds of labour belong with equal rights to all members of society'; that the instruments of labour are the monopoly of the capitalist class; that the emancipation of the working class demands the communal ownership of the means of production, co-operative control of labour and a just distribution of the proceeds of labour, and that such emancipation of labour must be the work of the labouring class, 'in contrast to which all other classes are only a reactionary mass'.

35

The Programme committed the party, 'by all legal means', to the 'establishment of the free state, and the socialist society, to destroy the iron law of wages by abolishing the system of wage-labour, to put an end to exploitation in every form, to remove all social and political inequality'. It demanded the 'establishment of socialistic productive associations with state help under the democratic control of the labouring people' and such things as universal, equal and direct suffrage, direct legislation by the people, a people's army, the abolition of all exceptional laws, administration of justice by the people and free education. For the present, it called for the greatest possible extension of political rights, a single progressive income tax, unrestricted right of combination and factory legislation.

German socialism as represented by the Gotha Programme could hardly be called revolutionary, or even Marxist. Indeed, the Programme angered Marx and Engels. They had looked to the Germans to spearhead the Marxist cause but faced a temporary retreat. They considered that unity had been bought at too high a price, in that it favoured the Lassallians who were, in their opinion, on the way out. Marx went so far as to send a detailed critique of the Programme to Bracke, eventually published as the *Critique of the Gotha Programme* in 1891. In his 'screed', as he called it, Marx criticized the Programme line by line. He attacked it for declaring labour to be the source of all wealth whereas nature is just as much the source, for restricting its attack to the capitalists when the landlords should have been included, for implying that in a socialist society the worker would receive the full value of his product when, in fact, deductions have to be made for social use, for calling the bourgeoisie reactionary when it had been revolutionary in attacking feudalism, for accepting Lassalle's theory of the iron law of wages instead of his own theory of surplus value, for accepting the patronage of the state in establishing producer cooperatives rather than the working class being made responsible for its own emancipation, and for treating the state as an independent entity instead of recognizing that it was based on the economic sub-structure. He also criticized the Programme for speaking of the state as if it were a democratic republic whereas it was feudal and militaristic. He added that even in a democratic republic, the class struggle still existed and had to be fought.

Engels, in a letter to Bebel, said that every word in the Programme, which had, moreover, 'been composed in a flat and flaccid style', could be criticized. Engels asserted that neither he nor Marx could give their support to a party established on the basis of the Programme, the result of the 'bending of the knee to Lassallianism on the part of the whole German proletariat'. He argued that fusion on the terms of the Programme would not last a year, that the resultant break-up would leave the Lassallians the stronger and the Marxists without their 'political virginity'. But having vented their anger and misgivings, Marx and Engels allowed Liebknecht to suppress the *Critique* in the interests of unity. The unification of the two parties went ahead and Marx and Engels gave it their help and support.

Though a lot of ink and anger had been spilt on account of the Gotha Programme, the disagreement and the Programme soon became irrelevant. The Programme soon ceased to represent the views of the majority but could not be altered because of Bismarck's Anti-Socialist Laws which drove the party underground for over a decade. When they expired in 1890 the party held a congress in Halle, changed its name to the German Social Democratic Party (SPD) and decided to prepare a new Programme. The Erfurt Programme, as it came to be called, was adopted in 1891, at a time when the party could boast nearly one and a half million votes and thirty-five members in the Reichstag.

The Erfurt Programme eliminated the last remnants of Lassallianism, eradicated all demands for state-aided producer cooperatives and pledged the party to Marxism. It began by emphasizing the tendency towards capitalist concentration, the increase in the size of the proletariat and the 'army of superfluous workers', increasing misery, oppression

37

and exploitation and a sharper and more bitter class war 'between bourgeoisie and proletariat which divides modern society into two hostile camps'. The Programme asserted that crises in capitalist society became more 'far-reaching and more ravaging' and furnished the proof that 'the productive powers of modern society have outgrown its control, that private property in the means of production is irreconcilable with the due application and full development of those powers'. To remedy this, the Programme argued that:

Only the conversion of capitalistic private property in the means of production – land, quarries, and mines, raw materials, tools, machines, means of communication – into common property, and the change of the production of goods into a socialistic production, worked for and through society, can bring it about that production on a large scale, and ever-growing productiveness of human labour, shall develop, for the hitherto exploited classes, from a source of misery and oppression, into a source of the highest well-being and perfect universal harmony.

It asserted that only the working class could emancipate itself, that this could only be achieved by political struggle and that it was the task of the SPD to help the development of class organization and consciousness, and lead the workers to their goal. Furthermore, it proclaimed the interests of the working classes in all countries to be the same and declared the SPD to be '*one* with the class-conscious workmen of all other countries'.

In immediate terms, the Erfurt Programme called for universal, equal and direct suffrage, proportional representation, biennial parliament, direct legislation by means of the mechanisms of proposal and rejection, local self-government, election of magistrates, and such things as free legal assistance and medical care. For the immediate benefit of the workers it advocated the eight-hour day and the prohibition of the employment of women and children, and, where possible, night work.

This, then, is the first Programme of a party organized on

a mass basis and dedicated to Marxism. Yet nowhere in the Programme is there so much as a hint of violence or revolution to achieve its aims. Its tone is that of a party desiring peaceful constitutional progress towards socialist objectives – and many of them could be more correctly described as liberal. There was, as George Lichtheim has observed, a 'yawning gap between its theoretical analysis and its practical demands'.[1] It was silent about the class character of the state and the need for force to overthrow it. Indeed, Liebknecht, who had asserted in 1869 that socialism was a question of force and attacked what he called the illusion that universal suffrage was 'the miraculous key that would open the doors of public power to the disinherited', now argued that although the Reichstag was primarily of value from a propagandist point of view, this did not mean that parliamentarianism should be condemned, and he repudiated the use of violence. Liebknecht, as George Bernard Shaw wrote, 'had become a parliamentarian but his marxism ... prevented him from becoming a statesman. He still covers every compromise by a declaration that the Social Democrats never compromise.'

Though revolutionary slogans had, of necessity, to be kept in the background if the newly legalized party was not to be faced with another bout of repressive legislation, there was some doubt as to whether revolution was really in the minds of any but a few of the SPD leaders. The party never became what it appeared and pretended to be. In his 1895 introduction to a new edition of Marx's *Class Struggles in France*, Engels called the SPD 'the most numerous, most compact mass, the decisive shock-force of the international proletarian army'. The most numerous and compact it certainly was, but its 'shock-force' was never used, except as an army for peaceful electioneering. And the exigencies of electioneering made it necessary for the party to advocate and emphasize immediate reforms. Before long the capture

1. George Lichtheim, *Marxism: An Historical and Critical Study*, p. 262.

of a parliamentary majority had almost become an end in itself.

In the main, the leaders of the SPD believed that a socialist majority in the Reichstag would introduce socialist measures. Nor did they see the existence of the capitalists as an obstacle. Kautsky, for example, could ask:

> The capitalists and their followers are but an insignificant little bunch. How could they, then, under universal suffrage, hold up the transition to socialism?

The difficulty lay in determining how the majority was to be achieved. On the one hand there were those, like Lieb-knecht, who, whilst advocating the fighting of elections, urged that the party should adopt a negative attitude to the work of parliament and the state. On the other hand, there were those like George von Vollmar, who wanted the SPD to adopt a constructive policy in parliament as a way of obtaining electoral support. The latter course had to recommend it the social legislations of Bismarck which indicated, at least, that the state was capable of introducing measures of some benefit to the working class. Moreover, the developing trade unions, uninhibited by revolutionary phraseology and distrustful of a future that was indeterminate, increasingly looked to the SPD for support for industrial legislation.

This policy was not without its difficulties. It posed the dilemma of whether the party should ally itself with other parties for electoral purposes, and in the work of parliament, in the pursuit of short-term objectives, or retain its independence and class character. In fact, whilst the party officially repudiated electoral alliances with bourgeois parties at national level, a number of arrangements were made at the local level.

A further complication in the quest for a parliamentary majority was the obstinacy of the peasants in refusing to disappear. The SPD regarded itself as a proletarian party and, following Marx, anticipated the gradual disappearance of the peasants as a consequence of large-scale capitalistic farming. Unfortunately for the party theorists, and especially Kautsky, the peasants refused to participate in the Marxist scenario. Instead of disappearing they increased in number. This, naturally, placed difficulties in the way of a party seeking electoral success by an exclusive advocacy of proletarian interests. The result, once again, was a compromise. Short-term measures for the benefit of the peasants became part of the electoral armoury of the SPD.

(a) Revisionism – Bernstein

The writings of Eduard Bernstein represent the first coherent critique of Marxism from within the Marxist camp, and the first sustained attempt to move the party away from its revolutionary Marxist theory to that of reformism. It is important, therefore, to have some appreciation of Bernstein's ideas. Long before the advent of Bernstein and revisionism, the SPD was gradually losing its revolutionary ardour and diluting its Marxism. Bernstein, 'the outstanding reformist theoretician of German Social Democracy in the twentieth century', as Peter Gay describes him,[2] simply rationalized and hurried along the process. Just as Marxism was the product of a German Jew, so also the first systematic attempt to revise Marxism came from a German Jew who had worked alongside Engels and was a member of the SPD.

Revisionism was the only important challenge to Marxism that developed within the SPD and it became one of the major philosophies of gradual and peaceful evolution towards socialism. But although Bernstein is rightly credited with being the main standard-bearer of revisionism, it is arguable that many had shot arrows tipped with its 'heresy' long before Bernstein appeared. Revisionism, of sorts, can be found in the later writings of Engels, especially the preface to the 1895 edition of Marx's *Class Struggles in France*. Vollmar, too, had given a series of speeches in the early

2. Peter Gay, *The Dilemma of Democratic Socialism*, p. 19.

1890s in which he advocated 'slow, organic evolution' and supported immediate reforms like labour legislation. He had aroused controversy by his demand that the party support nationalization within the existing state. However, Vollmar was easily warded off by Liebknecht and Kautsky. Bernstein proved to be a different proposition. With Diderot, he could say 'everything must be examined, everything must be shaken up, without exception, without circumspection'.

Influenced by Fabian socialism (Engels characterized him as having 'Fabian-Enthusiasm'), and English democracy and tolerance, by the evidence of rising prosperity which appeared to invalidate Marx's prediction of increasing misery, and the failure of the peasants, small holders and petit bourgeoisie to disappear, Bernstein contributed a number of articles to *Neue Zeit*. These were debated at the 1898 Stuttgart party congress after which Kautsky suggested to Bernstein that he write a comprehensive statement of his convictions. The result was *Evolutionary Socialism*, 'the bible of revisionism', published in 1899. From being a political exile in England, Bernstein was catapulted into the forefront of controversy: a controversy that was to align him against Kautsky of the orthodox centre and Rosa Luxemburg of the radical left. It was a controversy that not only dominated the policy discussions of the SPD but also intruded into the deliberations of the Second International.

At first Bernstein's criticisms of Marxism were primarily directed against the prediction of the increasing impoverishment of the workers and its closely related contention that the crises of capitalism would grow more severe and lead to its collapse. Soon he went beyond this and attacked the core of Marxian socialism. In the hands of Bernstein revisionism was not the mild reformism of Vollmar or the tactical retreats of Engels, but a sustained and coherent onslaught on the philosophic, economic and political aspects of Marxism.

Having become sceptical of Marxism because events, in his eyes, had falsified some Marxist predictions, Bernstein was eventually led to abandon the whole structure. Even

the dialectic was abandoned as he believed it to be a cause
of the errors in that it encouraged idle speculation in place
of a search for knowledge of the empirical world. It was an
excrescence that had to be eliminated from socialist theory.
For the Marxist dialectic, which he called 'cant', he substituted evolutionism as the core of socialism, a linear concept of progress whereby social evolution became a gradual
growth into socialism with a decrease in class antagonisms.
For the vision of the revolution he substituted that of 'the
daily struggle of the workers, which proceeds and repeats
itself in spite of all persecutions. Workers grow in number,
in general social power, in political influence, and no party
can evade it.'

Bernstein explained the failure of Marx's predictions to
materialize by arguing that Marx had underestimated the
economic and social consequences of the operation of a free
political system on the mode of production. He argued that
Marx's theory of the influence of the substructure on the
superstructure was too simple, that men were motivated, in
part, by ideal influences. Whereas for Marx ideas were relative, for Bernstein they were objective and independent.
'The point of economic development that has now been
reached', he wrote, 'leaves the ideological, and especially the
ethical, factors greater scope for independent activity than
used to be the case.' While to Marx the socialist future was
necessary and inevitable, to Bernstein it was no more than
ethically desirable and, therefore, dependent on will. While
still calling and regarding himself a Marxist, he replaced
Marxist science with Kantian ethics. Moreover, the goal of
socialism is a never-ending task. In the words which caused
great bitterness: 'The goal is nothing, the movement everything.' Thus Bernstein relegated the importance of the final
collapse of capitalism and emphasized the striving for
limited and attainable ends.

In attempting to refute Marx's economic predictions,
Bernstein accepted that capitalism was undergoing a shift
towards concentration and centralization but argued that
small, independent enterprises continued in existence and

43

were, in fact, called into being by the demands of the large enterprises. Far from disappearing, both the middle classes and the number of property owners were increasing. He quoted the widespread increase in shareholding and income statistics that showed income to be rising and disputed the theory of the increasing misery of the proletariat. He argued that capitalism had not simplified class relations but differentiated them, as was shown by the rise of a new white-collar middle class. 'The structure of society has not become simplified. Far from it. Rather, both as far as income and economic activity are concerned, it has been further graduated and differentiated.' Even the proletariat is a mixture of divergent elements resulting from the differences of employment and income creating different life-styles and expectations. Bernstein logically went on to play down class warfare, put national loyalty above class loyalty, played down internationalism and emphasized community of interest and partnership.

More than anything else, Bernstein's critique of the theory of the inevitable collapse of capitalism demanded a fundamental change in the political tactics of the SPD. Although he affirmed that the working classes in the various industrialized countries were still subject to periodic trade cycles, he argued none the less that the general trend of capitalism was towards increasing prosperity and stability, and that disturbances interfering with this trend were becoming more mild and infrequent. Capitalism, he argued, was gradually overcoming the anarchy of the market through the growth of a world market, improvements in transportation and communications, the increased wealth of the industrialized countries, the increased flexibility of the credit system, and the rise of monopolies and cartels. All these, in his view, served to increase both the stability and adaptability of capitalism.

Bernstein's political tactics were the logical outcome of his philosophical and economic doctrine. Both led in the direction of a gradualist non-violent policy in recognizing that the state, as it existed, could be used for socialist ends.

This was further strengthened by his theory that socialism gradually permeates capitalism through the increase of social control over the economy and the development of democratic institutions. The growing political power of the proletariat leads to an increase in its participation in the formulation of national policy, the enactment of social and welfare legislation, and the growing power of the trade unions sets bounds to the arbitrary acts of employers. For Bernstein the working class and its political and industrial organization was just another, but more powerful, pressure group.

Thus Bernstein became the advocate of a non-violent revolution by means of a persistent economic and political struggle to widen the area of democracy. Once achieved, this would itself become the means of changing society. He went further still and argued that if the achievements of the socialist movement were inadequate, then it was the fault of the movement, not the system. To Bernstein, democracy was 'the means of the struggle for socialism and it is the form socialism will take once it has been realized'. In his hands the concept of socialism was redefined to mean the fight for social reforms and the abandonment of all thought of revolution and the dictatorship of the proletariat. Indeed, he argued that the SPD would increase its influence if 'it found the courage to emancipate itself from a phraseology which is actually obsolete, and if it were willing to appear what it really is today: a democratic-Socialist reform party'.

In his interesting book on Bernstein Peter Gay argues that if there had been no Bernstein, it would have been necessary to have invented him. Political and economic conditions around the turn of the century demanded a reformist doctrine. Revisionism was the rational recognition of an already existing state of affairs. The economic boom which lasted, with brief minor interruptions, from 1871 to 1914 seemed to invalidate Marx's prediction of collapse and probably sapped whatever will to revolution the proletariat might have had. And although the SPD had redrawn its programme on Marxist lines in 1891, it was by then actively

C

engaged in and committed to parliamentary electioneering. This, as Gay argues, and as Marx had argued, is the dilemma of democratic socialism. The final goal inevitably becomes obscured by the need for electoral success and, therefore, the advocacy of short-term reforms. Again, does the achievement of short-term reforms make the revolution unnecessary or bring it nearer? Whatever the answer, the SPD had compromised over electoral alliances with the bourgeoisie and sublimated its antagonism to the peasants and the Catholic Church long before Bernstein began his heretical writings. As Plamenatz wrote, no doubt with tongue in cheek: 'From 1891 until 1914 the leaders of the German Social Democratic Party were true Marxists; they were as much committed to Marxism and as eager to defend it as practical politicians could well be.'[3] Whilst the SPD retained its revolutionary-socialist slogans and rhetoric it agitated for liberal reforms. The revolution, as Cole wrote, was 'post-dated to electoral victory'.[4]

(b) The Orthodox Defence

Whatever Bernstein's views had done to party unity, his revision of Marxism did at least provide a plausible theoretical explanation of the situation of the German proletariat around 1900. It was popular in the South among people like Eduard David, Kurt Eisner and Ludwig Frank. It offered an alternative to Marxism similar to that being offered by the Fabians in England and the Possibilists in France. Indeed, the secretary of the SPD, Ignaz Auer, wrote to Bernstein that the party was already reformist but that, given its historic revolutionary literature, one does not openly say that it is reformist, one carries on with reformist practice. This 'official' recognition of the nature of the party

3. John Plamenatz, *German Marxism and Russian Communism*, p. 170.
4. G. D. H. Cole, *History of Socialist Thought*, Vol. III, Part 1, p. 320.

did not prevent Bernstein from being condemned by both the orthodox and radical wings of the party. As Daniel Bell has written in another context, 'For some movements, ideology is a pose, easily dropped; for others it is a bind.'[5] For the SPD its ideology was a bind, and Bernstein a nuisance for drawing attention to it.

The characteristic trait of the orthodox, as Alfred Meyer observed, 'was not a question of how the doctrine should be interpreted; the mark of orthodoxy was an emotional loyalty to the doctrine, in one form or another'.[6] Bebel, for instance, both called himself a revolutionary and concentrated the energies of his party on the struggle to win a parliamentary majority. Kautsky, the 'old war-horse of Marxian orthodoxy', the leading German Marxist theorist, and the man most responsible for the Erfurt Programme, also redefined the class struggle as a struggle to obtain parliamentary victory for the SPD. 'Only the bold', as E. H. Carr has commented, 'offered openly to "revise" Marx; the sagacious interpreted him.'[7]

Though he always insisted on the proletarian basis of the party and resisted all attempts to dilute the class war doctrine in order to enlist the support of other classes, Kautsky nevertheless envisaged the overthrow of the existing state and the proletarian conquest of political power in terms of a peaceful advance by parliamentary means. To Kautsky the advent of democracy meant that the proletariat had no need to overthrow the state, as Marx had thought; rather they had a vested interest in its maintenance. For Kautsky the 'workers' state' was one in which the political party of the workers, through its parliamentary majority, transformed society and introduced full democracy. This, in itself, was a thorough enough revision of Marx under the guise of an interpretation. Yet there was some substance for Kautsky's

5. Daniel Bell, *The End of Ideology*, p. 278.

6. Alfred G. Meyer, *Marxism: The Unity of Theory and Practice*, p. 130.

7. E. H. Carr, *Studies in Revolution*, London, 1962, p. 19.

view to be found in the writings of Marx and Engels. Marx, in extolling the virtues of the Paris Commune and universal suffrage, and Engels, in his criticisms of the draft of the Erfurt Programme, had said that the working class could come to power only under the form of a democratic republic. But whereas Bernstein abandoned Marxism, Kautsky claimed to have reinterpreted Marx and reached new conclusions.

Against Bernstein he argued that if the number of capitalists was increasing, as Bernstein alleged, then capitalism, not socialism, would be strengthened and the goal of socialism would recede. He asserted that Marx's theory of crises was about to be vindicated by events, that capitalism was not far away from a stage of chronic stagnation that would intensify the class struggle and which was foreshadowed by the colonial rivalries of the capitalist powers. Both Bernstein and Kautsky stressed the importance of the new middle class and argued that it was coming closer to the proletariat. But while Bernstein saw this in terms of the embourgeoisement of the proletariat, Kautsky anticipated the proletarianization of the bourgeoisie. The latter foresaw the result to be an exacerbation of class war, the former the development of social peace.

In general, the orthodox insisted on the inevitability of proletarian revolution, and argued that even if ownership was becoming more diffuse it was control that was crucial, and that this was being concentrated in fewer hands. And even if it were true that the proletariat was experiencing an increase in its living standards, it was relative impoverishment that was important. When all the rationalizations and arguments are put aside, it is clear that the orthodox valued and used Marxism as a propaganda weapon against the ruling classes, and the doctrine of the inevitability of proletarian revolution as a psychological weapon with which to exact concessions from the ruling oligarchy. Thus the threat of revolution became more important than its actual occurrence. This, at any rate, is the opinion of Alfred Meyer. If he is right then they were incredibly inept and stupid. Certainly, as he points out, their doctrine showed signs of political impotence.

(c) The Radical Challenge

There was nothing sterile, however, in the challenge of the radicals. Whereas Bernstein wanted the theory of the SPD amended to fits its practice, the young left-wingers wanted the practice to conform to its theory. Of these the most notable were Karl Liebknecht, Wilhelm's son, who, as James Joll observes, 'inherited his father's political romanticism without his commonsense',[8] and Rosa Luxemburg, 'pompous Rosa', as Lenin called her.

Rosa Luxemburg was by far the most profound and effective critic of revisionism. Her book *Reform or Revolution* (1888) contained the best and most systematic critique of Bernstein's theory. Of Bernstein's book she wrote:

It is of great historical significance for the German and International movements – it is the first attempt to give a theoretical basis to opportunist streams of thought within German Social Democracy.

Society, she argued, could only be transformed by revolution. She condemned Bernstein for abandoning scientific socialism for idealism and argued, like Kautsky, that contradictions within capitalism were growing more severe. Rather than bringing stability, the extension of credit contributed to the downfall of capitalism while the extension of monopolies and cartels indicated that capitalism was in its last stages. Indeed, the precondition for its collapse already existed in that the growth of the shareholding company, cited by Bernstein as an example of an increasing propertied class, was, in reality, the beginning of the socialization of production.

8. James Joll, *The Second International 1889–1914*, p. 100.

Luxemburg also attacked the political tactics of revisionism. In her view the trade unions could neither abolish exploitation nor obtain any control over production policy. Social reform would only be allowed where it was in the interests of the stability of capitalism and the protection of private property, and democracy was only endured on sufferance, and then only whilst it served the ruling class. To Rosa Luxemburg a socialist victory could only be achieved by a revolutionary seizure of power. Revisionism led to no more than a modification of the existing system.

Rosa Luxemburg adhered firmly to Marxism as a scientific method (she was what C. Wright Mills calls a 'plain marxist'), and expected crises on an international scale to break out in the foreseeable future. She resurrected a theory of spontaneity in which the workers made the revolution with the catalyst of the intellectuals, and advocated continuous revolutionary activity. In this she came into conflict not only with Lenin but also with the orthodox German Marxists who were trying to build a proletarian state within the existing capitalist state. Later, with Anton Pannekeok, she attacked the orthodox for their reformist practice, the party for being bureaucratic and the trade union leaders for being bourgeois politicians. She proposed the education of the workers by revolutionary activity, especially by means of the general strike, and opposed all ideas of a minimum programme and working for and within bourgeois democracy.

Luxemburg had demanded the expulsion of Bernstein from the party. Instead, his views were formally condemned by the party congresses of 1899 and 1903. Yet in spite of the strong language of the resolution condemning revisionism the party continued, in practice, to be a reformist party. But, as James Maxton once said, 'the man who cannot ride two bloody horses at once doesn't deserve a job in the bloody circus.' The circus was a comfortable one, and the SPD had a big stake in it. As Maurice Duverger wrote, the SPD 'constituted a veritable state more powerful than some national states'.[9] The SPD fought elections, it had 110 members in the Reichstag in 1912, and advocated immediate reforms. For all their professions of Marxist orthodoxy, Liebknecht and Bebel 'always remained within the ideological realm of democratic radicalism, as did their party as a whole. The notion that German Social Democracy, at any stage of its career, represented a threat to bourgeois society is a fantasy which no competent historian has found it possible to take seriously.'[10]

At the same time the SPD consistently disassociated itself from the work of parliament and the existing order. It opposed, for example, the nationalization of the Reichsbank on the grounds that it would increase the power of the capitalist state. The party refused to submit candidates for parliamentary office until 1912, when Philip Scheidemann was allowed to become Vice-President of the House. But even he was ousted for refusing to pay homage to the Kaiser. Still, in 1914 the party was waiting for the revolution and regarded itself as outside bourgeois society.

It was Marx who wrote that all political movements have been slaves to the symbol of the past. The SPD was a slave to the symbols of Marxism when it could have been leading the international socialist movement towards a more realistic conception of socialism. The tragedy of the revisionist debate was that it forced the party back on a rigid adherence to and defence of a policy which did not, and could not, correspond to its practice. They were not, however, alone in this. It also applied to the other Marxist parties based on the SPD model that were emerging.

9. Maurice Duverger, *Political Parties*, London, 1954, p. 66.
10. George Lichtheim, *A Short History of Socialism*, p. 233.

4
THE EMERGENCE OF
MARXIST POLITICAL PARTIES

Although by 1875 the Germans had established a socialist party it was not until the 1880s that Marxist socialist parties in other European countries took definite shape. In no respect could they compare with the Germans.

(a) Britain

In Britain, socialism as an organized movement had died with the Chartists in the early 1850s and what leaders the working class had, concentrated on building up the strength of the trade unions and securing the enactment of protective trade union legislation. What criticism there was of capitalist society found expression in the writings of individuals, of whom the most notable were Carlyle, Ruskin, and, later, Henry George and Charles Booth.

However, in 1881 the Democratic Federation was formed largely on the initiative of H. M. Hyndman, an orthodox follower of Marx in economic theory. An aristocrat, dedicated to the destruction of capitalism while earning his living by speculating in stocks and shares, Hyndman had been greatly influenced by Lassalle and wished to build a political party on the German model. Like Lassalle, he courted eminent politicians, Disraeli and Lord Randolph Churchill, and went to Marx for advice. As a result of the conversations with Marx he published *England for All: The Textbook of Democracy*, in 1881.

Though Marx had expressed doubts as to the feasibility of Hyndman's project, he nevertheless went ahead with his attempt to create a proletarian party that would continue the work of Robert Owen and the Chartists. The programme he formulated called for universal suffrage; triennial parliaments; equal electoral districts; payment of members; corruption and bribery of electors to be criminal offences; abolition of the House of Lords as a legislative body; Home Rule for Ireland; self-government for the colonies; and the nationalization of land. The last demand owed much to the influence of the land reformers, and especially Henry George's *Progress and Poverty* (1879). It was also the only demand that could be described as socialistic. Yet although the Federation in its early years was dominated by the demands for liberal political reforms and Home Rule for Ireland, it was not long before it adopted a socialistic programme.

A series of lectures by Hyndman were published under the title *Socialism Made Plain* in 1883. This became the basis of the Federation's programme of 1884, when it embraced Joseph Lane's Labour Emancipation League and changed its name to the Social Democratic Federation (SDF). The programme asserted that all wealth belonged to labour and declared the object of the SDF to be the establishment of a free society based upon political and social equality, and the emancipation of labour. It demanded the election of administrators, legislation by the people, abolition of the standing army, free education and justice, the nationalization of the means of production and distribution and, of course, Home Rule for Ireland. And to indicate that their collective head was not entirely in the clouds, the programme advocated the adoption of what Hyndman called 'stepping stones to a happier period' – an eight-hour day, better housing for workers and such things as nationalization of the land and state appropriation of railways and national banks. To propagate these views *Justice* was established the same year.

Throughout its existence the SDF was a mixed bunch composed of reformers and revolutionaries, as well as anarchists in its early period. Some advocated palliatives while others were strongly opposed to anything but a revolutionary policy, and there were frequent attacks on Hyndman for his autocratic control of the SDF, his Jingoism, anti-German feelings and anti-semitism. In 1884 there was a split in which the majority, including William Morris, Belfort Bax, Eleanor Marx and Edward Aveling, left to form the Socialist League. In 1896 another group seceded and formed the Socialist Union.

The secessions and frequent conflicts inevitably weakened the SDF, leaving it short of both intellectual and financial resources. But Hyndman somehow managed to keep the organization together, due no doubt to his belief both in the 'final clash' and in 'stepping stones', and his ability, as Tsuzuki remarks, 'to reconcile millenarianism with concessions to opportunism'.[1]

In spite of all its efforts the SDF was never very effective in promoting socialism, and still less in propagating the only form of Marxism to be found in England. It alienated the unions in its early period and only partially made up for this by its later support of strikes. It was, as Hobsbawm notes, 'the first modern socialist organization of national importance in Britain'.[2] But it was always a middle-class-dominated sect rather than a mass political organization. Its anti-religious attitude and the aridity of its socialism put off the working man. The dissensions and splits not only left it weak, and at times ineffectual, but also, as Cole says, left Hyndman 'cock of the walk in the SDF; but he had not much of a dunghill to crow from'.[3] Even after the help its members gave in the match girls' strike in 1888, the 1889 dock strike, the rise of new unionism, and the increased interest in socialism manifested by the formation of the Second International in 1889, it still had only 5,000 mem-

1. Chushichi Tsuzuki, *H. M. Hyndman and British Socialism*, p. 86.

2. E. J. Hobsbawm, *Labouring Men. Studies in the History of Labour*, London, 1964, p. 231.

3. G. D. H. Cole, *History of Socialist Thought*, Vol. II, p. 410.

bers in 1894, 9,000 in 1900 and not many more than 12,000 at its height. It could hardly compare itself to the SPD with its 100 members in the Reichstag and $4\frac{1}{2}$ million votes in 1912.

Nor was it any more successful in its forays into parliamentary elections, despite the help of 'Tory gold' aimed at splitting the Liberal vote. Nevertheless, it included among its members, at one time or another, prominent socialists like Ernest Belfort Bax, Harry Quelch and William Morris, and prepared the way for the Communist Party of Great Britain.

(b) France

While in Britain the socialists spent most of their time trying to win over the working class and the trade unions, in France the Marxists faced a working class organized into a plethora of rival socialist factions. The French working class had a long tradition of socialism of one sort or another. And although the tradition remained intact after the fall of the Paris Commune, French socialism in the 1870s could hardly be said to exist as an organized movement. Even in 1893 Engels could with justice call French socialists the 'scratch lot'.

Socialism in France was bedevilled by the backwardness of industry, political divisions and frequent splits. Socialism was indeed of little practical significance in French politics in spite of its long and revolutionary traditions. In the elections of 1889, for example, only seven socialist deputies, of various persuasions, were elected. The following year the German SPD received nearly twenty-five per cent of the vote and elected thirty-five members. Unlike the German party, the French never became wholeheartedly Marxian, though they were more revolutionary than the British. Again, while in Germany the trade unions were regarded, and often (though not always) acted, as the subordinate allies of the SPD, and in Britain were to be instrumental in the founding of the Labour Party, in France they developed their own philosophy and programme and remained aloof from politics.

Jules Guesde was probably more responsible than anyone else for the organizing of a French socialist movement. The 'Apostle of Socialism', as he was called, emerged from a youth spent dabbling with anarchism, and imprisonment for sympathy with the Paris Commune, as the main advocate of Marxism in France. In this he was helped by Paul Lafargue, the 'last Bakuninist' according to his father-in-law, Marx. Guesde was the most important leader of the Fédération des Ouvriers Socialistes de France, founded in 1880 with the help and approval of Engels. Like Hyndman in England, Guesde wanted to create a workers' party on the German model and, like Hyndman, visited Marx for advice.

To Guesde, socialism was inevitable through the concentration of capital. He saw the primary task of the proletariat to be the overthrow of capitalism. He made little of immediate reforms and thought parliamentary agitation to be important for purely propagandist purposes. The object of the workers' party was to be 'a kind of recruiting and instructing sergeant preparing the masses for the final assault upon the state, which is the citadel of capitalist society'. Like the orthodox German Marxists, he rested his hopes for revolution exclusively on the proletariat, viewed the trade unions as useful only in so far as they acted as schools for socialists, expected the peasants to disappear, refused to collaborate with the bourgeois parties and remained aloof from both the Boulangist and Dreyfus affairs, which he thought of as disputes among the bourgeoisie, irrelevant to the proletariat.

The party, which changed its name to the Parti Ouvrier Français after a split with the Possibilists in 1882, was however beset by internal strife and from the beginning of the 1890s had to fight against the practical reformers on the right and the syndicalists on the left. At the same time it was prepared to engage in electoral alliances with the other socialist parties. This proved particularly successful in the municipal elections of 1896. The unity of the socialist groups (they could hardly be called parties) resulting from this, on the basis of Millerand's Saint-Mandé Programme, lasted only a short time. Ironically, it was broken by Millerand's acceptance of office in the Waldeck-Rousseau Ministry.

In 1898 the Marxists, the Blanquists and the Communist Alliance joined forces to form the Parti Socialiste de France, a loose federation against those socialists prepared to support Millerandism. The party urged the necessity for a national and international class struggle for the conquest of political power and the expropriation of propertied classes. It declared itself to be the party of revolution, rejected all compromises with the bourgeoisie and demanded the socialization of the means of production and exchange. It also declared that it would put through reforms of benefit to the working class whilst refusing to take any action that would prolong the existence of bourgeois society. Partly as a result of this more intransigent policy it had only twelve deputies after the election of 1902, compared with the thirty-two of its socialist right-wing rivals. Only in 1905 was some semblance of unity achieved when the Section Française de l'Internationale Ouvrière was formed under the leadership of Jaurès. From this point on the party became essentially parliamentarian, and further discussion belongs to Chapter 5.

(c) Belgium

The French Marxists fought elections like their German mentors. But while the SPD could claim to represent the German Left, the Parti Socialiste de France could never realistically claim to represent the French Left. In Belgium, on the other hand, the Parti Ouvrier Belge, formed by Caesar de Paepe, Édouard Anseele and Louis Bertrand in 1885, could claim to be more representative of Belgian socialism. But though it had a Marxist flavour it was also greatly influenced by anarchist theory. For this reason, if no other, it is worth a brief glance. The Brussels Programme, for example, while it called for 'collective appropriation' to secure 'for every human being the greatest possible sense of freedom and well-being', also, and unlike the Erfurt Programme, emphasized the need to develop altruistic feelings and a sense of solidarity. It had a list of immediate demands such as universal suffrage and factory legislation but it also, and this is its distinctive feature, advocated the creation of autonomous 'Legislative Councils' to represent the functional interests of society, the devolution of power, public services to be administered by special autonomous commissions and a regulatory function for the trade unions in industry. Indeed, the Belgians viewed the commune as the basic unit of social and political organization, though they recognized the necessity of some services being provided centrally.

Like the other European parties, the Belgians became concerned with the winning of seats. Like them it was therefore forced into the pressing of immediate reforms, and in attempting to attract the peasant vote. Unlike them it attempted to build up the cooperatives, sick and welfare societies and trade unions as a means, not of educating the workers in the realities of class conflict, but of improving immediate conditions. Parliamentary action, as Cole points out, was treated as 'only one of a number of instruments for furthering working-class claims'.[4] It was also opposed to the German conception of a centralized party and a centralized state. In this it followed the conception of socialism as outlined by Emile Vandervelde. Vandervelde conceived of socialism as the reconstruction of society with the aid of cooperatives, trade unions and cultural agencies. And although he was a Marxist in accepting the Marxian theory of surplus value, he nevertheless denied that of the disappearance of the middle classes, increasing misery and the polarization of classes.

4. ibid., Vol. II, Part 2, p. 628.

(d) The United States

The 1870s in the United States was a period of severe depression with high unemployment, wage cuts and riots. Of the thirty or so national unions in existence in the early 1870s, only eight or nine were left by 1878. The National Labor Union, set up by William Sylvis in 1866 with a programme of producers' cooperatives and an eight-hour day, and which sent A. C. Cameron to the First International, disappeared in the depression.

Nevertheless, socialist influence was developing in the late 1870s, mainly among German immigrants who wielded great influence in the German Trades' Assembly in New York. The Germans, indeed, accounted for over a quarter of the total immigration between 1871 and 1895. There had, of course, been various socialist and reformist organizations, excluding utopians, earlier than this. Joseph Weydemeyer, the first active exponent of Marxism in the United States, had established the American Workers' Alliance in New York in 1853 with the object of forming an independent labour party. Ira Steward had started an agitation for the eight-hour day which he saw as the beginning of the transformation of society and F. A. Sorge, the secretary of the First International when it was moved to the USA, helped found the German Workingmen's Association in New York in 1867. However, all these had disappeared as separate movements by the mid 1870s. But the Universal German Workmen's Association, established by followers of Lassalle in Chicago in 1869, lived to become the Illinois Labor Party in 1874, with a policy of producer cooperatives set up with state aid and the public ownership of banks and transportation. The same year a group of New York Marxists established the Social Democratic Workingmen's Party of North America and these two, with other groups, formed the Workingmen's Party of the USA in 1876. This became the Socialist Labor Party (SLP) in 1877 with a long list of immediate demands.

The SLP, in which Germans predominated, insisted that the emancipation of the workers must be brought about by their own efforts. In the face of the opposition of the trade unions that had helped to establish the party, it decided to concentrate on socialist propaganda. In 1879 it elected four aldermen to the Chicago City Council and endorsed Henry George in 1886 for the mayoralty of New York. Daniel de Leon, a lecturer in law at Columbia, joined the party in 1890 after having supported George in his election campaign, been a member of the Knights of Labor and Bellamy's Nationalist Movement. The latter advocated a system of state socialism and complete economic equality. De Leon became editor of the party's organ *The People* in 1892 and, with the aid of Lucien Sanial and Hugo Vogt, advocated the organizing of trade unions under socialist leadership in opposition to the American Federation of Labor (A F of L). Whereas Samuel Gompers argued that 'The way out of the wage system is through higher wages', de Leon reproached the trade union leaders for working for 'grovelling "improvements" or hunger-aggravating crumbs' and assailed the 'pure and simple' trade union leaders he characterized as 'labor fakers'. In pursuit of the policy of bringing the trade unions under socialist leadership, the SLP set up the Trades and Labor Alliance in 1895 as a federation of trade unions and socialist bodies aimed at supplanting the conservative A F of L, the officials of which de Leon described as 'essentially hired men of the capitalist class'. But after an initial spurt it soon petered out.

De Leon was the pioneer of socialism in the USA, but, as Marx said of John Stuart Mill, his eminence was due to the flatness of the surrounding landscape. He viewed the state through Marxist eyes, opposed reformist socialism and consequently attacked Gompers and the A F of L for their strictly trade union preoccupations. In pamphlets like *The Burning Question of Trade Unionism* (1904) he preached revolutionary industrial unionism and advocated a policy of dual unionism whereby revolutionary trade unionists should attempt both to create their own revolutionary trade unions and capture the reformist collective-bargain orientated unions.

De Leon described the USA as the most developed capitalist country and thought it inconceivable that other countries might start building socialism first. 'No other country', he wrote, 'is ripe for the execution of Marxian revolutionary tactics.' But de Leon's tactics were not exactly Marxist. He believed in the need for a double attack on capitalism. The party should participate in elections and aim at electoral victory and the trade unions at industrial unionism. With the winning of political power the party would vest all authority in the unions and divest itself, and all political institutions, of authority. For de Leon this was the inauguration of the classless, stateless society. 'The political movement of labour', he wrote, 'that in the event of triumph would prolong its existence a second after triumph, would be a usurpation.' He saw no need for a dictatorship of the proletariat but rather anticipated the changeover to be accomplished peacefully due to the cowardice of the capitalists.

When the moderates, led by Morris Hillquit and Henry Slobodin, left the SLP in 1899, de Leon eliminated all the immediate demands, like a decrease in hours and the nationalization of mines, transport and communications under workers' control, from his party's programme. He proclaimed a revolutionary policy in 1900 and paved the way for the Industrial Workers of the World, but which eventually turned against him. 'He made many enemies and little headway.'[5] Inhabiting the backwaters of American life, the SLP was never comparable to the major European parties and was largely irrelevant to American political life. Its presidential candidate in 1900, for instance, obtained just 35,000 votes, less than some British MPs obtain in a single constituency. But then for de Leon participation in elections was never more than a propagandist exercise. It is

5. H. Wayne Morgan, ed., *American Socialism 1900–1960*, New Jersey, 1964, p. 2.

fortunate that he took this view. To have looked for success would have led to even more disappointment. The reasons for the 'failure' of socialism to take firm root in the USA I discuss elsewhere.

5

THE REFORMIST SOCIALISTS
TO 1914

So far we have concentrated on those who believed that
revolution was the road to power and the socialist society.
The Marxists and the anarchists were not, however, the
only ones to claim the title socialist. They have monopolized
the attention of the world and its scholars, due no doubt
to their colourful language and dramatic activities, but there
were many who thought and taught that socialism could be
achieved by the reform of the existing socio-economic and
political system. These reformist socialists existed in most
countries which had a tradition of socialism. In many
they were influential, often more so than the Marxists,
and in some they were more successful in terms of mass
and electoral support and in the reforms that they
accomplished.

These were the socialists that Lenin was to describe as
'enemies of the people'. They were enemies of the people
because they deluded the people into believing that fundamental changes could be brought about by piecemeal social
reform over a long period of time. Lenin and the revolutionaries, of course, had, in a phrase of Bagehot's, 'inherited from their barbarous forefathers a wild passion for
instant action'. To them it was inconceivable that a socialist
society could be built without first destroying the existing
system. The reformists were, perhaps, temperamentally and
physically unsuited to the storming of barricades, or lacked
the imagination to be inspired by a vision and the capacity
for faith in the coming of a new epoch. 'In many instances,
in fact, reformism is no more than the theoretical expression
of the scepticism of the disillusioned, of the outwearied, of

those who have lost their faith; it is the socialism of non-socialists with a socialist past.'[1]

Yet it could also be argued that it was the reformists who were the realists, before realism became a term of abuse, who were prepared here and now to get down to the humdrum job of actual reform, who eschewed the once-for-all solution, however attractive, because it was long-term and because, as they knew, in the long run we are all dead. The revolutionaries sacrificed the present for the future. The reformists were concerned with the present leaving the future as something that politicians make pompous speeches about.

The reformists are today's scapegoats, not for anything specific, just for everything; unfashionable and considered effete and, worse, mere careerists. Yet they have, if we have to calculate in these terms, as many monuments to their credit as have the revolutionaries, except that they lack the monument made of the blood of the countless victims of revolution. Nor, despite the impression that may have been created in previous chapters, have the revolutionary socialists always had things their own way. So often revolution has been the checkmate of reform and reaction the gainer.

The reformist socialists differed from the Marxists not only in not drawing their inspiration from Marx but also in their conception of capitalist society and the state. As with the Marxists, the reformists regarded capitalist society as moving inevitably towards the creation of large-size industries, but they regarded them also as becoming inevitably publicly owned. To them capitalist society was one in which the workers could progressively increase their standard of living by means of trade unions, cooperatives and political action. To the reformists the state was not so much the instrument of one class for the oppression and exploitation of another as an instrument that could be manipulated in any direction by those who gained control over it.

The reformists tended, therefore, to repudiate the theory

1. Robert Michel, *Political Parties*, New York, 1915, pp. 211–12.

of class war and to emphasize, as a first step, the imp
of the democratization of the franchise and the ed
of the workers in socialism so that once having got the vote,
they would use it for socialist candidates and policies. In
this way, it was thought, the state could be used for socialist
ends though the change would be evolutionary rather than
revolutionary. Logically, then, the reformists were democrats and libertarians, hostile to ideas of a coup d'état or
dictatorship of the proletariat. In some cases democracy and
socialism were considered to be synonymous and many,
forced to make a choice between the two, would have
chosen democracy.

In reality the distinction between the revolutionaries and
the reformists is arbitrary. It turns, of course, on the definition of revolution and many of the reformists' proposals for
the reconstruction of society could be described as revolutionary. In general the distinction is used to differentiate
means rather than ends. Again, both the revolutionary and
reformist socialists participated in the bourgeois electoral
system and many of the self-styled revolutionaries hoped for
and anticipated a peaceful socialist revolution.

It is not possible here to trace or examine all of the various
reformist movements and ideas. It is, however, both necessary and possible to indicate the kind of alternative that
existed in a number of countries to the revolutionary doctrines of Marxism and anarchism.

(a) Britain – the Fabians, the I L P, L R C and the Labour Party

The stronghold of reformist socialism was, and remains,
Britain. Indeed, in Britain the reformist socialists came to
socialism almost by accident. This is true both of the
Fabians and the Labour Party, neither of which began as a
specifically socialist organization. Formed in 1884, the
Fabian Society (FS) did, however, contain a number of
socialists who had become disillusioned with the Marxist

Social Democratic Federation, particularly because of its attitude to revolution, its involvement in street demonstrations and its acceptance of 'Tory gold' to finance its parliamentary candidates. Soon after its formation, the Society was joined by such eminent socialists as Sidney Webb, George Bernard Shaw, Graham Wallas, Annie Besant and William Clarke. Even so, most of their early proposals were of a radical nature rather than socialist and were taken, as McBriar points out, from the programmes of the Radical Clubs.[2] Nor did they ever formulate a comprehensive socialist plan but rather concentrated, perhaps as a result of the influence of the Webbs, on an analysis of specific institutions and in proposing specific remedies.

'Fabianism', as Alexander Gray has written, 'was begotten by highbrows in the drawing rooms of London';[3] highbrows who preferred analysis to action. But the highbrows were not above fighting.

In the Fabian Cabinet [George Bernard Shaw wrote] there was considerable strife of temperaments; and in the other Socialist societies splits and schisms were frequent; for the English are very quarrelsome. I believe that some of my own usefulness lay in smoothing out these frictions by an Irish sort of tact which in England seemed the most outrageous want of it. Wherever there was a quarrel I betrayed everybody's confidence by analysing it and stating it lucidly in exaggerated terms. Result: both sides agreed that it was all my fault. I was denounced on all hands as a reckless mischief-maker but forgiven as a privileged Irish lunatic.

Whilst most political groups started with slogans, the Fabians started with a study of the work of Robert Owen, Proudhon, Lassalle and English political economy. The approach to politics which they adopted owed much to the influence of John Stuart Mill and Jeremy Bentham but, as Max Beer points out, for the latter's principle of the greatest

2. A. M. McBriar, *Fabian Socialism and English Politics 1884–1918.*

3. Alexander Gray, *The Socialist Tradition from Moses to Lenin,* p. 385.

happiness of the greatest number they substituted the 'greatest efficiency of the greatest number'[4] and set up what became, in effect, an 'Institute for social engineering'.[5]

The first pronouncement of Fabianism was the *Fabian Basis* of 1887 but which represented more a consensus of opinion than a profession of faith. After declaring that the FS consisted of socialists (and they were a motley crowd) it went on to declare that the society

aims at the re-organisation of Society by the emancipation of land and industrial capital from individual and class owner-ship, and the vesting of them in the community for the general benefit [and works] for the extinction of private property in land and of the consequent individual appropriation, in the form of rent, of the price paid for permission to use the earth.

The Fabians extended the Mill–George theory of rent as being an unearned increment to other factors of production besides land. But whilst they wanted the unearned incre-ment appropriated by the community, they never intended that the worker would receive the 'full value of his product'. Instead, they advocated the establishment of a basic mini-mum, though Shaw for a time argued that there should be equality of wages.

To achieve its objectives the *Basis* declared that the Society looked 'to the spread of socialist opinions, and the social and political changes consequent thereon' and sought to achieve this by the 'general dissemination of knowledge as to the relation between the individual and society in its economic, ethical and political aspects'. Marx had thought in terms of a revolution being necessary to sweep away the existing state before a new society could be erected. The Webbs almost believed that it could be accomplished through after-dinner conversations with Liberal ministers. Certainly, they believed that they could be more effective in disseminating their views by permeating the Radical

4. Max Beer, *History of British Socialism*, Vol. II, p. 276.
5. ibid., p. 287.

Clubs, the Liberal Party and, later, the Labour Party than they could by a propagandist campaign. Indeed, they viewed with distaste the forming of the Independent Labour Party. Their aim, as Beatrice Webb made plain, was not to organize the unthinking persons into socialist societies but to make thinking persons socialists.

The most comprehensive and distinctive statement of the Fabian approach to politics is to be found in *Fabian Essays* (1889) to which the most important member of the society contributed and which established socialism as respectable and a best-seller. Yet, comprehensive as they were, the essays omitted any mention of trade unions, cooperatives and international affairs.

The job of the Fabians, as the essays made clear, was to adapt socialism to democracy. The only problem they saw was that of finding the means by which the state could be used to introduce social reforms. Instead of constructing a grand design, they pointed to specific evils, potential remedies and attempted to educate the public in the desirability and practicability of their measures. Accordingly, they placed great emphasis on knowledge and research, produced numerous tracts on contemporary problems and established the Fabian Research Department in 1912. 'They may not', as Alexander Gray commented, 'have had much faith in the class war but they believed in the production of an ample supply of controversial ammunition, and in the virtue of keeping it as dry as possible.'[6] Socialism to the Fabians was what the ordinary man would want if he were rational. They had great faith in the rationality of the electorate. They had not, of course, the experience of elections as we have today, nor the sociological evidence on the motivations of voters.

The Fabians were never confronted with the choice between reform and revolution that had divided the Chartists before them, the Social Democratic Federation (SDF) in Britain and the Social Democratic Party in Germany in the 1890s. Indeed, they were, in the main, in favour of

6. Alexander Gray, op. cit., p. 388.

the retention of a constitutional monarchy. Nor did they accept the doctrine of class war and the imminent socialist revolution but instead set out to introduce immediate social reforms, and they were not particular as to the agency for their introduction. The immediate objective of the FS was the democratization of society and the socialization of industry, or, more correctly, economic rent. To achieve this they advocated not the establishment of a political party but the 'permeation' of all organizations so that their ideas would become generally accepted. The 'people' already possessed the political rights the Chartists had demanded and longed for; the difficulty lay, and still lies, in persuading them to use them for socialist ends. Thus, unlike Marx, the SDF and the continental Marxists, the Fabians appealed not to a class but to the conscience of all classes. Their original purpose, as Adam Ulam has pointed out, was that 'of convincing public opinion as a whole, rather than indoctrinating a class'.[7] It was not class consciousness they wanted to awaken; they wanted to stir the conscience of all classes.

To the Fabians, socialism was a logical, necessary and inevitable development of the trends towards the concentration of capital; an evolutionary progress to be built on the existing political and social institutions and brought about by the pressure of the electorate. Fabian socialism was, as Max Beer remarked, 'everyday politics for social regeneration'.[8] What they meant by socialism was that there should be a national minimum below which the state should not allow its citizens to fall. As a part of this they argued that there should be an extension of the factory acts for the protection of workers, reduction in hours, establishment of pensions, improved housing and a widening of educational opportunities and facilities. But they also conceived of socialism as being a movement towards the ownership and control of vital industries by a democratic parliament and

7. A. B. Ulam, *Philosophical Foundations of English Socialism*, New York, 1964, p. 77.
8. Max Beer, op. cit., Vol. II, p. 281.

the expropriation of all forms of economic rent for the benefit of the community – what William Morris called a 'collectivist bureaucracy'. Yet this was unfair. The Fabians did not think primarily of state control so much as control by the municipalities. 'Gas and water socialism' as its critics described it, was to the Fabians a means of social and economic amelioration. In their system there would be a great role for the local authorities, the state being responsible only for national services. Nor did they ever anticipate or advocate the complete elimination of private enterprise.

Eduard Bernstein, who admitted to having been influenced by the Fabians in outlining his own conception of socialism, condemned Fabianism as 'a series of socio-political measures without any connecting element that could express the unity of their fundamental thought and action'.[9] He would, however, have agreed with Sidney Webb when he wrote that 'the movement to socialism is a continuing process: there is no frontier over which we must pass to enter the promised land'.

It has been argued by Hobsbawm that the Fabians had no place in the British political tradition. They were out of rapport with the Left and the liberals and always suspicious of the trade unions. Part of a middle-class reaction to the breakdown of mid-Victorian certainties and the rise of new strata, new structures, the 'middle-class socialism of the Fabians reflects the unwillingness, or the inability of the people for whom they spoke, to find a firm place in the middle and upper class structure of late Victorian Britain'.[10] Provocative and interesting as this interpretation is, it understates the contribution of the Fabians to the development of British socialism, their influence in getting the idea of a welfare state generally accepted and the continuing influence that Fabian thought exercises in the Labour Party. Though it may be a questionable contribution to have made

9. Quoted in Peter Gay, *The Dilemma of Democratic Socialism*, p. 162.

10. E. J. Hobsbawm, *Labouring Men: Studies in the History of Labour*, London, 1964, p. 268.

to the evolution of British socialism, they were certainly instrumental in ensuring that it bypassed Marx.

As with the Fabian Society, so with the Independent Labour Party (ILP). Its main impetus was an aversion to the evils of capitalism rather than a vision of the socialist society. Like the FS it was pragmatic and stressed the need for immediate reforms rather than engaging in theoretical formulations about the coming utopia. As the *ILP News* said in October 1897: 'The Social Revolution is accomplished by patient toil.' Reforming practice was important, theory could be left till later. Moreover, its inspiration was ethical and owed more to Carlyle, Ruskin and the Bible than to explicit socialist theoreticians. Nor was the idea of class war important. 'Socialism', as James Kier Hardie said, 'makes war upon a system, not upon a class.'

The original impetus for an independent working-class political party came from Hardie. A 'super-cunning Scot' according to Engels, Hardie had strongly protested at the TUC in 1887 against the labour representatives in the House of Commons identifying with the Liberal Party. After having been turned down by the Liberal Party, he stood as an Independent Labour candidate in 1888 and a few months later helped to form the Scottish Labour Party. The manifesto of the Party called for the 'formation of a distinct, separate and *Independent Labour Party*, which will rally at the polls the forces of the workers and of those who sympathize with our efforts'. Among other things, its programme called for the nationalization of railways, land and minerals, an eight-hour day and state provision for insurance for sickness, old age and death.

In England the Labour Union had been established in 1890 in Bradford, led by Robert Blatchford, the editor of the popular and influential *Clarion* and author of the bestsellers *Merrie England* (1894) and *Britain for the British* (1902). Soon after, similar bodies with a policy of working-class political independence were set up in Colne Valley, Salford, London and Manchester. At the general election of 1892 Hardie, 'the member for the unemployed', John Burns and Havelock Wilson were successful. British labour was stirring itself and had not, it seemed, made an inauspicious start. But then, two years earlier the German party had obtained nearly a million and a half votes and thirty-five members in the Reichstag. In 1893 a national conference at Bradford set up the Independent Labour Party (ILP). Although the delegates to the conference had rejected the name Socialist Labour Party, they adopted a socialist programme which called for the collective ownership of the means of production, distribution and exchange. In practice, however, the party emphasized immediate demands like the eight-hour day, abolition of overtime and piece-work, relief for the unemployed, free education and old age pensions. The party differed from the Social Democratic Federation in having a strong ethical basis to its demands, a philosophical basis which could only be described as humanitarian, and in being internationalist and pacifist. It differed from the Fabian Society in wanting a socialist society because it would be more just rather than because it would be more efficient. Yet socialism was a vague notion of a society that would be harmonious, where the motto, in Kier Hardie's words, would be 'each for all, not each for self'. Like the SDF and the FS the ILP had a predominantly middle-class leadership.

In its early years the ILP concentrated on attempting to obtain the support of the trade unions, which it viewed as a likely source of funds for electioneering. But although the flexible socialism of the ILP was ideal for this purpose, many of the older trade union leaders were still firmly wedded to the Liberal–Labour alliance and opposed socialism. They were content to be the 'tail of the great Liberal Party', as Engels had described the working class in 1881. Thus many ILP parliamentary candidates found a hostile reception awaiting them in strong trade union areas. By 1899 attitudes had changed enough for a resolution at the Trades Union Congress to be passed which instructed its Parliamentary Committee to invite the cooperation of all working-class organizations to 'devise ways and means for the securing of an increased number of Labour members to the next Parliament'. Though few of those who voted for the resolution anticipated its consequences, and many expected little in the way of action, a committee composed of representatives of the TUC, SDF, FS and the ILP convened a conference for February 1900 which elected a Labour Representation Committee (LRC) with an affiliated membership of nearly 400,000. The 'tail' was gradually being sawn off and was soon to eat its body.

Even so, as Cole pointed out, 'it was still a long way off constituting a party'.[11] There was no central fund for fighting elections nor even a programme on which to fight them. The demand that parliamentary candidates should undergo a political test was rejected; the sole objective of the LRC was to get Labour members into parliament. A programme could wait. All that the LRC could manage in the way of a programme was a declaration of its willingness to 'co-operate with any party which, for the time being, may be engaged in promoting legislation in the direct interest of Labour'. Indeed, many of the members of the LRC were Liberals and a few were Tories. What came to the aid of the LRC was the more militant opposition of employers to trade unionism and a series of court cases that shattered the rights trade unionists believed that they enjoyed. Thus in 1903, after the Taff Vale decision, its membership rose to over 800,000, though the SDF had left in 1901. In 1903 the 'party' emphasized its separation from the other parties. Nevertheless, from 1900 to 1906 the fortunes of the LRC and the Liberal Party were so intertwined that, as Philip Poirier remarked, the history of the LRC is a 'case study in political opportunism'.[12] In 1906, for example, when it changed its name to the Labour Party, only twenty-nine of its fifty candidates were successful and then due largely to the pact between Ramsay MacDonald and the Liberal Chief

11. G. D. H. Cole, *History of Socialist Thought*, Vol. III, Part 1, p. 187.
12. Philip Poirier, *The Advent of the Labour Party*, Preface.

Whip as to the seats that the party would fight. The party was more successful in the 1910 election, returning forty M Ps; but this too was largely due to the adherence of the miners' M Ps who had formerly sat as Liberals.

Socialism for the Labour Party was not a matter of real debate. Indeed, it was deliberately kept in the background for fear of alienating the trade unions. Not until 1908 did the party adopt some semblance of a socialist policy when it expressed the opinion that the time had arrived for the party to have as a definite objective 'the socialization of the means of production, distribution and exchange'. This was, however, no more than an opinion and MacDonald, its leader after 1911, still wanted accommodation with the Liberals. Nor was class war important. The class war, MacDonald wrote in *Socialism and Society* (6th edition, 1908) was 'both inaccurate as to the facts it assumes and misleading as a guide to action'. Moreover, he went on:

Socialism marks the growth of a society not the uprising of a class. The consciousness which it seeks to quicken is not one of economic class solidarity, but one of social unity and growth towards organic wholeness. The watchword of Socialism, therefore, is not class consciousness but community consciousness.

The Labour Party was in its theory and practice what the German SPD had become in its everyday politics: a party of social reform emphasizing immediate demands. The only fixed principle that kept the party together was the desire to increase the number of working-class representatives in parliament. This, too, proved to be difficult. The independence of the party was hard to preserve in a parliament in which the Liberal government was introducing reforms like the Trades Dispute Act (1906), Old Age Pensions Act (1908), National Insurance Act (1911) and the Trade Union Act (1913). The Labour Party, as Henry Pelling has observed, had 'either to support the Liberal policy or risk criticism as opponents of practicable reform'.[13] It chose to sup-

13. Henry Pelling, *A Short History of the Labour Party*, p. 19.

port the Liberals and in so doing gave fuel to light more brightly the growing criticism of the increasing syndicalist movement. Syndicalism and industrial unrest attracted the main attention of the party in the years immediately preceding the outbreak of the First World War – the period that has been described as one of 'labour unrest'.

Although British socialists did not distinguish themselves at international socialist conferences and included supporters of the Boer War like Bernard Shaw in their ranks, they were, in the main, disposed towards disarmament and the Labour Party protested in 1912 against what it called the anti-German policy of Sir Edward Grey, the Foreign Secretary. When the party had to decide its attitude to the vote on war credits, MacDonald urged neutrality and resigned from the chairmanship of the parliamentary Labour Party when the party refused to make a pronouncement. When Germany invaded Belgium, Arthur Henderson and the majority of the party supported the government, while the ILP sent 'sympathy and greetings to the German socialists'. Thereafter most of the members of the parliamentary Labour Party rallied round the flag. The Labour Party and the TUC called for an industrial truce and Henderson, the new leader of the party, entered the War Cabinet in 1916. Only MacDonald and his ILP colleagues propagandized against the war, aligning themselves with the Liberals in the Union of Democratic Control which demanded the democratic control of foreign policy and an international organization to encourage and maintain peace and disarmament.

(b) France – the Possibilists, Independent Socialists and the Unified Party

In France reformist socialism was represented by the Possibilists, or 'opportunists' as the Guesdists called them, led by Paul Brousse, a former anarchist who had evolved a gradualist theory of socialism on lines similar to those of the Fabians in England. Like Guesde and the Marxists, however, he believed in the existence of class war and advocated the collective ownership of the factors of production. But, in opposition to the Guesdists, he promoted a policy of working for immediate reforms. 'I prefer', he said, 'to abandon the principle of all or nothing which generally leads to nothing at all, and to split our demands into what is possible.' Socialists should not wait for the workers' state to take over industry but should, through the municipalities, take them over when they became ripe for socialization. Thus he stressed the important role which the trade unions could play in obtaining reform rather than treating them as mere schools for socialists, urged the importance of local municipal politics and conceived of a national party built up from local foundations. Because, no doubt, of his anarchist past, he strongly opposed the centralizing tendencies of the Guesdists.

Thus in 1882 a split occurred in the Fédération des Ouvriers Socialistes de France with Brousse retaining control of the organization but changing its name to the Parti Ouvrier Socialiste Révolutionnaire. The Guesdists, according to Brousse, were domineering and authoritarian. Yet the Possibilists were also afflicted by dissensions. As the party, in which various strands of opinion were allowed to exist, moved towards a more gradualist and reformist policy, so the left wing under the leadership of Jean Allemane developed a policy of direct trade union action, the repudiation of parliamentary action and alliances with the bourgeoisie. Nonetheless, Allemane was elected to the Chamber of Deputies in 1902. The Allemanists broke away from the Possibilists in 1890 and formed the Parti Ouvrier Socialiste Révolutionnaire – the Possibilists by then having dropped the last word from their title.

In addition to the reformists led by Brousse, there were the Independent Socialists grouped around Bénoît Malon and his journal *Revue Socialiste*. Malon had helped Guesde found the Parti Ouvrier but left to form the Société pour l'Économie Sociale in 1885 as a research organization on lines similar to those of the Fabian Society. A believer in evolutionary socialism, though a former revolutionary and half-Marxist, he believed that socialism could only be achieved by a broad movement of the whole of society, not by a class or party. He thus attempted to create a circle of socialist economists and philosophers independent of the political parties. Adherence to socialist principles was expected but so also was freedom of political action and thought. Though never large, his group included Alexandre Millerand, Clovis Hugues, René Viviani and Jean Jaurès among its professional middle-class supporters. As with the Fabian Society, the Independent Socialists put forward specific proposals for the gradual socialization of industry, the protection of labour and advocated anti-colonialist measures and were strong supporters and defenders of liberty. Unlike the Fabians, they acted more as a loose parliamentary group than an extra-parliamentary organ.

By 1896 there were six national socialist parties in France, all competing for the allegiance of a working class smaller than that of Britain or Germany. Even by 1911 there were only one million organized workers compared with the three million of Britain and Germany. The parties did, however, often reach agreement on electoral tactics and at least refrained from opposing each other in the run-off elections. As a result they had a considerable success in the municipal elections in 1896.

It was at a banquet to celebrate these victories that Millerand attempted to define a minimum common programme to which all socialists could subscribe. The Saint-Mandé Programme, as it came to be called, was (as such things inevitably are) extremely vague and ambiguous. All socialists could subscribe to it without troubling themselves as to what socialism meant. Millerand proclaimed that no one was a socialist who did not accept the necessary and progressive substitution of social property for capitalist property, and the objective of socialism as an increase in liberty and diffusion of property. Millerand saw the socialization of industry developing out of capitalist monopoly as industries became ripe; there was no need to wait for a complete workers' victory. Essential services would gradually be taken over and, like the Fabians, he stressed the importance of the municipalities in this process. Also like them he put his faith in universal suffrage and the use of the vote by the workers for socialist ends. He emphasized the gradual and constitutional means by which socialism would be introduced and declared himself to be at once an internationalist and a patriot. Later, in *Le Socialisme reformiste français* (1903) he argued that socialists should form alliances with the bourgeoisie to win elections and implement reforms, should work within the Republic and democracy, and advance to socialism by piecemeal legislation. This openly reformist doctrine was also allied to his liberal idea that there should be collaboration in industry between the workers and owners rather than conflict, the arbitration of disputes rather than strikes.

In the euphoria of electoral success, the parties entered into loose alliances and were aided in this by the Dreyfus affair which they saw as a threat to the Republic. The Dreyfus affair led to the formation by the socialist parties of a Joint Vigilance Committee to defend the Republic in 1898. But before the dust of the affair had settled, Millerand accepted office in the Waldeck-Rousseau ministry. He defended his action as being necessary to save the Republic, though he had not consulted the Joint Vigilance Committee or the Independent Socialists. Defended by Jaurès and his fellow Independent Socialists, he was denounced by the Guesdists and Blanquists. His action caused a great stir in international socialist quarters but Millerand was not expelled from the socialist group until 1904. He went on to become one of the most reactionary Presidents of the Republic.

Millerand's action in accepting office in a bourgeois government, and one moreover that included General de Gallifet, responsible for the suppression of the Paris Commune, led to a realignment of the socialist parties with the

Independent Socialists, Broussists and Allemanists forming the Parti Socialiste Français, which supported the Waldeck-Rousseau ministry, and the Guesdists forming the Parti Socialiste de France. The former were, however, stronger in the Chamber of Deputies in 1902, with thirty-two seats compared to the twelve of the latter.

The two main parties joined forces in 1905, forming the Parti Socialiste Unifié – Section Française de l'Internationale Ouvrière (SFIO), on the basis that whilst the party would pursue reforms, it would be a party of class war and revolution – 'While pursuing reforms the socialist party is not a party of reform but of class war and revolution' – and would refuse to support governments which prolonged the bourgeois order – 'The deputies must refuse the government any support which would prolong bourgeois domination.' In fact the party became more reform-orientated, declared itself to be reformist in 1908 and participated in electoral alliances with the radicals from 1905 onwards. Although organizational unity was achieved, there was little in the way of a common policy. Indeed, it would have been surprising if one had existed, given that the unified party included an extreme republican Right, an extreme Left led by Gustave Hervé, and such politically incompatible figures as Guesde, Vaillant and Jaurès. Nonetheless, unity proved successful in electoral terms. The number of deputies increased to fifty-four in 1906 and seventy-five in 1910. In the latter year, however, the extreme Right broke away to form the Parti Républicain Socialiste, which declared itself to be resolutely and exclusively reformist. While it had thirty-five deputies in the Chamber, including Briand, Millerand, and Viviani who were often in ministries, it had little organizational strength in the country.

Jaurès was the leader of the unified party, its most outstanding figure and of great influence in international socialist counsels. It was only his adept political 'opportunism' that kept together the diverse elements that made up the party. As Molotov said of Harold Macmillan, Jaurès was always making compromises, and they were always good

ones. Given the nature of French socialism and the circumstances in which Jaurès had to operate, good compromises
were necessary if there was to be any common action by the
socialists. And although he used Marxist phraseology and
defended the theory of surplus value against Bernstein he,
like Bernstein, placed great stress on the ethical aspect of
socialism and on democracy, though he was not averse to the
use of illegal means when necessary. Like the Fabians he
saw collectivization as the natural consequence of radical
reform. Like the agrarian theorists in the German party he
did not want to lose peasant support by a rigid adherence to
Marxist orthodoxy. He did not envisage the disappearance
of the peasants but saw them existing alongside cooperatives,
and he advocated measures for alleviating their position.

From 1905 to the outbreak of war it was Jaurès, the
moderate and former independent socialist, who was most
active in the efforts to prevent war by all means, from parliamentary activity and public demonstrations to a general
strike and insurrection. In this respect he was to the left of
Guesde who would do no more than recommend a refusal
to vote war credits and who now argued, in spite of what
Marx had taught, that the workers had a fatherland and
ought, therefore, to be prepared to defend it. Guesde became a minister in the War Coalition. The line taken by
Jaurès and Vaillant was endorsed by the SFIO and Jaurès
elaborated his anti-war policy in *L'Armée nouvelle* (1910).
In this he argued for the replacement of conscript armies by
citizens' armies which could, if necessary, be used against
a government, especially a militaristic one. The line taken
by Jaurès was not so much antipatriotic as anti-colonist and
anti-militarist, but his proposal for a citizens' army was
somewhat naïve in view of the increasing professionalism of
armies.

Jaurès was still actively attempting to obtain the international cooperation of socialists to prevent the outbreak of
a European war when he was assassinated in 1914. Soon the
SFIO with its 103 deputies went over to support the
government and the war.

(c) The United States and the American Socialist Party

In the United States a group led by Morris Hillquit and Henry Slobodin left the Socialist Labour Party (SLP) in 1899 and formed an organization which, with Eugene Debs's Social Democracy and other groups – 'little weeds' according to Daniel de Leon – developed into the American Socialist Party (ASP) in 1901. The ASP had more in common than had the SLP with the European socialist parties and included the collectivists of Wisconsin, progressive trade unionists and middle-class Marxist theorists like Hillquit. After 1901 it became the only representative in the United States of parliamentary social democracy.

The strongest section of the party, the Wisconsin socialists, were, as Cole pointed out, of the opinion that the USA was democratic and needed only the electorate to be educated in socialism for a mass socialist party to capture the state and introduce reforms and socialization.[14] They were state socialists but were prepared to temper their language and adopt popular proposals so as to attract support, but they were not prepared to work with progressives.

Like its European counterparts, the ASP grew into a nationwide electoral machine while the SLP increasingly turned away from parliamentary politics. Yet the ASP could hardly compare with the European parties in terms of electoral success. It never elected more than one representative, Victor Berger, to Congress but it did obtain representation in the Assemblies of some states and controlled Milwaukee and Wisconsin. In the Presidential elections of 1900 Debs received 100,000 votes; in 1904 400,000; a few more in 1908 and 900,000 in 1912 when he ran with Emil Seidel, the socialist mayor of Milwaukee. Debs preached a militant class-struggle form of socialism and was always on the left of the party. Though its most influential leader and spokesman, he took little part in factional fights or policy discussions. He could not, therefore, prevent the slow drift of the party to the Right, its domination by

14. G. D. H. Cole, op. cit., Vol. III, Part 2, p. 805.

middle-class intellectuals and its transformation, mainly under the influence of the Milwaukee 'sewer socialists', into a party of reform. Debs, as Lord Birkenhead said of Austen Chamberlain, always played the game, and always lost. And the same could be said of the ASP.

Right up to 1912 the party refused to ally itself with other parties and was incessantly attacked by the SLP and the American Federation of Labor (A F of L), though there was always a significant socialist minority in the latter. There were talks of unity between the ASP and the SLP prompted by the Second International, but de Leon never regarded it with favour and the leaders of the ASP were as reluctant to face de Leon 'as could possibly a fallen angel have been expected to face the Lord of Hosts'.[15] 1912 represented the peak of its strength, with newspapers and organizations in nearly every state, but it lost almost as many members and supporters after that date as it had gained before. At the outbreak of the war in Europe, the party urged US neutrality and in a presidential campaign in 1916, based on opposition to the war and militarism, it obtained thirty per cent fewer votes than it had received in 1912. When the United States entered the war the party declared its opposition and called upon the 'workers of countries to refuse to support their governments in their wars'. It advocated opposition to all military legislation and supported demonstrations and petitions. As a consequence of this attitude the party was prosecuted, its press suppressed and Debs imprisoned.

The reasons for the 'failure' of American socialism have been much debated and remain obscure. Amongst them was undoubtedly the hostility of the Catholic Church, which weeded out the Irish who were the mainstay of the unions. The lack of trade union support was also no doubt due to the fact that the workers were more interested in their economic struggles with their employers than in overthrowing a state which was, in any case, democratic. The

15. Henry Kuhn and Olive M. Johnson, *The Socialist Labor Party During Four Decades*, p 85.

government, as Cole put it, 'was not so much an enemy to be fought as an orange to be squeezed'.[16] The changing social structure of American society also played a part. Egalitarianism was, as Count Keyserling observed, a surrogate for socialism. Moreover, the lack of working-class homogeneity due to the influx of immigrants and the existence of the Negro inhibited united working-class political action and the unions, especially as represented by the A F of L, reflected the narrow and exclusive concern with the interests of a group rather than political action for a class. Indeed, like good trade unionists they sold their votes for political favours. Besides this there was the bickering between the ASP and the SLP and the hostility of Gompers who could tell the socialists: 'Economically, you are unsound; socially you are wrong; industrially, you are an impossibility.'

A further difficulty in the way of an increase in socialist strength was the refusal of the parties to compromise and traffick with the capitalist parties. Their national programme of 1904 declared:

The Socialist programme is not a theory imposed upon society for its acceptance or rejection. It is but the interpretation of what is, sooner or later, inevitable. Capitalism is already struggling to its destruction.

And, as Bell comments, the socialist party and Debs waited.[17] He might have added that they waited in vain.

The American socialist movement was, as Max Beer commented, 'a hole-and-corner affair of mixed Eastern immigrants – Jews, Germans, Slavs and Finns – with an infinitesimal proportion of American-born intellectuals'.[18] American socialism was and remains largely an imported doctrine dominated by the ideas of Fourier and Owen in the first half of the nineteenth century and varieties of Marxism and French syndicalism in the second half and the first decade of the twentieth century. The Americans never produced a

16. G. D. H. Cole, op. cit., Vol. III, Part 2, p. 814.
17. Daniel Bell, *The End of Ideology: On the Exhaustion of Political Ideas in the Fifties*, p. 285.
18. Max Beer, *Fifty Years of International Socialism*, p. 109.

socialist theorist of any significance. Henry George was never really a socialist, Edward Bellamy, the author of *Looking Backward* (1887) – called by William Morris a 'horrible cockney dream' – no more than a popularizer of other men's ideas and Eugene Debs an organizer and leader rather than a theorist. The best critique of American capitalism was Thorstein Veblen's *Theory of the Leisure Class* (1899), but he was no socialist and had no programme. The ASP did, however, attract numerous 'sentimental middle-class socialists' to its cause and their books, like Frank Norris's *The Octopus* (1901), Upton Sinclair's *The Jungle* (1906) and Jack London's *The Iron Head* (1907), probably did more to improve working-class conditions than all the agitation of the ASP.

Reformist socialist parties were also established successfully in other parts of the world. In Scandinavia and Australia, indeed, they were far more successful than in the United States. In Scandinavia parties were established in Denmark (1879), Norway (1887) and Sweden (1889). Their original programmes, however, were adaptations of the programmes of the German social democrats and had strong Marxist overtones. Yet they did not seek or advocate an immediate violent revolution but rather saw their political, social and economic objectives, once achieved, as bringing about a complete remodelling of society. In practice, they soon became increasingly reformist, mainly because they were not persecuted by the state, found access to parliament comparatively easy and, once there, found the social aims of the liberals ones that they could share and help to achieve. Thus socialism, for them, as for the Fabians and Millerand at the time of the Saint-Mandé Programme, meant a gradual evolution of the tendencies always at work in capitalism. They all supported progressive legislation. By 1915 the Swedish party had become the largest in the Lower House, and the Danish party joined the Radical cabinet in 1916.

Perhaps more remarkable was the growth of the moderate Australian Labour Party. While the Marxist and reformist parties in Europe and America were collecting votes, the Australian Labour Party was forming a government. In 1891 the Labour Electoral League obtained one third of the seats in the New South Wales state legislature and obtained a quarter of the seats in the first federal parliament in 1901, when the Labour Party was formed. Three years later the party formed the government, for a short period another minority government in 1908 and, with Andrew Fisher as Prime Minister, a majority government in 1910. Like the British Labour Party, the ALP drew its main strength and support from the unions, emphasized reforms designed to improve working conditions and put forward measures for social reform. It was also, unlike the British Labour Party, nationalistic. It advocated the raising of tariffs to protect wages, the restriction of coloured immigration to protect white employment and racial purity, the introduction of military service and the creation of a navy. With policies like these it is not surprising that it attracted many diverse elements into the party and could count on the support of a wider cross-section of the electorate than the more distinctively socialist parties of Europe. Indeed, socialism was less important to them and kept even more in the background in the programme of the Australian Labour Party than it was in the British Labour Party.

(d) The Second International

With the growth of the socialist parties in the 1880s it was not surprising that they should attempt, once again, to form an International. The Germans, the British trade unionists and the French Possibilists decided, almost simultaneously, in 1887 to launch a new International. Typically, the British thought in terms of an international conference to urge claims for the eight-hour day, while the Germans wanted an international socialist congress. After a dispute as to who should call the congress, the French Possibilists and Guesdists both organized congresses which opened on 14 July

1889, the hundredth anniversary of the storming of the Bastille. Incongruously, Hyndman attended the Possibilist congress and William Morris the Marxist, but delegates drifted from one to the other, and the anarchists disrupted both. Of the two, the Marxist congress was the most representative of the organized socialist parties. The French and Germans dominated the proceedings and Édouard Vaillant and Wilhelm Liebknecht were elected joint presidents.

Resolutions were passed at the Marxist congress calling for the eight-hour day and improved working conditions, condemning the existence of permanent armies, and calling for national defence to be undertaken by the people in arms. Resolutions also laid down that socialists should work for universal suffrage, participate in elections and use the first day in May as an occasion for a demonstration of the international solidarity of the working class. This last resolution was, however, interpreted in vastly different ways. The French and Austrians interpreted it to mean a complete stoppage of work, the Germans as an occasion for evening meetings and the British for a procession and picnic on the first Sunday in May.

The subject of the May Day demonstration, and the associated question of the political general strike, was also debated at the United Brussels Congress in 1891 and at Zurich in 1893, but in practice each country went its own way. It was, as James Joll comments, a 'depressing augury for the future of co-ordinated international socialist action';[19] this was especially so as the May Day strike had in 1891 been linked to the maintenance of international peace. But then the Zurich Congress had rejected a motion calling for a general strike in the event of war.

The other congresses of the 1890s added little to the development of socialist theory. They did serve to emphasize the 'respectability' of the socialists and the emphasis they placed on constitutional political action. The fanatical bearded quack image of the socialist was being eradicated and the socialist leaders looked as if they were ready to be

19. James Joll, *The Second International 1889–1914*, p. 54.

received into the drawing-rooms of the Establishment, albeit as quaint curiosities. The French and the Germans brought their internal disputes before the International; the French in 1900 to have the Millerand affair papered over by a motion of Kautsky's allowing the participation of socialists in bourgeois governments as an exceptional measure, and the Germans in 1904 with the revisionist heresy all wrapped up for condemnation.

After 1904 the International, in common with its separate parties, became preoccupied by the question of the attitude that socialists should adopt in the event of war. The instructions laid down by Marx were explicit enough. The fact that the International had still to strike an attitude was indicative of its fidelity to Marxism, or perhaps, more correctly, nationalism. In 1907 Gustave Hervé proposed that a declaration of war be met by revolt and a general strike, but Guesde preferred to put his faith in a socialist victory at the polls which would make the issue irrelevant, or so he believed. The Germans reiterated their panacea of the abolition of standing armies and announced their pious intention to do all in their power to prevent war. Jaurès and Vaillant, on the other hand, advocated a people's army and, while asserting that a nation had a right to defend itself, advocated the use of strikes and insurrection. Rosa Luxemburg, 'one of the last two men remaining in the German Social Democratic Party', as she called herself, went further. For her, strikes and insurrection should not be regarded merely as the way to prevent war but also as the way to overthrow capitalism. But the Germans, whatever the protestations to the contrary, had a vested interest in the maintenance of their electoral machine, and refused to be committed to any specific form of action. And as they were powerful, influential and, so it was believed, true Marxists, a compromise was reached. The International contented itself with a call for a decrease in armaments, the abolition of standing armies and action by socialists to prevent war.

When war came, not only were the socialists unable to prevent it, but many were undecided as to whether or not it ought to be prevented. Discussions between French and German socialists proved inconclusive. The German Social Democrats were eventually to vote for the war credits, only fourteen of the 110 members of the party in the Reichstag distinguishing themselves by voting against in the pre-liminary party meeting. Only the radicals, led by Luxemburg and Liebknecht, were to be found consistently oppos-ing the war, though they were later joined by Bernstein and Kautsky. The Germans rallied to the defence of Ger-many against Russia, the French to protect themselves against Germany and them all from each other. Of the social democratic parties of Europe, only the inconsequen-tial Serbian and Russian parties voted against the war.

With the vote of the social democratic parties for the war budgets of their respective countries, the International fell. The social democratic leaders joined their respective gov-ernments, even Hyndman offering his services as a spy, and their followers, with some notable, heroic and futile ex-ceptions, fought for their countries. As C. Wright Mills put it, 'In so far as they were composed of working classes, they killed off one another.'[20] Socialism, let alone revolutionary ardour and internationalism, was replaced by blind patriot-ism. The only thing they had succeeded in nationalizing was socialism.

Even so, the International did have some value. It was an international force for the spread of socialist ideas and managed to bring about the unification of the French parties. Nevertheless, Sidney Hook must be given the last word. In discussing the costs of revolution he wrote:

If the Second International had been true to its pledged faith in 1914 and had been organised for social revolution, it is unlikely that the costs would have come as high – to mention only the most conspicuous item – as twenty-five millions of dead and wounded.[21]

20. C. Wright Mills, *The Marxists*, London, 1963, p. 135.
21. Sidney Hook, *Towards An Understanding of Karl Marx*, Lon-don, 1933, p. 240.

6

THE ANARCHIST CHALLENGE TO SOCIALIST ORTHODOXY

Throughout the period from the beginning of the First International to the outbreak of the First World War, the social democrats, whether Marxist or explicitly reformist, were constantly harrassed and frequently embarrassed by the activities of the anarchists. Until the Russian Revolution the anarchists represented the most important challenge to the predominance and smug complacency of the social democrats who were content to continue to amass members and votes and wait, in Andrew Sinclair's phrase in another context, for 'the red flag at the end of the rainbow'. Until the advent of Lenin they were the only real revolutionaries. More important, they specifically rejected any attempt to work through political institutions to achieve their aims, renounced political parties and competed with the social democratic parties for their members. In France, where anarchism took the form of syndicalism, they were particularly successful in weaning the working class from the socialist parties, though they had successes elsewhere. In many countries the anarchists were more influential and popular than the orthodox Marxists and were often responsible for the failure of effective social democratic parties to develop.

The anarchists we are concerned with are not the individualist anarchists like Max Stirner or Benjamin Tucker, but the collectivist anarchists who believed in collectivities and associations and whose doctrines represented the most fundamental criticism of the state.

(a) Kropotkin

After the death of Bakunin Prince Peter Kropotkin became the leading international anarchist theorist, personality and advocate of anarcho-communism. It was Kropotkin who made anarchism semi-respectable, which was no good thing. It became the ideological dress, for a season, of the frequenters of polite London drawing-rooms. Certainly Kropotkin eliminated the colourful, violent and revolutionary image of anarchists created by Bakunin and replaced it with a doctrine that was a clear, reasoned and plausible alternative to capitalist society. Utopian it no doubt was, but it also pointed out the deficiencies of modern society. Like Rousseau, Kropotkin did not solve the problems thrown up by modern industrial society, but he did awaken an awareness of their existence.

Bakunin was primarily a conspirator and agitator. Kropotkin was pre-eminently a philosopher and prophet. Unlike Bakunin he was not possessed of a destructive urge. Rather, as George Woodcock wrote, 'it was the positive, constructive aspect of anarchism, the crystal vision of an earthly paradise regained, that appealed to him, and to its elaboration he brought a scientific training and invincible optimism'.[1]

A close friend of Élisée Reclus, with whom he founded *Le Révolte* in 1879, he had joined the Bakuninist section of the First International, worked with Jules Guesde in Paris and had been profoundly influenced by the idyllic life of the Jura Swiss. It was his experience among them, he tells us, that made him an anarchist.

The basis of Kropotkin's philosophy, like that of John Locke, was the belief that society was natural to man and, in addition, that men lived best in small face-to-face groups. These, he believed, developed man's propensities to mutual aid and democracy. To Kropotkin it was a law of nature that men cooperated. He repudiated the theories of competition and struggle as the way in which men had and would develop and he asserted instead that primitive

1. George Woodcock, *Anarchism*, p. 172.

societies furnished numerous examples of man's instinct to cooperate and of his innate sociability. In his view man's basic virtues had been corrupted by the institutions of society, by capricious capitalists *à la* Hobbes, and by an apathetic people willing to give power to governments. *Mutual Aid* (1902²) was an attempt to show that, contrary to the Darwinian theory of evolution, those societies that survived were those that had been the most cooperative.

Thus the society he imagined, worked for and advocated in pamphlets like *The Conquest of Bread* (1892³), *Fields, Factories and Workshops* (1898), and most important of all *Mutual Aid*, was to be based on a foundation of self-organizing and -governing communities. Only in this way could man's better instincts be encouraged and a new morality created. Like Bernstein, though for different reasons, he denied the validity of Marx's prediction of the increasing concentration of capital and argued that small businesses were always springing up. To Kropotkin small businesses were both happy and economic, and provided the variety and choice of occupation he believed, along with Marx, to be necessary for a full life. Like Marx, he did not share William Morris's distaste for, and pessimism about, the introduction of machinery but saw it as a means of ending the drudgery of work. He believed, however, that scientists would only use their ability to decrease the burden of work if they had experience of manual labour. He avoided the difficulty that Marx, his followers and successors had in trying to fit the peasants into their political theory by advocating a combination of agricultural and industrial enterprises.

Kropotkin was the advocate of anarcho-communism. In elaborating his theory of society he, in common with other anarchists and socialists, started from the premise that the heritage of humanity is collective and must, therefore, be enjoyed collectively. Private property was to be abolished as it had created inequalities, class distinctions and antagon-

2. London, 1972.
3. London, 1972.

isms and a selfish morality. He proclaimed the slogan of 'Prosperity for all as an end, expropriation as a means'. The task of the social reformer was thus destructive. He had to destroy the existing system of property and the coercive power of the state; the state because it was

a society of mutual insurance between the landlord, the military commander, the judge, the priest, and later on the capitalists, in order to support each other's authority over the people, and for exploiting the poverty of the masses and getting rich themselves.

With the accomplishing of the destruction of the state, Kropotkin, like Bakunin, believed that man's natural impulses would lead them to construct a new, more natural society lacking in coercive instruments. As with Bakunin and Marx, he believed that revolution would be necessary to eliminate the existing state. But though at first he advocated violent means and was prepared to sanction the activities of the propagandists by deed, in his later years he became more genteel, as befitted his stature in respectable society, and he stressed the evolutionary aspects of social change. By the 1890s, for instance, he could assert that anarchism could be achieved 'by the ripening of public opinion and with the least possible amount of disturbance'. He was fortified in this belief by what he considered to be a growing trend of voluntary organizations gradually taking over the administrative functions of the state. In fact, the opposite appears to have happened with the state gradually assuming responsibility for functions formerly provided by voluntary associations.

Though revolution was the short-term objective, it was not to end in the establishment of a revolutionary government. To Kropotkin this was a contradiction in terms. The aim of the revolution was to abolish government. When this had been achieved, the powers of the government would initially be vested in the commune, a local voluntary association uniting all social interests and representing the groups of individuals directly concerned with them. The commune would gradually extend itself and establish social and economic relations with other communes so that a new social structure would emerge replacing the coercive apparatus of the state with cooperation. In the commune goods and services would be freely available to all who needed them. The wage system would be abolished and the only incentive to work would be the consciousness of useful achievement. For Kropotkin,

Common possession of the necessaries of production implies the common enjoyment of the fruits of common production; and we consider that an equitable organisation of society can only arise when every wage-system is abandoned and when everybody contributing to the common well-being to the full extent of his capacities, shall enjoy from the common stock of society to the fullest possible extent of his needs.

It is this notion of distribution that distinguishes Kropotkin from Proudhon and Bakunin, and makes him an anarcho-communist. It was, of course, a principle of distribution that went back at least as far as Sir Thomas More and Gerrard Winstanley. Kropotkin believed that the trend towards his ideal society could be discerned in the fact that water, libraries, museums and the like were free and used according to need.

Like Bakunin, however, he allowed a role for public opinion in forcing the recalcitrant, whom we today call the work-shy, to work. It is perhaps strange that those who strut proudly under the banner of liberty should, in the end, allow the individual to be regulated by the capricious and arbitrary opinion of a 'public', the potential tyranny of which was so well demonstrated in John Stuart Mill's *Essay On Liberty*. But this apart, as Camille Pissarro wrote, Kropotkin's ideal society, even 'if it is utopian, it is in any case a very beautiful dream'.

(b) Revolutionary Syndicalism

In France the energies and intellectual activities of the anarchists were absorbed in the syndicalist movement which, under the leadership of Fernand Pelloutier, became an influential and powerful movement controlling the Confédération Générale du Travail between 1902 and 1914. Syndicalism brought anarchism back from the effete middle class to the working class and revolution. No one bothered to tell them, however, that it was the middle class, not the working class, that was prepared to storm the barricades. It also meant that for the first time the working class became self-sufficient in its ideology and practice. As with the other anarchist theories, syndicalism, or revolutionary syndicalism as it is more correctly called, was more of a rejection of existing organizations and ideas than the formulation of constructive and coherent proposals for a future society.

Revolutionary syndicalism was a spontaneous creation of the French trade unions. For this reason it is more a theory implicit in the practice of the French unions than a philosophy handed down by some armchair theorist (though George Sorel attempted to perform this role). Had it been the creation of a single theorist, then it might not have suffered from the ambiguities and discrepancies that it did – though this, admittedly, is no guarantee. Be that as it may, the theory of syndicalism has to be found in the conference reports and pamphlets of the trade unions and the debates and speeches of its leaders. 'There is', F. F. Ridley has observed, 'no shelf of books to serve as a basis of study',[4] though he has now provided a lucid account of the emergence and principles of the doctrine.[5]

The syndicalists accepted the Marxian notion of class war but did not bother themselves with its economic or philosophical proof. For them its existence was manifested by the daily battles between employers and workers. As Levine wrote, 'The class struggle was a fact, not a theory in need of proof; a fact manifested every day in the relations

4. F. F. Ridley, 'Revolutionary Syndicalism in France: The General Strike as Theory and Myth', *International Review of History and Political Science*, Vol. III, No. 2, December 1966, p. 17.

5. F. F. Ridley, *Revolutionary Syndicalism in France: The Direct Action of its Time.*

between employers and wage earners; a fact inherent in the economic organization of existing society.'[6] In common with Marx, they accepted that no reforms of the system could eradicate the exploitation of the workers. At best they would be palliatives dulling working-class consciousness. Exploitation could only be diminished by the destruction of the state and with it the existing economic, social and political system. Yet, whereas the Marxists were prepared to accept the help of the bourgeoisie (indeed most of them came from it), the syndicalists rejected the bourgeoisie. With Marx they saw the state as an instrument for the domination and exploitation of one class by another. They differed from Marx in not regarding the dictatorship of the proletariat as a state different from any other.

The syndicalists had exhibited a profound distaste for bourgeois intellectual sympathizers, those who came to the aid of the working class with their hearts on their sleeves and overdrafts at the bank. They believed that the bourgeoisie could have no more than a passing interest in working-class problems, fraternized with the reactionary middle class, were easily seduced by the aristocratic embrace and soon betrayed socialism. There was nothing new in this fear or distaste of intellectuals. In 1899 Waclaw Machajck, in his *Evolution of Social Democracy*, had anticipated James Burnham and Milovan Djilas in arguing that the discontented intellectuals were in embryo the new ruling class of a socialist society and, therefore, the new exploiters of the workers. Perceptive as they undoubtedly were in this, the syndicalists were insistent on retaining the working-class leadership of their movement and the virginity of their proletarian morality and values. As Sorel wrote, 'all our efforts should aim at preventing bourgeois ideas from poisoning the rising class'. To him the class war was not merely an economic war, it was also one between two opposed civilizations.

Political action, too, was rejected as an avenue of working-class emancipation. 'The aim of the syndicates', Émile

6. L. Levine, *The Labor Movement in France*, 1912, p. 119.

Pouget wrote, 'is to make war on the bosses and not to bother with politics.' To the syndicalists the working class was betrayed in parliament by the necessity for bargains and compromises to be made with the bourgeois parties. Bargains and compromises were, in any case, eschewed by Sorel in favour of action and irrationality. As early as 1888 a congress of syndicates meeting at Bordeaux had repudiated political action by the workers and called for direct action by means of the general strike. This was the beginning of the division between political and trade union action that was so characteristic of syndicalist doctrine. Socialists could not accept responsibility for governing the state if they were not also prepared to become its defenders. With William Godwin they could say, 'Electioneering is a trade so despicably degrading, so eternally incompatible with moral and mental dignity, that I can scarcely believe a truly great mind capable of the dirty drudgery of such vice.' And if politics and parliamentarianism were to be shunned, then so also were political parties. Political parties cut across class lines and were, as Lagardelle pointed out, heterogeneous, whereas a class was the product of history drawn together by economic interest and necessity rather than ideology. Political parties watered down their programme so as to attract votes and in doing so lost their class and revolutionary character. They were also, and perhaps this is what really rankled, dominated by bourgeois intellectuals. They had, of course, the evidence later presented in Robert Michel's *Political Parties* (1912) exposing the oligarchical nature of parties which made nonsense of party democracy. More dramatically, they had the example of Alexandre Millerand, Aristide Briand, once a powerful advocate of the use of the general strike, and René Viviani before them, as well as the Socialist Party's defence of the bourgeois republic during the Boulangist and Dreyfus affairs. Nor did the system of political democracy escape the condemnation of the syndicalists. It brought reforms, they knew, but they knew also that these dulled the workers' appetite for revolution, blurred class conflict and distracted the workers from the class war.

Yet, whilst they formally repudiated political action and proclaimed their political neutrality, they nevertheless pursued reformist ends, worked for concessions from the state, engaged in compromises and had, themselves, a political doctrine that contained both a critique of existing society and a vision of the future.

For the parliamentary game the syndicalists, at least in their words, substituted the policy of direct action. As the emancipation of the workers was not being accomplished by the 'democratic process' then it had to be accomplished by the workers themselves, though Sorel and Griffuelhes, sticking to the long-established socialist tradition of élitism, believed that they would need to be led by a 'conscious minority'. And the action they knew best and could use most effectively was industrial action. First, the unions would need to be organized on industrial lines. This would strengthen their fighting capability and increase their sense of solidarity and working-class revolutionary consciousness. Whereas industrial action had previously been used for reformist ends and as a complement to political action, it was now to be used for revolutionary economics and political objectives. A whole panoply of weapons were at the disposal of the workers – work-to-rule, go-slow, shoddy work, boycott – all subsumed under the category of sabotage. Given the nature of the capitalist system, sabotage was a good thing for, as G. D. H. Cole wrote, 'to do good work for a capitalist employer is merely ... to help the thief to steal more successfully'.[7]

Best of all was the strike weapon. It highlighted the conflict between the interests of the workers and employers. As Levine commented,

The strike brings the workingman face to face with the employers in a clash of interests. A strike clears up, as if by a flash of lightning, the deep antagonisms which exist between those who employ and those who work for employers. It further deepens the chasm between them, consolidating the employers

7. G. D. H. Cole, *Self-Government in Industry*, London, 1917, p. 235.

on the one hand, and the workingmen on the other, over against one another. It is a revolutionary fact of great value.[8]

Strikes had two main functions: to obtain concessions from, and therefore weaken, the capitalists and their system, and to develop working-class consciousness. Strikes educated the workers in the realities of capitalism, emphasized their solidarity and kept alive hopes for the revolution. The syndicalists envisaged a long series of strikes, each gradually weakening capitalism, increasing working-class revolutionary consciousness and culminating in the general strike which would overthrow capitalism.

Called 'general nonsense' by the Guesdists, the general strike meant different things to different people at different times. At one time it was conceived of as no more than a peaceful cessation of work. In its more extravagant form the workers and their families would go for a picnic in the Bois de Vincennes and there await the downfall of capitalism. Others realized the impracticability of this rosy dream and of the necessity for the workers to seize food supplies. From this it was an easy step to see the general strike as the beginning of insurrection. Some, however, thought that the general strike would break out spontaneously or would develop from a long succession of strikes. Others thought in terms of a general command issuing a proclamation for a general strike. Whatever they thought, to them all the 'general strike was the curtain that would go down on the old society and rise for the new'.[9]

There was not, of course, anything particularly original about the idea of a general strike. William Benbow in England had once thought of it as a Grand National Holiday and it had been almost incessantly debated in the early congresses of the Second International as a means, on American initiative, of securing the eight-hour day. What was original was that to Sorel and others it was no more than a myth, an expression of will with which to influence action and sustain

8. L. Levine, *Syndicalism in France*, London, 1911, pp. 126–7.
9. F. F. Ridley, *Revolutionary Syndicalism in France: The Direct Action of its Time*, p. 149.

hope. For Sorel, the idea of the general strike provided 'a body of images capable of evoking instinctively all the sentiments which correspond to the different manifestations of the war undertaken by socialism against modern society'. It was a commitment to action, it gave meaning and purpose to the daily, dull economic struggles of the workers. It was a way of affirming that revolution through the avenue of politics was discredited, that socialism would not be achieved by evolutionary means. As Daniel Bell wrote, it functioned as a 'bastardized version of the doctrine of salvation'.[10] A myth it remained. The general strikes of 1912 and 1914 were total failures. Indeed, it is arguable that the syndicalists were never really convinced of the desirability of the general strike. At least they seemed to spend more time talking about it than planning and organizing for it. It may well be, as Ridley has suggested, that their revolutionary élan was no more than a rationalization for their ineffectiveness in everyday politics. Certainly the occurrences of direct action were spasmodic, ill-prepared, and manifested more of a frustration with the system than an organized attempt to overthrow it.

Though sure in their own minds of their ultimate salvation, the syndicalists were singularly uncertain as to the structure of the new society. As with the anarchists in general, so also with the syndicalists; the future was something that would take care of itself. Yet they were more emphatic than most anarchists in insisting that the future should be left to the future. After all, their philosophy was supposedly one of action, not thought; the future society would be created by action not theorizing.

Nevertheless, there were some who were prepared to commit themselves to principles if not to details. It was argued that the trade unions, by encroaching on employers' prerogatives, would eventually take over industry and the state. The trade unions were both the instruments of revolution and the embryo of the new society. In the words of

10. Daniel Bell, *The End of Ideology: On the Exhaustion of Political Ideas in the Fifties*, p. 282.

99

the Charter of Amiens (1906) the trade unions 'will be in the future the group responsible for production and distribution, the foundation of the social organization'. Fernand Pelloutier had a clearer idea. He saw the future society as a federal grouping of producers, as did James Guillaume. Industries would be run and managed by the producers on behalf of its owners, the latter being the communes. Delegates from the various industries would make up the local commune and these would federate at a larger level of administration. Though this was to be workers' control in action many, like Malatesta and Emma Goldman, detected signs of a new bureaucracy arising and a consequent loss of individual autonomy. Malatesta, in particular, pointed to the difficulty of trying to reconcile the different interests of the workers and he feared that the trade unions would be a means whereby the stronger workers would coerce the weaker. By the time of the First World War, the syndicalists had come to accept the state. Trade union leaders had been invited into the corridors of power and, like most of those so invited, found them not at all distasteful.

Largely as a result of French influence the Confederación Nacional de Trabajo was established in Spain in 1911 and organized strikes all over Spain between 1917 and 1923. As has already been pointed out, large areas of Spain came under the control of the anarchists after the Franco rebellion in 1936. For once, anarchism seems to have been successful, for a time. Collectives were established in Aragon, Levant and Castile. In *The Tragedy of Spain* Rudolf Rocker quotes the Swiss socialist, Andres Oltmares, as saying that after the revolution the Catalonian workers' syndicates accomplished in seven weeks as much as France did in fourteen months of world war. He went on to say:

As a Social Democrat I speak here with inner joy and sincere admiration of my experience in Catalonia. The anticapitalist transformation took place here without their having to resort to a dictatorship. The members of the syndicates are their own masters, and carry on production and the distribution of the products of labour under their own management with the advice of technical experts in whom they have confidence. The enthusiasm of the workers is so great that they scorn any personal advantage and are concerned only for the welfare of all.[11]

They were, however, soon crushed by the communists and the fascists.

In the United States the Industrial Workers of the World (IWW), or Wobblies, was founded in 1905 mainly as a result of the opposition of the militant trade unionists to the reformist collective-bargain-orientated policy of the American Federation of Labor, but also to attempt to organize the non-union workers, create industrial unions and unite the working class in opposition to capitalism. As the first sentence of the preamble to its constitution announced: 'The working class and the employing class have nothing in common.' It advocated class war and the abolition of the wage system.

The main support for the IWW came from the Western Federation of Miners led by Bill Haywood, an advocate of direct industrial action and for whom 'industrial unionism is socialism with its working clothes on'. Both Eugene Debs and Daniel de Leon belonged for a time, though Debs resigned because of the IWW's lack of interest in political action and de Leon, who thought the trade unions should be an independent arm of the political movement, headed his own splinter group from 1908 on. Thus in 1908 there were two groups calling themselves the IWW. Even so, the group led by Haywood did not entirely repudiate political action, though they did accord it a lower priority than did de Leon.

Haywood wanted one big union encompassing all workers organized on a class basis and subject to central direction. This was to be the central planning agency of the new society. The centralized power of capitalism, he argued, had to be fought by a centrally organized working class. His faith lay in the unskilled worker:

11. Quoted in Noam Chomsky's *American Power and the New Mandarins*, London, 1969, p. 118.

I do not care a snap of my finger whether or not the skilled workers join the industrial movement at the present time. When we get the unorganised and the unskilled labourer into the organisation the skilled worker will of necessity come here for his own protection. As strange as it may seem to you, the skilled worker today is exploiting the labour beneath him, the unskilled man, just as much as the capitalist is.

In spite of the rivalry between the two groups, the hostility of the more orthodox trade unionists, the socialists, the employers, the state and its forces, and the periodic witch-hunts that were directed against them, they nevertheless led successful strikes in 1909 and 1912. By the beginning of 1914, however, they had both virtually disappeared as an industrial force.

Revolutionary unionism was not new to Britain. It had been advocated for a time in the 1830s. But the workers' control or syndicalist movement of the beginning of the twentieth century owed a great deal to the influence of the French and American movements, especially as interpreted by James Connolly and Tom Mann. Described by Max Beer as having 'a golden heart and mercurial brain',[12] Mann, like Haywood in the United States, and unlike the French syndicalists, accepted that political action could be useful to the working class. At the same time he argued that

there is no possibility of achieving economic freedom, not of taking any step towards that end, unless the workers themselves are conscious that what they suffer from, as a class, is economic subjection and consequent exploitation by the capitalists.

Mann advocated the formation of industrial unions, the abolition of the wage system and workers' control of industry. However, some British trade unionists wanted one big union on the American model, while others wanted them to have more freedom and spontaneity on the French model.

In *The Industrial Syndicalist* Mann argued that the existing unions were moribund, had accepted the philosophy of

12. Max Beer, *History of British Socialism*, Vol. II, p. 358.

liberal capitalism and worked for peace between employers and workers. Moreover, they were unsuited for the fight with capitalism by being organized on craft lines. Instead, he urged the need for a sharpening of the class war, the abandonment of collective agreements, conciliation and politics. He wanted unions to amalgamate into industrial unions, form a General Federation of Trade Unions and make frequent use of the strike for revolutionary means.

The syndicalists opposed what they considered to be the panacea of nationalization. It was, they argued, inadequate in that the workers would still remain wage slaves. Thus the mines for the miners was put forward as an alternative in *The Miners' Next Step* (1912) published by the Unofficial Reform Committee of the South Wales Miners. They urged the adoption of a militant policy on the part of the unions to make the mines unprofitable, so that the workers could take over and introduce workers' control. Other workers were advised to do likewise and so work towards the collapse of capitalism.

For a time syndicalist views were influential in most unions and particularly among the miners, railwaymen and engineers. Syndicalist ideas were propagated by the Socialist Labour Party in Scotland and the Plebs League, but it did not last long as an organized force. It suffered from the profound hostility of the Webbs and their ilk, who had a preference for a 'discreetly regulated freedom'. The Webbs, and many like them in the Labour Party and the trade unions, argued that the workers did not want even so much as a share in management, let alone control, and could not be trusted to run it efficiently if they did. Chartering a line followed by Hugh Clegg and the Labour Party today, they wanted no more than that trade unions should be recognized in industry and the system of collective bargaining strengthened and extended. After all, syndicalism was too violent a doctrine for the cautious English. It is, however, a doctrine that has become fashionable again – both among the New Left and prominent trade union leaders like Jack Jones and Hugh Scanlon.

(c) Guild Socialism

Of more influence in Britain was the doctrine of guild socialism which began effectively around 1912. The collectivist socialists were mainly interested in the organization and control of industry by the workers. The syndicalists emphasized the importance of the producer, the guild socialists made room in their theory for the consumer. A very English compromise, it can be viewed as an adaptation of the extreme continental doctrine of revolutionary syndicalism to English conditions and thought. And just as the syndicalists were predominantly workers, and indeed denounced intellectuals, so the guild socialist movement was predominantly middle-class and intellectual. Most of its theorists and supporters were ex-Fabians, writers and academics and there was even an occasional leader of the church.

As the guild socialists Reckitt and Bechhofer wrote in *The Meaning of National Guilds* (1919), we shall find in guild socialism,

the craftsmen's challenge and the blazing democracy of William Morris; the warning of Mr. Belloc against the huge shadow of the servile state and, perhaps, something also of his claim of the individual's control over property; the insistence of Mr Penty on the evils of industrialisation and its large scale organisation, and his recovery and bequest to us of the significant and unique word 'guild'. We should find something of French syndicalism, with its championship of the producer; something of American industrial unionism, with its clear vision of the need of industrial organisation; and something of Marxian socialism, with its unsparing anlaysis of the wage-system by which capitalism exalts itself and enslaves the mass of men.

If we are to believe this assessment of its adherents, then guild socialism was extremely eclectic, to say the least. Certainly, the guild socialists were influenced by the writings of Morris, Ruskin and Carlyle, with their detestation of industrial society and disappointment at the decline of crafts-manship and their assertion of the dignity of labour. A. J. Penty's *Restoration of the Guild System* (1906) was also in-fluential but few of the more erudite guild socialists accepted Penty's pessimism about industrial society or accepted the need, as he saw it, to return to the organization and spirit of the medieval guilds. Nevertheless, journals like the *New Age* and writers like S. G. Hobson, A. R. Orange and later G. D. H. Cole attempted to recreate the structure and spirit of the guilds of the middle ages in contemporary society. There was, however, another trend in political theory that went hand in hand with, and influenced, guild socialism. Guild socialism was easily accommodated to the fashionable theory of political pluralism developed and popularized by writers such as Ernest Barker, J. N. Figgis, A. D. Lindsay and H. J. Laski, but which had its origins in the writings of Maitland and Otto von Gierke. Pluralists like Figgis argued that associations like trade unions which had not been created by the state, whose interests were indepen-dent of the state, had legal personalities. It was not too difficult to go on from this and argue that they should, there-fore, take over the function of the state.

There were, however, many variations in the theory and many changes in doctrine. There were differences over the role of the state and whether the guilds should be local or national.

The guild socialists started from their perception of the position of the worker in industry. To them the worker in a capitalist society was a wage slave, a commodity to be bought and sold on the open market like any other com-modity; he was degraded and used. They argued that only the elimination of the capitalist employer could rescue the worker from his commodity status. Under the capitalist system he received wages, which was what the capitalist was forced to give; under the guild system he would re-ceive pay, his entitlement for services rendered. This is a somewhat facile distinction, yet the motive behind it is clear enough. Service and dignity in work was to replace the profit motive and commodity status. They argued further that it was a mockery to give the workers political democracy whilst at the same time subjecting them to a servile state in industry where, after all, they spent the major part of their time. Producers ought, they affirmed, to be allowed to exercise direct control over production while the proper sphere of the state was to look after the interests of men as consumers. If political democracy was to become real, then there needs also be industrial democracy. As S. G. Hobson asked:

> Is it not abundantly clear that a community, four fifths of which is rendered servile by the wage system, cannot possibly slough off the psychology of servility and claim to be a community of free men politically whilst remaining servile economically?

Like the Marxists and the syndicalists, the guild socialists accepted the doctrine of class war. To Cole it was a 'monstrous and irrefutable fact' and, like the syndicalists, they had little time for political action. Politics, and the bargains and compromises which are its necessary and inevitable feature, obscured the reality of the class struggle. Political democracy accepted, indeed it concentrated, the wage system and for this reason the guild socialist vehemently opposed the first Insurance Act which, like other reforms, only gilded the chains around the workers. Political action was ineffectual because the working class did not vote as a bloc. If they did, it would still take too long through legislative means to introduce the new society, the state was unsuitable for the job and there was, in any case, always the danger of counter-revolution.

The guild socialists did not, however, express the same distaste for reason and the intellectuals as did the syndicalists. Given that their leaders were all intellectuals and, most of the time at least, semi-rational, they could hardly do so. The vilification the syndicalists reserved for intellectuals the guild socialists reserved for the collective socialists. Indeed, the guildsmen, and Cole in particular, seemed to spend more time and take a greater delight in knocking the Fabians than in abusing the capitalists. But then those who suffer from unrequited love (and Cole had attempted to seduce the Fabians to guild socialism) are usually the most bitter opponents of their former objects of adulation. 'Collectivists', Cole wrote in *Self-government in Industry* (1917) 'may take their choice: they are knaves, who hate freedom, or they are fools, who do not know what freedom means, or they are a bit of both.'

The burden of the guild socialists' complaint against the collectivists was that state socialism was undemocratic and did not alter the position of the worker in industry. The collectivist socialists thought in terms of higher wages and improved working conditions but dismissed what Cole called the 'problem of giving to the workers responsibility and control, in short, freedom to express their personality in the work which is their way of serving the community'. Without being able to participate in the running of industry the workers would be little better off than they were under capitalism and would remain stunted and frustrated individuals. State socialism to Cole was no more than 'the sordid dream of a business man with a conscience'.

Certainly, the collectivists made little reference to or allowance for, workers' control in their plans for nationalization. The Fabians never made any provision, and indeed the Webbs spoke out against workers' control, saying that the workers did not want it and, if they did, were not trained for it. Another Fabian, Annie Besant, explicitly rejected workers' control of industry for a time, and Philip Snowden believed it to be inconsistent with efficiency. Most trade union leaders and the Trades Union Congress (TUC) also rejected the demand, although their grounds for doing so were that it would blur the role of the trade unions in industry if they or their members were also to become the owners and managers. What might be called the anti-democratic stand in socialist thinking on industry has been one that has been generally adopted since by the leaders of the Labour Party and the TUC. For example, Cripps in the 1940s still argued that the workers were incapable of running industry, while politicians like Anthony Crosland thought that industrial democracy could be more effectively introduced by an extension of collective bargaining.

Nonetheless, the warnings of the guild socialists came home to roost in the late 1940s and early 1950s, when nationalization was introduced for a number of industries. In spite of the high and exaggerated hopes of the workers and trade union leaders, nationalization soon came to be seen as the same old dog with a new collar.

The traditional concept of the state was also criticized by the guild socialists. To Cole it was a 'coercive power, existing for the protection of private property'. Moreover it was, the guild socialists argued, assumed to be all-inclusive, representing men's total interests, whereas in fact men had a multiplicity of interests that were not, and could not be, adequately represented by a territorial form of representation. Representation should be functional, not universal. To the guild socialists the state was just another association among many others whose true purpose was to represent the interests of consumers *qua* consumers. Unlike the anarchists and the syndicalists, they did not envisage the abolition of the state; they would be content with its castration.

In the guild socialist schema the state would be reduced to a subordinate role in society with the mystique of sovereignty shattered. Many of the functions it now performed would be taken over by the trade unions themselves turned into guilds. First, however, the trade unions would need to be reorganized. They had to become industrial unions organizing all grades of workers, including the managers and technicians. Hence the guild socialists encouraged amalgamations, the elimination of craft unions and the siting of the union branch in the factory so as to make it a more effective fighting union and the nucleus of the future guild organization. Given the relatively slow pace of union reform, even under the external threats imposed by governments in the late 1960s and early 1970s, the guild socialists were somewhat blasé about the ability and willingness of the trade unions to reform themselves, amalgamate and recruit the non-manual worker, especially as even today the trade unions have in membership little more than one third of the total workforce.

But suspending disbelief, as one has to if their proposals are to be followed through, the next step in the guild socialist programme was for these new powerful industrial trade unions gradually, in a Fabian manner, to take over the control of industry. This, as Hobson and Orage wrote in *The Bondage of Wagery* (1913), would be a 'period of thrilling interest'. Strikes were a part of the armoury for gradually taking control. They were educative and desirable in that industrial peace was a sham but the guild socialists were not prepared to go so far as to advocate violence in the manner of their more romantic colleagues in France. Rather they were more pragmatic and to that extent realist. They advocated the method of encroaching control, defined by Cole as

a policy directed to wresting bit by bit from the hands of the possessing classes the economic power which they now exercise, by a steady transference of functions and rights from their nominees to representatives of the working class.

Hobson believed that the encroachment over the control of industry would start with the trade unions gaining control over the supplies of labour to industry and receiving and distributing the workers' income. From this beginning they would proceed to full control. Cole thought that workers' control would start with factory discipline becoming the prerogative of the unions, who would gradually extend their power to the appointment of foremen, the hiring and firing of workers and their payment.

Though they were opposed to nationalization, they did see it as a stepping stone to the guild society. Although the workers might well make it impossible for the capitalists to run industry, it would be some time before the workers

E

would be in a position to run industry themselves. Nationalization was, therefore, considered to be a temporary situation in which the state had eliminated the capitalists and
prepared the way for the eventual take-over by the workers.
Yet, as Stanley Glass observes, they had 'an unrealistic view
of the government's probable reaction to their plans', assuming, as they often did, that it would stand aside while
the workers took over. And, as he continued, 'The belief
that a section of organized labour could impose its will on
the country's rulers was naïve – as the events of 1926
showed.'[13]

More naïve and muddled was their conception of the
future guild society. Hobson conceived of each industry
being run by a national guild formed out of the trade
unions and chartered by the state. There would be, he believed, fifteen in all, mutually exchanging their products.
The community would own and lease out land, buildings
and machinery and receive rent in return. In return for
their charter from the community the guilds would be required to provide an efficient service to the community and
provide for their members in injury, sickness and unemployment. A Supreme Guild Council formed out of the
T U C would determine overall economic policy, coordinate
the activities of the guilds and act as a conciliator in disputes. The government would be relegated to dealing only
with foreign policy, defence and internal security. Most
guild socialists thought of the guilds as being independent
of the government, legislating for themselves and electing
their officials and managers.

The role of the state, or the organization that was to be
supreme, occasioned great difficulty among the guild socialists. They all agreed that the state was a territorial association and concerned with everyone as consumers, and that it
must act in partnership with the guilds, but they were undecided as to the correct relationship it should have with the
latter. In *Social Theory* (1920) Cole argued for consumer

13. S. T. Glass, *The Responsible Society: The Ideas of Guild
Socialism*, pp. 58–9.

associations and producer guilds joining together in a joint congress as the supreme organ of government. In *Guild Socialism Restated* (1920), his final version, he envisaged the country divided into rural and urban areas, each governed by an indirectly elected commune composed of equal representatives of producers and consumers. The commune would levy taxes and be responsible for the local economy and the preservation of law and order. In this way he believed that individuals would be more active in the determination of decisions that affected them than they were under a system of territorial representation.

Critics have argued that the guild state would be static and would suffer from occupational and geographical immobility of labour. The theory assumes a fairly static economy and fixed industrial boundaries. Moreover, as the Webbs pointed out, there would be little to stop the more powerful guilds from acting selfishly and seeking and obtaining the highest return for their products. They would be 'by the very nature of their membership, perpetually tempted to seek to maintain existing processes unchanged, to discourage innovations . . .' The answers of the guildsmen, as of all utopians, is that with their new system a new social ethic would develop which would ensure that the interests of the nation would be served by the guilds without recourse to external sanctions. It was Cole who later admitted guild socialism to be 'a good deal of nonsense'.

In spite of the middle-class nature of its leadership and its utopian character, the guild socialists were a particularly effective propagandist group. Many unions took up their ideas. Guilds were formed in the building industry and the Union of Post Office Workers continued to advocate the formation of a Post Office Guild in the 1950s. But perhaps more important than their grandiose schemes for the reorganization of industry is their affirmation that the worker is due for more consideration and respect than he is given. Only now are there some half-hearted attempts to give the workers a more effective voice in industry.

7
LENIN –
THE REVOLUTIONARY CHALLENGE
TO SOCIALIST ORTHODOXY

Leninism represents the second major challenge to the social democrats and it was a challenge that was far more important in practical terms than that posed by the anarchists. Indeed, many of the latter were eventually to throw in their lot with him. Lenin castigated the social democrats for their lack of revolutionary ardour, and many other things besides, and through his creation of the Third International and the policy it followed, initiated the first major ideological and organizational break in the international socialist movement.

In his *Philosophical Notebooks* Lenin wrote: 'After half a century, not a single Marxist had understood Marx!' Whether or not this was true, whether or not Lenin himself understood Marx, it not at issue here. What is true is that Lenin turned Marxism back to its revolutionary aspects, so long neglected by the Marxists of the West. The Social Democrats of Germany, he told Max Beer, had turned Marx's teaching into an academy while to him it was 'an arsenal, replete with arms for the revolution'.[1] The Marxists of western Europe, including the Germans, subordinated the revolutionary aspects of Marxism and concentrated, in practice, on achieving short-term advantages for the workers and building a socialist majority in parliament. Lenin, as Axelrod said of him, was 'occupied with the revolution twenty-four hours a day ... has no thoughts except the thought of the Revolution, and ... even when he goes to sleep, dreams only of the Revolution'.

1. Max Beer, *Fifty Years of International Socialism*, p. 150.

Throughout his adult life Lenin was actively preparing for revolution. Like many previous revolutionaries he was constantly forming new sects, engaged in conspiracies and the writing of revolutionary pamphlets, especially against those self-professed Marxists he believed to have deviated from what he considered to be orthodoxy. Yet Lenin, though his understanding of Marxism was close, was probably the most thoroughgoing revisionist of them all. Lenin's mind, as Bertram Wolfe has written, 'was political before aught else, and dipped into the body of Marxist generalizations only occasionally for guidance or polemics'.[2] He relied heavily upon the voluntarist, insurrectionist Marx of before 1850, the Marx of the tradition of Blanqui. And he found in Marx's writings always what he sought, as so many did before him and so many more have since.

This is not necessarily to say that Lenin was consciously selective in his quotations from Marx or deliberately fraudulent in his expositions of Marxism. In a sense his orientation to the revolutionary elements of Marx's thought was dictated by the circumstances in which he found himself. Given the autocratic nature of the Russian régime, it was only natural that Lenin should look to revolution to overthrow it and that in his search for means and theoretical justification it was the revolutionary aspects of Marxism that appeared more relevant than the learned discourses of the mature Marx on maturing capitalism. In a real sense Lenin was inhabiting the same kind of environment that Marx was in western Europe before 1848, 'the moment', as George Lichtheim has it, 'when an autonomous socialist labour movement had begun to emerge in Europe from the matrix of the democratic revolution'[3] but which had bypassed Russia.

Hence there is relatively little to be found in Lenin's writings on the theories of price, value or dialectical

2. Bertram D. Wolfe, *Three Who Made a Revolution*, p. 256.
3. George Lichtheim, *The Origins of Socialism*, London, 1969, p. vii.

materialism which convulsed his western colleagues with orgasms of intellectual debate. Most of his writings are concerned with a specific historical event, even though it be no more than the then unpublished *Credo* of the little-known Katherine Kuskova in favour of economism, to which he felt constrained to reply in *A Protest of the Russian Social Democrats*. Indeed, his writings have a specificality and historical relevance that is difficult to find in any other writer. He concerned himself with the revolutionary aspects of Marxism, the training of professional revolutionaries and the techniques of revolution. In these works his hardheadedness and practicality show through. It is only when he leaves off to write about philosophy or the structure of the proletarian state of the future that he becomes sloppy and utopian.

(a) The Role of the Party and Revolutionary Tactics

To Lenin revolution was an art. In *What is to be Done?* (1902) he stressed the need for a party with an advanced theory to be the vanguard of the masses. Though he had been influenced by the writings of Alder and Kautsky in the 1890s, his party was not to be built on the German model. Whilst the Marxists of the world, including the Russians led by Plekhanov, envied and attempted to emulate the mass party of the German Social Democrats, Lenin insisted on the need for the establishment of an élite corps to agitate and lead the masses. The pamphlet was, in fact, an attack on the theory of economism and the semi-anarchist ideology implicit in the theory of spontaneity. The Economists wanted to develop trade unionism and work for immediate reforms. Against them he argued that trade union organization would not lead to the spontaneous acceptance of socialism by the workers. To concentrate on an economic struggle through the medium of the trade unions would mean that the workers would remain the slaves of capitalism, whereas the objective was to destroy it. 'Socialist consciousness', he wrote, 'cannot exist among the workers. This can only be introduced from without.' Left to itself the working class would develop no more than trade union consciousness. Socialism, to Lenin, was too important to be left to the workers.

To Marx 'the emancipation of the working class is the work of the working class itself'. Lenin, on the other hand, regarded the socialist consciousness of the workers as an extraneous element injected into the working class by radical intellectuals. The conscious element was the professional revolutionary organized on military lines, working day and night for the revolution and infused with the revolutionary spirit of the populist heroes. It was to the professional revolutionaries that control of the workers' movement should be entrusted. Lenin asserted that no movement could endure without a stable organization of leaders to give it continuity, that the need for such an organization became more urgent the more the masses were drawn into the revolutionary struggle, that such an organization must consist of professional revolutionaries and that by these means the police would have difficulty in destroying the organization while its continuity, existence and success would mean that more of the workers would be drawn into the struggle.

What Lenin proposed was a highly centralized hierarchical structure for the new party. The commands of the centre would be implemented by the local organs, after they had discussed them. And though he attacked the intelligentsia for being 'sluggish in their habits', they were to be the new revolutionaries, diluted only by 'exceptional working men'. It is hard to decide who was the greatest revisionist of Marx, Lenin or Bernstein. Was it not Marx, after all, who had said that the striving of the workers for socialism was a spontaneous product of the economic conditions under which they worked and lived? And was not Lenin, in his theory of the necessity for intellectuals to inject socialist consciousness into the working class, accepting Bernstein's observation that the working class had lost, if it had ever possessed, revolutionary class consciousness? Moreover, the

logic of Lenin's argument is that there must be a leader.
This, to say the least, is something of a novelty in Marxist
theory. It did, however, pave the way for a general secretary
to straddle the party and the state. As George Lichtheim has
observed:

> The Leninist model in fact amounted to the political expro-
> priation of the proletariat and its subjection to a dictatorial
> machine operated by the Bolshevik leadership: a leadership
> which was essentially self-constituted and irremovable.[4]

It was to be revolution from above, and it was.

But Lenin was not without critics. Of these Trotsky was
the most outstanding. Trotsky was not a man of the party;
he was far too intelligent and arrogant to be led and was not,
in any case, particularly interested in getting involved in
the mundane and unglamorous task of creating the necessary
administrative structure for a successful revolution. Trotsky
thought of himself, and was thought of by others, as an
aristocrat of revolution and of having an historic role to
fulfil. As Bruce Lockhart wrote in 1918, 'He strikes me as
a man who would willingly die fighting for Russia provided
there was a big enough audience to see him do it.'[5] Ironically,
he did die fighting for the kind of Russia he wanted, but it
was with a pen and he had only the hired assassin for an
audience.

But this is to move more ahead of our theme. In 1903
Trotsky denounced Lenin as the 'party disorganizer', and at
the Second Congress of the Russian Social Democratic Party
held the same year he sided with Martov against Lenin. In
Our Political Tasks (1904) he portrayed Lenin as Robespierre, repudiated his conception of a revolutionary party
and denied that socialist theory had to be injected into the
working class. 'Lenin's methods', he wrote, 'lead to this: the
party organization at first substitutes itself for the party as

4. George Lichtheim, *Marxism: An Historical and Critical Study*,
1961, p. 337.

5. Quoted in Edmund Wilson. *To the Finland Station*, London,
1968, p. 434.

a whole; then the Central Committee substitutes itself for the organization; and finally a single "dictator" substitutes himself for the Central Committee.' Yet in his *Autobiography* he wrote of the 1903 debate, 'I did not fully realize what an intense and imperious centralism the revolutionary party would need to lead millions in a war against the old order.'

Trotsky was not alone in failing to realize this. Both Rosa Luxemburg and Plekhanov severely criticized Lenin's organizational model. Luxemburg repudiated it altogether and put her faith instead in the revolutionary initiative and spontaneity of the masses. Plekhanov, who was credited by Lenin with having reared a whole generation of Marxists, wanted a mass party on the German model. He accused Lenin of being an 'autocrat', though that was yet to come, of aiming at 'bureaucratic centralization' and 'transforming party members into cogwheels and screws', which was true. *What is to be Done?*, he said, represented an 'organizational utopia of a theocratic character' and he argued that Lenin was 'confusing the dictatorship of the proletariat with the dictatorship over the proletariat'. But then, as E. H. Carr said, Plekhanov 'remained to the end doctrinaire and academic'.[6]

Against these criticisms Lenin defended himself in *One Step Forward, Two Steps Back* (1904). In this he argued that the task of the party was to educate the workers to 'its own level of consciousness'. He stressed the importance of organization, and a strictly hierarchical organization at that, and the need for the minority to be subordinate to the majority and them all to the central committee. The élitism is evident. So also is the embryo of the dictatorship over the proletariat. Yet Lenin had the *Manifesto* to support him. After all, it had asserted that the communists were the most advanced and resolute section of the working class and that their party constituted the vanguard of the workers' movement. Lenin was doing no more than making explicit the implicit logic of the Marxist revolutionaries but which they

6. E. H. Carr, *Studies in Revolution*, London, 1962, p. 117.

sublimated because of their democratic and libertarian scruples. Certainly, Lenin's insistence on the need for professional revolutionaries and his pessimistic view of the revolutionary and socialist consciousness of the working class was, and remains, more realistic than Luxemburg's belief in spontaneity. It was also more successful than Plekhanov's brand of genteel Marxism, the Marxism that frowned upon the amorality and expropriations sanctioned by Lenin. 'Nice guys finish last', Leo Durocher tells us. Lenin finished first. Luxemburg was eliminated in a badly planned and led uprising and Plekhanov begged for charity.

Nevertheless, Lenin's conception of the party as a narrow dedicated band of professional revolutionaries led from the centre was defeated at the Congress of the Russian Social Democratic Party held in London in 1903. Martov's draft of Article One of the party statutes defining membership according to support for the party was preferred to Lenin's definition which restricted membership to activists. Though he had written that the minority should be subordinated to the majority, Lenin ignored the decision, lost control of the party newspaper, *Iskra*, and held his own Bolshevik congress in 1905. The injunction of the French Radical deputy who laid down that 'the main task of a great party is the same as that of a good stomach; not to reject but to assimilate' was not one which recommended itself to Lenin. But then the Russian Social Democratic Party was hardly a party and it was certainly not great.

Lenin's conception of the party was accepted by the Sixth Congress of the party in 1917. At the Second Comintern Congress in 1920 it was laid down that the basis of party organization should be 'democratic centralism' – the subordination of the lower party organs to the higher party organs. Until a decision had been reached debate and criticism were acceptable, but all attempts to organize any opposition were branded as fractionalism. Certainly, Lenin's conception of the party, and his ability through all the schisms and quarrels to make it a reality, was vindicated by the Goddess Success in 1917. Bakunin had written in 1869 that if 'the workers of the West delay too long it will be the Russian peasant who will set them an example'. It was Lenin, rather than the peasant, that set the example of revolution to the proletariat of the West, though Bakunin would not have approved of the resultant élitist government.

More than anything else it was Lenin's control of a well-organized and disciplined party, his willingness to compromise and carry the party with him, that enabled him to outmanoeuvre, or rather outbid, his more numerous Menshevik and Social Revolutionary rivals in 1917; aided, of course, by his deep awareness of peasant grievances and his willingness, if only for a short time, to offer all things to all men and appropriate the Social Revolutionaries' policy on land ownership.

This opportunism was a basic part of Lenin's teaching on the role of the party and the tactics and techniques of revolution. The 'greatest engine-driver of revolution', as Trotsky called him, Lenin was not above making radical changes in his policy and tactics if they appeared to him to serve the revolutionary cause. Rationalization from Marxism would come later.

Lenin had an unquestioned and unwavering dedication to the final goal of revolution but managed, at the same time, to be extremely flexible in his choice of means. Tactical considerations took into account the objective conditions and opportunities. As he announced in September 1917, 'The task of a revolutionary party is not to renounce compromise altogether but to be able to remain loyal to its principles during all the compromises that may be necessary.' There was but one principle – the need for revolution; there were many compromises. He showed his own ability to compromise in his relations with the Menshevik leaders and, for example, strung along with Struve in writing for *Iskra* when, as early as 1899, he had decided that Struve was 'ceasing to be a comrade' and later called him 'Judas Struve'. At the Tammerfors Conference in December 1905 he argued in favour of participation in the first Duma and then, in deference to the opposition of the more extreme

activists, he publicly endorsed their opposition to participation and their insistence on insurrectionary tactics. In
1906 he advocated guerrilla tactics, but once again performed a volte face and advocated participation in the
elections to the second and third Dumas.

Similarly, before the revolution he advanced slogans
urging the election of officers in the army and the ending of
strict discipline, but once the Bolsheviks were in power he
recruited ex-Tsarist officers and became an advocate, with
Trotsky, of firm discipline. In 1918 he argued that as the
petit bourgeois are 'beginning to turn towards us, we
ought not to turn away from them just because we used to
have a different slogan in our pamplets, we ought to rewrite
these pamphlets ... and say that we're not afraid to use
conciliation as well as coercion'. Yet he continued to argue
for the necessity of violence and passed over the terroristic
activities of the Cheka. The same inconsistency can be seen
in his attitude to the various nationalities and religious sects
in Russia. Whilst exhorting his followers to be sensitive to
their sensibilities, he also authorized acts of violence and
expropriation against them.

Both before and after the revolution Lenin seems to have
been guided by expediency more than anything else. It is
not surprising that he should have been considered by many
to be inconsistent and irresponsible. But, to be fair, he was
always attempting to reconcile the requirements of practical
politics with his stated goals. It was no doubt as distressing
to him as it was disconcerting to his followers and colleagues
that he often had to engage in intellectual acrobatics. Yet,
in all the changes of front which he made, he always had
adequate rationalization to hand. His critics were condemned as either dogmatists or extremists. Lenin seemed
to think he destroyed people with labels.

In the same way as he developed a new concept of the
vanguard of the proletariat, so also he developed a new
theory of the proletarian revolution. In *Two Tactics of
Social Democracy in the Democratic Revolution* (1905) he
wrote: 'To wish to attain socialism by other ways, without

passing through the stage of political democracy, is merely to arrive at ridiculous and reactionary conclusions, in the political as well as in the economic fields.' He added:

We cannot jump out of the bourgeois-democratic confines of the Russian revolution, but we can vastly extend its boundaries, and within those boundaries we can and must fight for the interests of the proletariat, for its immediate needs, and for the conditions that will make it possible to prepare its forces for the complete victory that is to come.

Thus, in 1905, he seemed in this respect to be an orthodox Marxist. He anticipated a bourgeois revolution preceding the final overthrow of capitalism by the proletariat. After noting that democratic changes would not undermine capitalism but would allow the bourgeoisie to rule as a class, he went on to say:

It does not at all follow from this that the democratic revolution cannot take place in a form advantageous mainly to the big capitalist, the financial magnate, and the 'enlightened' landowners, as well as in a form advantageous to the peasant and the workers.

Yet there is some doubt as to what Lenin meant by the bourgeois-democratic revolution. He had argued that the bourgeois was not liberal and was incapable of 'waging a decisive struggle against Tsarism'. He argued that because of this the onus was on the proletariat and the peasantry to lead the bourgeois revolution and set up the 'revolutionary-democratic dictatorship of the proletariat and the peasantry'. Because, so far as Lenin was concerned, the proletariat was the only consistently revolutionary class, it was called upon to play a leading part in the general democratic movement in Russia. This did not seem to mean that Lenin in 1905 intended or anticipated the proletariat to proceed immediately to the dictatorship of the proletariat.

Trotsky was more specific. As Bertram Wolfe rightly notes, 'if Lenin provided the party machine and the conspirative bent and concentration on power, it was Trotsky who provided the central doctrine and the actual military-political strategy of the armed conquest of power.'[7] This was the doctrine of 'permanent revolution', beginning as a dictatorship of the working class and ending in world revolution. In his *The Period up to the Ninth of January* (1905) Trotsky argued that revolution depended upon the assumption of leadership by the industrial proletariat. He stated his belief that the revolution would begin with a general strike, the occupation of the towns and the establishment of a revolutionary administration. At the same time, there would need to be propaganda amongst the peasants and soldiers to prevent them from destroying the revolution. His experiences as leader of the St Petersburg soviet in 1905 led him to argue that the soviets would be the future administration for towns and that they would collaborate to form a new socialist government.

Trotsky argued that, because of the weakness of the bourgeoisie in Russia, the proletariat would need to be the pacesetter of the revolution. Thus, in *Results and Prospects* (1906) he argued that 'In a country economically backward, the proletariat can take power earlier than in countries where capitalism is advanced.' He went on to assert that in Russia power would pass to the proletariat which would 'appear before the peasantry as its liberator'. Trotsky was more realistic and logical than either Lenin, or the more orthodox Marxists who thought in terms of a bourgeois revolution occurring before the proletariat could come into its own. Trotsky realized that the main burden of the revolutionary struggle would devolve on the proletariat, that this would force it into taking power and that it was naïve to believe that it would then voluntarily relinquish it to the bourgeoisie.

For Trotsky the revolution in Russia would pass direct from its anti-feudal to its anti-capitalist stage. But though Russia would be the first, it could not be successful on its own. Though he believed that at first the peasants would

7. Bertram D. Wolfe, *Strange Communists I Have Known*, London, 1966, p. 197.

accept a subordinate role and the revolution be initially secured by encouraging them to seize land, he also believed that after the revolution the peasants would come into conflict with the proletariat. The temporary success of the revolution could only be made permanent by help being forthcoming from the European proletariat in a governmental form. The Russian socialist revolution could not last unless, in Trotsky's words, it was 'the initiator of the liquidation of capitalism on a world scale'.

This was the second leg of Trotsky's theory of permanent revolution. To be successful the revolution would need to pass from a national to an international revolution. If the final outcome was not world socialism, if the revolution failed to spread from Russia, then the Russian revolution would fall prey to a conservative Europe or become thwarted in backward Russia. It was indeed a 'sensational suggestion' that, contrary to accepted Marxist orthodoxy, an economically backward country like Russia might reach revolution and socialism before western Europe.

The events of 1917 clarified Lenin's thinking on the subject of revolution. On his return to Russia he issued his *April Theses* which called for 'no support for the Provisional Government' and advocated the establishment of a Soviet Republic which would prepare the way for the transition to a proletarian government. He became an advocate of the theory of permanent revolution; the telescoping of the bourgeois and proletarian revolutions, a proletarian-socialist revolution supported by agrarian upheaval. The 1917 takeover by the Bolsheviks cut off the incipient bourgeois parliamentarianism. The aim, as Lichtheim observed, 'had shifted to full-blooded Communism in the sense of the 1848 *Manifesto* and Marx's pamphlet on the Paris Commune'.[8] So much for Marx's dictum that 'no social order ever disappears before all the productive forces for which there is room in it have been developed'. Lenin's decision to bypass capitalism and leap straight into socialism was not, however,

8. George Lichtheim, *Marxism: An Historical and Critical Study*, p. 342.

new. Leaving aside Trotsky's theory of permanent revolution, the idea that capitalism could be bypassed in Russia was a particular feature of Russian thought and could be found in the writings of Herzen and Bakunin, among others.

(b) The Dictatorship of the Proletariat and the Leninist State

'Leninism', wrote Stalin, 'is the theory and tactics of the proletarian revolution in general, the theory and tactics of the dictatorship of the proletarian in particular.' Indeed, Lenin went further. For him 'a Marxist is one who *extends* the acceptance of the class struggle to the acceptance of the *dictatorship of the proletariat.' The State and Revolution* (1917) is his most detailed exposition of the new order to be created by the proletarian revolution. Using the model of the Paris Commune, he argued that the revolution will destroy the bourgeois state and put the dictatorship of the proletariat in its place.

First he deals with the pattern of revolution as laid down by Marx and Engels, always emphasizing their insistence on the need for revolutionary violence to overthrow the capitalist state. He argues that when Engels wrote about the abolition of the state, he was referring to the bourgeois state which would be smashed by the revolution. When Engels wrote that the state would 'wither away' this was to be interpreted as referring to the proletarian state and which would be a longer process. First, the capitalist state is 'smashed' and a new state, the dictatorship of the proletariat, established. Even though Lenin could say that 'we Marxists are opposed to all and every kind of state', he was nevertheless aware of the need for and insisted upon, maintaining the apparatus of the state so as to break down the resistance of the bourgeoisie and other counter-revolutionaries. As he wrote in *The State and Revolution*:

The proletariat needs the state, the centralized organization of force and violence, both for the purpose of crushing the resistance of the exploiters and for the purpose of guiding the great mass of the population – the peasantry, the lower middle class, the semi-proletariat – in the work of economic socialist reconstruction.

He wrote in *The Proletarian Revolution and the Renegade Kautsky* (1918): 'The revolutionary dictatorship of the proletariat is power won and maintained by the violence of the proletariat against the bourgeoisie, power that is unrestricted by any laws.' That when it was established it was not the dictatorship of the *proletariat*, that the proletariat had not won it and that the violence of the dictatorship was used as much against the proletariat, the social democrats and the peasants as it was against the bourgeoisie, was conveniently glossed over. It was a dictatorship unrestricted by law, the latter being no more than an instrument of power. 'The dictatorship signifies ... unlimited power which rests upon force and not upon law.' It was Kautsky who pointed out in the *Dictatorship of the Proletariat* (1918) that the emphasis on dictatorship implied that its supporters had not yet obtained a majority. Once more, Marxist doctrine was relegated to the rubbish-heap of history.

Lenin's insistence on the need to smash the capitalist state, though in Russia one could hardly be said to exist, led him to attack those like Bernstein and Kautsky who, in their different ways, hoped to reach the Marxist utopia without recourse to force. Kautsky and Bernstein were 'opportunists', class collaborators and, what was worse, among those who argued 'defence of Fatherland' as an excuse for their wartime activities. This, as Lenin rightly but unrealistically pointed out, was 'tantamount to the utter betrayal of socialism'. As with the Economists in Russia and the Fabians in Britain, they recognized and accepted the existing state where, as Marx had long ago taught, their objective should be to destroy it. To those who retorted that Marx had allowed exceptions to this general rule, Lenin's riposte was that things had changed since Marx had written this.

Lenin was an uncomfortable 'ally' of the social democrats of the West. Indeed, he and they seemed to spend as much time and ink vilifying each other as they did the capitalists. The western Marxists had long ago accommodated themselves to their respective economic and political systems whilst retaining their Marxist revolutionary rhetoric. Now Lenin had to spoil it all by showing up the contrast between their words and deeds. Had this defence and advocacy of the revolutionary Marxism been muted and insignificant, it might not have mattered. That it was loud and forceful caused embarrassment to the social democrats and a quick search on their part for quotations from the liberal-humanist Marx and Engels to throw back. That it came from a man soon to be vindicated by events made them even more uncomfortable.

But at least they could take solace in the fact that Lenin's ideas of how the proletarian state would be administered were as utopian as his Jacobinical ideas for the seizure of power had proved successful. Lenin exercised what Reinhold Neibuhr called 'the strategy of fleeing from difficult problems by taking refuge in impossible solutions'. *The State and Revolution* was indeed a call for a return to primitive democracy. The dictatorship of the proletariat would not be 'a state in the ordinary sense of that word'. As the oppressors would be many, and the oppressed few, there would be no need for the complicated machinery of the bourgeois state. It would not require a special army or police force but would instead rely on the armed masses. In fact, it relied on the Cheka.

The 'first or lower phase' of the dictatorship of the proletariat, socialism, will still exhibit differences of wealth, of men being paid according to their work rather than need. But as the means of production would now belong to the whole of society and the workers be employees of the state, the exploitation of man by man would be abolished.

The means of production are now no longer the private property of individuals [Lenin wrote in *The State and Revolution*]. The means of production belong to the whole of society.

Every member of society, performing a certain part of socially-necessary labour receives a certificate from society that he has done such and such a quantity of work. According to this certificate, he receives from the public stores of articles of consumption a corresponding quantity of products. After that deduction of the proportion of labour which goes into public fund, every worker, therefore, receives from society as much as he has given it.

Bourgeois law, 'which gives to unequal individuals, in return for an unequal (in reality) amount of work, an equal quantity of products', remains.

Even so, officials would be paid at the level of workmen's wages. The great majority of the functions of the state have become so simplified, according to Lenin, basing himself on Marx, that they amount to no more than registration, checking and filing, tasks that any workman can perform. Business runs itself with control exercised from below by soviets of workers, soldiers and peasants and with officials elected and subject to recall.

The state will wither away, the highest phase of communist society will be reached, when society has realized the formula 'From each according to his abilities; to each according to his needs.' However, this is dependent upon the elimination of the division between mental and manual labour, on a gigantic development of the forces of production and the observance of the elementary rules of social intercourse and voluntary work on the part of the people. *The State and Revolution* is a strange utopian dream of a man generally credited with hardheaded realism and ruthlessness. How far off the higher phase was Lenin did not profess to know, though in 1920 he had guaranteed, albeit to a group of no doubt idealistic students, that it would be twenty years. But then revolutionaries, above all, need a dream to sustain them through the long days and nights spent in dreary quarrels and debate in even drearier surroundings. The dream, however, was short-lived.

The utopian schemes of *The State and Revolution, The*

Impending Catastrophe and How to Combat It (1917), and *How to Organize Competition* (January 1918) were revised in the face of reality in his *Immediate Tasks of the Soviet Government* (April 1918). In this work Lenin recognized the value of experts and the necessity of integrating specialists into the administration. As Adam Ulam has commented, 'The Revolution was hardly one week old, the ink on his *State and Revolution* was hardly dry, when Lenin chose to remonstrate with the workers that pay differentials and the privileged position of the specialist was a necessary thing.'[9]

In order to produce we need the engineers and we greatly value their work. We shall willingly pay them well. We do not as yet desire to deprive them of their privileged positions.

He used ex-Tsarist military officers in the Red Army, some of them being on the Brest-Litovsk delegation and on the Supreme Military Council, though Voroshilov, among others (but not Trotsky), was against their use. To cap it all in 1921 the New Economic Policy was launched, encouraging peasant private enterprise, private trade, the leasing of nationalized factories to private entrepreneurs, and the seeking of the help of foreign capitalists. Gorky could well call it the 'Old Economic Policy'. There can be little doubt that Lenin was willing to forget that he had ever written *The State and Revolution*. It is known that he was angry with Bukharin for publishing extracts from it. Yet whilst in flight after the abortive July Revolution, Lenin had written a note to Kamenev asking him to finish it off if he should be caught and killed.

Lenin rationalized these radical departures from his professed aims by arguing that they were necessary but temporary evils. Necessary they may have been, temporary they were not. His short-term objective of a state administered by the workers has yet to be realized and looks even more distant now than it did in 1920; that is, of course,

9. Adam B. Ulam, *Lenin and the Bolsheviks*, p. 498.

unless we define as workers those who manage and control the party. But as Bukharin said in 1923, in anticipation of Milovan Djilas, 'Even a proletarian background, the most calloused hands, and other equally remarkable qualities are no guarantee against transformation of the privileged proletarian elements into a new class.' In fact, the party was already then what it is now: a party of bureaucrats manipulating the workers behind a façade of democratic institutions. Lenin had argued for a centralized party; now he urged the total organization of life by the party. Instead of the utopian vision of early 1917, he now sought to 'organize everything; take everything into our own hands'. Soon the identification of the party with the proletariat was complete, verbally at least. In 1920 Lenin could proudly announce that 'not a single important political or organizational question is decided by any state institution in our republic without the guiding hand of the Central Committee of the Party'. Zinoviev in 1923 could say without embarrassment:

The hegemony of the proletariat is impossible without the hegemony of the Communist Party. The dictatorship of the party which it has created and which stands at its head. The history of the Russian Communist Party is the history of the Russian working class.

That the working class had not created the party was forgotten. That middle-class intellectuals had created it to eliminate the middle class was never said. To say a new class had arisen was heretical.

Soon the party became the state, and a repressive authoritarian state at that. Once again the Tsars were in the saddle. Plekhanov had long ago warned, in *Socialism and the Political Struggle* that it would be dangerous for a revolutionary socialist party to seize power in a backward country like Russia. It would, he argued, be faced with the dilemma of failing to build socialism because of the ignorance of the workers, or of establishing an authoritarian communism. Plekhanov, unfortunately, lived to see his prediction come true. Bakunin did not, but he had issued the same warning much earlier:

According to the theory of Mr Marx, the people not only must not destroy [the state] but must strengthen it and place it at the complete disposal of their benefactors, guardians and teachers – the leaders of the Communist Party, namely Mr Marx and his friends, who will proceed to liberate [mankind] in their own way. They will concentrate the reins of government in a strong hand, because the ignorant people require an exceedingly firm guardianship; they will establish a single state bank concentrating in its hands all commercial, industrial, agricultural and even scientific production, and then divide the masses into two armies – industrial and agricultural – under the direct command of the state engineers, who will constitute a new privileged scientific-political estate.[10]

In itself, the existence of a new class may be defensible. Yet the history of the Russian revolution and its subsequent development bears out Noam Chomsky's observation that 'One who pays some attention to history will not be surprised if those who cry most loudly that we must smash and destroy are later found among the administrators of some new system of repression.'[11]

(c) Imperialism and World Revolution

Lenin not only returned to the revolutionary Marx but also claimed to have updated Marx with his theory of imperialism; an attempt to explain why revolution had not occurred as Marx had said it would. Elaborated in *Imperialism, The Highest Stage of Capitalism* (1916) it owed a great deal to the Englishman J. A. Hobson's *Imperialism* (1902). Yet what to Hobson had been preventable by a quick exercise of liberal conscience was, to Lenin, an inevitable feature of historical development.

10. Quoted in Noam Chomsky, *American Power and the New Mandarins*, London, 1969, p. 62.
11. ibid., p. 18.

Lenin defined imperialism as 'capitalism in that stage of development in which the domination of monopolies and finance capital has taken shape; in which the export of capital has acquired pronounced importance; in which the division of the world by the international trusts has begun, and in which the partition of all the territory of the earth by the greatest capitalist countries has been completed'. This is not just the concentration of capital as foreseen by Marx but one in which the industrialists have become subservient to the international banks. For Lenin it represents the highest stage of capitalism, the final stage of parasitic and decaying capitalism, 'the eve of the proletarian social revolution'.

Lenin's argument is that capitalism has become monopolistic but, more important, power has also been transferred from the industrialists to the banks and finance houses and which now operate internationally. The formation of trusts and cartels has led to a reduction in profitable opportunities in the home countries and a falling rate of profit, as Marx predicted. What Marx did not see clearly enough was that the capitalists would have outlets in international expansion. New outlets were and are sought in other parts of the world. Hence, there begins a rivalry for the partition of the world among the competing capitalists. Whilst at first friendly, the conflict over the division of the spoils eventually leads to war – the 1914–18 war being, in Lenin's view, the first imperialist predatory war.

To Lenin's way of thinking imperialism would lead to socialism through war. The inherent contradictions that Marx believed he discerned in capitalism, Lenin saw as being transferred to a global scale. Moreover, the emergence of the phenomenon of imperialism explained the continued existence of monopoly capitalism for which Marx had predicted catastrophe. It explained the continued accumulation of capital through its ability to sell products to and obtain cheap raw materials from what we now call the underdeveloped world. Worse than this, imperialism enabled the capitalists in the industrialized countries to buy off the revolution for a time by increasing the standard of living of their workers at the expense of those in the under-developed countries. This prevented the increasing im-poverishment of the proletariat so essential for the enact-ment of the Marxist drama. Engels had used the theory of the 'labour aristocracy' to explain the lack of revolutionary spirit among the English workers. Lenin used it to explain the lack of revolutionary feeling among the workers of western Europe.

The superficial neatness of the theory does not, however, stand up to even a cursory examination of the facts. Far from capitalism stagnating, it has expanded; far from the rate of profit falling in the West, it has increased and with it general prosperity. And both increased still further after the western industrial countries had relinquished what had been called the 'white man's burden', a phrase which, in itself, indicates that some, at least, of the western capitalists saw their colonial exploits in a different light from that of Lenin. But then Lenin, with Marx's backing, could claim this to be no more than a rationalization for economic self-interest. Yet 'the Common Market', as Alec Nove has written, 'would seem to fit the prophecy about a vision of European states, but far from drawing industrial production from overseas as tribute, the industrialized countries have vastly expanded their own production, and they have expanded their export of goods more rapidly than that of capital. Lenin's vision of imperialism as the last stage of a dying capitalism was evidently mistaken.'[12]

However, this did not prevent Lenin and his followers from drawing lessons from the theory. Not only did it offer a convenient explanation for the failure of Marx's predic-tion with which to silence his critics but it also led to a reassessment of the theory of revolution. If capitalism in its new form became an international system, then the revolu-tion too would have to be international. What was required

12. Alec Nove in *Lenin: The Man, the Theorist, the Leader; A Reappraisal*, ed. Leonard Schapiro and Peter Reddaway, pp. 200–1.

was a common front of the exploited of the world against the exploiters. In the middle of a world war in which social democrats were busily bayoneting social democrats, Lenin blandly asserted that the 'workers have no country'.

In 1905 he had argued that a condition for the success of the Russian revolution would be the assistance of the western proletariat. In 1917 too, in *Letters from Afar*, he re-iterated the view that by itself the Russian proletariat could not bring the socialist revolution to a successful conclusion in Russia without the help of the European proletariat. This was combined with a belief in the inevitability of revolution in Europe. In the preface to *The State and Revolution* he had confidently asserted that 'it is clear an international proletarian revolution is preparing'. Certainly, at the conference of anti-war radicals held in 1915 and 1916 he had tried to prevent the socialists moving towards pacifism and urged the policy of revolutionary defeatism. The war, in line with his thinking on imperialism, was the harbinger of revolution. 'Who,' he asked, 'profits by the slogan of peace?' And he answered: 'Certainly not the revolutionary proletariat. Not the idea of *using* the war to *speed up* the collapse of capitalism.' As Ulam ironically noted, 'He overlooked the fact that the lives of millions of human beings also could have "profited" by the "slogan of Peace".'[13]

(d) The Third International and World Communism

The Third International, or Comintern, was founded in 1919 to organize world revolution. It was a logical outcome of the policy that had been advocated by Lenin at Zimmerwald in 1915, when he had been outvoted, and Kienthal in 1918 when he had won, urging the creation of a new International pledged to world revolution. It was to exclude all those who opposed this policy and was to make no attempt to unite the reformists and revolutionaries. The Third

13. Adam B. Ulam, op. cit., p. 399.

International had as its purpose the mobilizing of the revolution, against both governments and social democrats.

The organizational model of the International derives from Lenin's *What is to be Done?* What he wrote there concerning the organization and tactics of the Russian Social Democratic Party was now transplanted to the work of the International. Lenin wanted it to be a small body of professional revolutionaries engaged in winning over the support of the international proletariat. It was to be the directing organ of world revolution. In contrast to the loose organization of the Second International, it was to be based on the fundamental principle of 'subordinating the interests of the movement in each country to the general interests of the International Revolution as a whole'. The plan was for the masses to be awakened to their true interests. They would then form soviets by which they would gain and maintain power. There was no talk of communist parties, only of the International Communist Party.

In fact there was some substance for the belief in the idea of imminent European revolution. There were upheavals in central Europe, three eastern European empires had been broken up, and the general disillusionment with war and the inevitable disruption to social and economic life made fertile ground for revolutionaries to plough. Lenin could perhaps be forgiven for believing that it was 1848 all over again, but this time on better terms for the proletariat. But in spite of this, the International in 1919 was composed only of small sects founded by Moscow in Hungary and Austria, slightly larger self-founded small sects in Germany, Holland and Britain, and a few mass parties in Bulgaria, Italy and Norway. The latter, however, whilst formally adhering to the International, went their own way.

In April 1920, before the meeting of the Second Congress of the International, Lenin published *Left Wing Communism, An Infantile Disorder*. In this he criticized the western communists for refusing to cooperate with the social democrats against the bourgeois parties and he laid down the strategy to be adopted by communists towards socialists.

The communists were not to cut themselves off from the social democrats or the trade unions. Rather they were to infiltrate and collaborate with all working-class organizations whilst retaining their own organization and doctrinal purity. They should be prepared to manoeuvre, make temporary alliances and compromises. As he asked his readers:

> To carry on a war for the overthrow of the international bourgeoisie, a war which is a hundred times more difficult, protracted and complicated than the most stubborn of ordinary wars between states, and to refuse beforehand to manoeuvre, to make use of conflicts of interest (even though they should be temporary) among one's enemies, to refuse to temporise and compromise with possible ... allies – is this not ridiculous in the extreme?

This was essentially the policy endorsed by the Second Congress of the International held in July the same year. The Congress urged the formation of communist parties and for legal parties to have underground sections. Communist representatives in parliament were to be regarded as 'scouting parties' facilitating the task of revolution. The communist member of parliament should not be a legislator but an agitator of the Party, directly responsible to it, whether it was lawful or illegal, and not to his constituents.

The Congress also adopted the Twenty-One Points laid down as conditions of admission to the International. These were:

> The press of the party should be under the control of the central committee and be used to expose the bourgeoisie and the reformists;
> Reformists should be removed from all responsible positions in the labour movement;
> Every party should have an underground organization;
> The party should attempt to disorganize the army of its country;
> The party should work among the peasants;
> The party should fight against patriots and pacifists in the labour movement;
> The party should split off from the reformists (which

included the 'notorious opportunists' Kautsky, Longuet and MacDonald);

Communists should help in the revolutionary movements in the colonies of their respective countries;

Communists should work within trade unions for the over-throw of reformist leaders;

The party should support the Red International of Labour Unions;

The party should subordinate its parliamentary group to the party central committee;

The party should subordinate itself to the central com-mittee;

The party should carry out periodic purges of its member-ship;

The party should support the Soviet Republic;

The party should submit its programme for approval by the Comintern;

The party should subordinate to Comintern decisions;

The party should call itself a Communist Party;

The party should publish all important documents of the Comintern.

Finally, the last three points dealt with the way in which those parties wishing to join the Comintern should split with other parties. Those wishing to join must accept the twenty-one points at an extraordinary Congress to be held within four months; at least two thirds of the central com-mittees of those parties wishing to join must have voted for affiliation and those members of the parties who voted against acceptance of the twenty-one points must be excluded from their parties before the latter would be admitted to the Comintern.

Reading the twenty-one points, one cannot, as Ulam said, 'determine whether the main task of the communists is to fight capitalism or their former socialist comrades'.[14] But then the International had already announced that 'the world was hurrying towards proletarian revolution at break-neck speed' and, as the experience of the Russian revolution indicated, the social democrats were often troublesome in

14. ibid., p. 658.

that they often had scruples about revolution and its means, Yet, far from the revolution hurrying along, it was taking one step forward and two steps back. Still, Lenin maintained the optimistic belief that the Russian revolution could be transplanted to Germany. In the middle of the civil war in Russia he insisted on the Red Army advancing to Warsaw and was foolish enough to set up a Polish Revolutionary Committee, destined to become the Polish Government but which was composed of men completely out of touch, if not also sympathy, with the Polish working class. He insisted too that the Red Army should reach the German frontiers as soon as possible, though it failed to do so.

By the time of the Third Congress in 1921 there were communist parties in Germany, France, Italy, Norway, Sweden, Poland, Britain – it had two M Ps in 1923 – Chile, the United States, Uruguay, and Argentina. The Third Congress accepted that revolutionary fervour was dying down, endorsed the New Economic Policy and changed the tactics of the international communists. Attempts at armed insurrection were to be postponed. Whereas a few months previously the communists had been enjoined to split their labour movements, they were now urged to adopt the slogan 'To the Masses'. What this meant was that the once-dreaded curse of economism was sanctified with respectability. The masses were to be won by an appeal to their immediate interests. The communists were to work in a 'United Front' with their more respectable social democratic rivals whilst at the same time attempt to embarrass them by greater militancy. The aim of the policy, as Radek described it, was to convince the socialist rank and file that 'their leaders do not want to fight, not even for a piece of bread'. Thus, the communists found themselves accused either of opportunism or, if they retained their organization and theoretical purity, of sectarianism. Whatever they did they were confused and confusing and always likely to be accused of being wrong.

The Fourth Congress of the Comintern in 1923 called on the proletariat of the world to show solidarity with Russia.

Their watchword was to be defence of Russia. Given that they were to believe that strengthening Russia meant weakening capitalism, this was a logical strategy. Yet as the Dutch communist, Hermann Gorter, wrote:

> The Communist Parties in western Europe and throughout the world that retain their membership of the Russian International will become nothing more than a means to preserve the Russian Revolution and the Soviet Republic.

And this is precisely what happened. While the Russians preached the need for world revolution and charged the Comintern and the Red International of Labour Unions with creating foreign revolutionary movements, Russia participated in a basically capitalist international order. It signed the Treaty of Rapallo with Germany in 1922 and an Anglo-Soviet Trade Treaty in 1924. The Russian government, even when apparently anticipating the outbreak of world revolution, was more concerned with promoting its own national interests than stimulating and organizing international revolution. The International as an effective force was doomed when international revolution failed to materialize. Though it continued in existence, and to be directed by Moscow, it was, as Lichtheim remarks, 'merely a loose congeries of satellite organizations whose leaders were occasionally assembled in Moscow to have their separate . . . activities properly co-ordinated'[15] – and then for the defence of Russia.

Not all communists were prepared to accept without question the leadership of the Russians. Paul Levi, a leader of the German Communist Party, in *Our Way* (1921) blamed the Russians for the unsuccessful rising in Germany while another German, Arkady Maslow, argued that by introducing the New Economic Policy the Soviet Union had forfeited its right to the leadership of the international revolutionary movement, and he advocated the forming of a Western European International. Tranmael in Norway took much the same line. But such was the prestige of the

15. George Lichtheim, *A Short History of Socialism*, p. 249.

Russian leaders that few others were prepared to disassociate themselves from what, after all, had been the first and only successful Marxist revolution.

Although he calumniated and slandered those whom he considered to have deviated from strict Marxist orthodoxy, Lenin produced a more profound revision of Marxism than anyone else had done previously. 'Lenin', Kenneth Minogue has written, 'was the first really talented revisionist of Marxism, and after his time the history of Marxism is the history of the men who showed the theory who was boss.'[16] As Trotsky wrote in *Our Political Tasks*, Lenin's conception of political organization was essentially Jacobinical and led straight to dictatorship. He wrote of the withering away of the state but, as Leonard Schapiro points out,

it is now plain that the reverse had been happening. Between 1917 and 1953, there was a progressive extension of the weapons of control, repression and interference in the life of the individual; and even today there is found in the Soviet Union a greater degree of state control and intervention, and probably also of police power, than in any state not founded upon the doctrines of Lenin.[17]

Yet it would be unfair to blame Lenin entirely for this. Certainly he adopted authoritarian methods immediately after the revolution, but then it is difficult to see how else it could have survived, especially during the period of War Communism. Engels had at one time insisted on the need for the revolution to maintain power by violence and terroristic methods and Marx, in a letter to Domela Nieuwenhuis in 1881, asserted that 'a socialist government does not come into power in a country unless conditions are so developed that it can above all take the necessary measures for intimidating the mass of the bourgeoisie sufficiently to gain time – the first desideratum – for lasting action.' There

16. Kenneth Minogue, 'Che Guevara', in *The New Left*, ed. Maurice Cranston, London, 1970, p. 25.

17. Leonard Schapiro and Peter Reddaway (eds.) op. cit., p. 11.

is also evidence to suggest that Lenin would have allowed more intra-party democracy and individual freedom than Stalin tolerated.

Yet there is no denying the major revisions of Marxism, the frequent changes of front and the sacrificing of principle to expediency. Lenin became converted to the Parvus–Trotsky theory of permanent revolution when he had asserted it to be foolish and he sponsored and masterminded the Bolshevik seizure of power when he had been consistently claiming it to be impossible. Whereas Marx emphasized social revolution and envisaged the political revolution as its climax, Lenin viewed political revolution as being most important. For Lenin the social revolution followed, not preceded, the political revolution.

Even so, Lenin's revision of Marx is difficult to assess. Marxism, in Sidney Hook's phrase, is after all an 'ambiguous legacy'. Like Bernstein, Lenin always called himself a Marxist; only they inhabited different worlds and meant different things. At the same time Lenin's inordinate insensitivity to 'deviations' and criticisms might have reflected his intellectual insecurity. He was always at great pains to present his revolutionary activity as conforming to Marxism. He defended it against charges of Blanquism and went so far as to insist, in 1917, that the soviets were the 'direct and immediate organizations of the *majority* of the people', when this was patently untrue. He argued that objective conditions had made insurrection the order of the day and while this may have been true, they were not the objective conditions as outlined by Marx. Nor indeed were they the objective conditions of the Lenin of *Two Tactics*, where they were equated with the degree of capitalist development. In 1917 they were redefined as the class consciousness and mood of the masses.

Lenin, it could be argued, thought of nothing else but revolution and had as an overriding passion the desire for power. Marxism then became for him a convenient set of useful slogans with which to galvanize the masses but which were discarded when other, more dramatic, slogans were needed in 1917. Certainly, it is difficult to find in his writings a glimmer of feeling for the oppressed that is to be found in the writings of Marx. When he thought or wrote about socialism, rather than revolution, it was utopian and soon forgotten in victory. Austere and self-effacing he no doubt was; a Marxist he was not. When he had to choose between Marxism and what he thought to be politically desirable, Marxism always lost.

And yet in spite of this the base of socialism shifted from western Europe, where it had been invented and nurtured, to Russia. From the time of the Russian revolution until that of the Chinese, Russia became the home and acknowledged leader of socialism. That it was not a socialism to which the social democrats of the West could subscribe did not alter this. Russia made the running. It was the standard by which socialism came to be judged. At first the judgements were favourable, as witness the Webbs' *Soviet Russia: A New Civilisation*, but soon, as was to be expected, a more critical standard was applied and Russian socialism was often found wanting.

PART TWO

PART TWO

INTRODUCTION

Lenin had emphasized the revolutionary aspects of Marx's doctrine. After his death and the emergence of Stalin the Soviet Union embarked upon a more conservative course and began what was called the building of socialism in one country. For all practical purposes it was conveniently forgotten that Marxism was about international revolution. Certainly Stalin, and after him Khrushchev, paid lip service to the notion of world revolution and the need for the Soviet Union to aid would-be revolutionaries in the rest of the world, but in fact Soviet policy was dictated more by the perceived needs of Soviet national interests than the international brotherhood of the proletariat.

More interesting in terms of Marxist theory was the revisionist era in the Eastern bloc initiated by Khrushchev, and the lone path travelled by Yugoslavia. And just as the communist states were toning down their revolutionary phraseology, and introducing liberal reforms into their economic and political systems, so also the democratic socialist parties were shedding more of their socialist orthodoxy.

Socialism in Europe, it seemed, had reached maturity; though perhaps it would be more appropriate to describe it as a senile old age. Whether communist or socialist, they had certainly lost the idealism and militancy that had characterized the movement in the last decades of the nineteenth century and the early decades of the twentieth. The communists busied themselves with establishing peaceful coexistence with the capitalist world and the socialists with an accommodation to their bourgeois political and economic systems. It was left to the underdeveloped countries to give Marxism and socialism new life.

8

STALIN AND REVOLUTIONARY CONSOLIDATION

If Lenin took liberties with Marxism, they were as nothing compared to those taken by Stalin. The 'wonderful Georgian', as Lenin once called him, used Marxism, and more particularly Leninism, to disguise his own political manoeuvring. He never claimed that Lenin was wrong: only that, he, Stalin, could correctly interpret what Lenin meant, and Leninism meant what Stalin needed it to mean at any particular time. He was, as Antonio Gramsci has written in another context, persuaded that he was the repository of revealed revolutionary truth. A new, more powerful and infallible Pope resided in the Kremlin. Leninism was used by Stalin as a ragbag of rationalizations for his political stratagems and the Stalinist state. As a social and political system Stalinism, as Milorad Drachkovitch wrote, 'became the incarnation of the totalitarian state that orthodox Marxism had visualised as the final stage of capitalist barbarism'.[1]

The construction of, and rationalization for, the totalitarian state was Stalin's special contribution to Marxism. He added nothing to political thought and very little to party doctrine. In his period of underground revolutionary activity he did no more in his writings than repeat the theories and slogans of the established leaders of Marxism, only in a more pedestrian style. Marxism for him was, in Isaac Deutscher's phrase, 'a mental labour-saving device'.[2] To quote Deutscher again, he was 'the practitioner of the revolution, not its man of letters'.[3] Even his celebrated essay

1. Milorad M. Drachkovitch (ed.), *Marxism in the Modern World*, p. xiii.
2. Isaac Deutscher, *Stalin: A Political Biography*, p. 128.
3. ibid., p. 134.

The Problems of Nationalities and Social Democracy was certainly inspired by Lenin, who probably also outlined its essential elements. It could not be said of Stalin what Clarendon said of Hobbes, that he 'spent too much time on thinking'. He was the least imaginative and least original of self-styled Marxist theorists and, what was worse, his Marxism was of a soulless kind. But then there was work to do and little time for thought.

What Stalin did do was to establish a state machine, unparalleled in its control over social, economic and political life, and all the techniques of repression and terror necessary for its continued existence. He achieved his own establishment as a tyrant, if not godlike figure, through the annihilation of all of his political opponents on the right and the left. With J. A. McNeill Whistler he could say, 'I'm lonesome. They are all dying. I have hardly a warm personal enemy left.' For the intra-party democracy of the Leninist era, he substituted the rigid orthodoxy and adherence to his views based upon the fear of terror. He accomplished the mass deportation of whole families, the institution of show trials to disgrace old Bolsheviks, the introduction of torture to exact 'confessions', secret executions, mass terror and the rewriting of history to appease his own vanity and discredit his opponents. 'Stalin', as Trotsky said, 'revises Marx and Lenin not with the theoretician's pen but with the heel of the G.P.U.'

On the flyleaf of Lenin's *What is to be Done?* Lenin quoted Lassalle's dictum that 'a party becomes stronger by purging itself'. Stalin took the lesson to heart and gave it a new and terrible meaning. As Boris Souvarine wrote,

Stalin's originality lies in the combined use of trickery and violence, pushed to the furtherest extreme, to attain his ends, and above all in his capacity for extending the imaginable limits of tyranny and all that tyranny can mean in terms of inhumanity and immorality.[4]

4. Boris Souvarine, in Milorad M. Drachkovitch (ed.), op. cit., p. 98.

In his last testament, Lenin had questioned Stalin's ability to use power with caution. The years of Stalin's dictatorship more than fulfilled Lenin's fears. A little man in big boots, he trampled all opposition into the ground.

Yet, this is less than half of the picture. Stalin did more than create a police state. He not only substituted nationalism for socialism, he nationalized socialism. He abandoned the *Internationale* for a more patriotic anthem, disbanded the Comintern, reintroduced an officer corps and distinctions into the army, and made Peter the Great, Ivan the Terrible and Tsarist generals heroes of the Soviet Union. No doubt there was something of self-identification in this.

Lenin had emphasized, even to an extreme, the revolutionary content of Marxism. Stalin emptied Marxism and Leninism of their revolutionary content and concentrated on the building of a massive state power. He increased the power of the party, the bureaucracy and the police, and gradually reduced and eliminated all the democratic elements. But like most commentators on Stalin, I have concentrated on the most despicable achievements. He may well have succeeded in accomplishing with the greatest efficiency that which should never have been done at all, but he also accomplished a great deal that was necessary and might not have been achieved by a less dogmatic and domineering leader. To Stalin is owed the rapid industrialization of Russia before 1939, the rebuilding of the army, the preparation for the war he foresaw with Germany, Russian military success and the even greater degree of industrialization at the end of the war. It would not be altogether unfair to claim for Stalin the achievement of a revolution of far more importance than that carried out by Lenin. Lenin replaced one set of masters for another: Stalin brought Russia out of its barbarous past, albeit by barbarous means, and defended what elements of the revolution were left. That he was allowed so much power, and was able to use it in the way that he did, is also a reflection on the cowardice or shortsightedness of the other Bolsheviks. What Marx once said of Tsarist Russia applied to Stalin's relations with his colleagues. 'The Russian bear', Marx said, 'is certainly capable of anything as long as he knows that other animals he has to deal with are capable of nothing.'

(a) Socialism in One Country and the Stalinist State

The most distinctive feature of Stalinism is the doctrine of socialism in one country – what Trotsky called a 'petty-bourgeois doctrine'. The revolution had been successful and counter-revolution and foreign intervention defeated. Rather than embark upon revolutionary activity in the rest of the world, as Lenin had advocated and Trotsky consistently supported, the task Stalin set himself was the consolidation of the revolution in Russia. He did not agree with Trotsky's idea that Europe was ripe for revolution and socialism. Stalin had a more realistic attitude to, and awareness of, the capitalist powers of resistance and the apathy of the European proletariat. Unlike both Lenin and Trotsky, he believed in the possibility of a truce between Russia and the capitalist world – which, of course, may have been no more than a rationalization for his conservatitve policy of successfully accommodating Russia to the capitalist world. Certainly in 1925 he declared that he assumed that Russia would be isolated from the rest of the world for twenty years.

As early as 1917 he had argued against Preobrazhensky that:

> You cannot rule out the possibility that precisely Russia will be the country that paves the way to socialism ... The base of the revolution is broader in Russia than in western Europe, where the proletariat stands alone against the bourgeoisie. With us the working class is supported by the poor peasantry ... We ought to discard the obsolete idea that only Europe can show us the way.

Yet in early 1924 he seemed to be at one with Lenin and Trotsky in not anticipating the success of socialism in Russia without western European revolution. Then he argued that 'for the final victory of socialism, for the organization of socialist production, the efforts of one country, particularly of a peasant country like Russia, are insufficient.' The special meaning he attached to 'the final victory' was only made clear, or only became clear to him, later.

Although acceptance of the doctrine of socialism in one country was to become the test of loyalty to the party and state, it was first advanced as a tactic against Trotsky in the jostling for power in 1924. It was a doctrine used to attack Trotsky for disloyalty while pretending to be a contribution to the debate about the viability of the theory of permanent revolution.

'While Stalinism came to represent the reality of the Soviet régime, Trotskyism stood for the utopian side of communism: belief in an imminent world revolution.'[5] Trotsky never disputed the need to start on the task of building socialism in one country. He even favoured proposals for increased industrialization. Indeed, even Lenin, at the end of his life, came very near to accepting that Russia could build socialism without help from the western proletariat. Trotsky did not go this far. What he argued was that special circumstances had enabled the revolution to occur in Russia but that it could not become socialist whilst Russia was backward and isolated. Revolution was needed elsewhere and it was therefore the duty of Russia, if only out of self-interest, to promote it. Against Stalin he argued that Russia could be neither socialist nor secure without the help of the advanced countries after they had had proletarian revolutions. Russia's entrance into the world economy would make her economically vulnerable or she would be invaded. As he wrote in 1940:

The complete victory of the democratic revolution in Russia is conceivable only in the form of the dictatorship of the proletariat which would inevitably place on the order of the day not only democratic, but socialist tasks as well, would at the same time give a powerful impetus to the international social-

5. George Lichtheim, *A Short History of Socialism*, p. 262.

ist revolution. Only the victory of the proletariat in the west could protect Russia from bourgeois restoration and assure her the possibility of rounding off the establishment of socialism.

In *The Revolution Betrayed* (1936) he condemned the doctrine of socialism in one country as repudiating Marxism in asserting that men could seize power and then use it to transform the legal, political and economic structure of society.

For Trotsky the first duty of the Bolsheviks should be the fomenting of world revolution. If they did not, then nothing could prevent the decay of the Russian revolution. He believed that if they concentrated on the building of socialism and ignored the necessity for world revolution either there would be a social revolution made by bureaucrats with the objective of giving themselves a more solid power base – they would destroy the socialist system of property and reintroduce private property – or there would be a political revolution that would destroy the newly emerging bureaucracy and restore a real and true dictatorship of the proletariat.

In his *Foundations of Leninism* (1924) Stalin put forward two formulations which were later used to support the doctrine of socialism in one country. First he argued that, as a result of capitalist imperialism, any country could become ripe for socialism irrespective of its degree of industrialization. Secondly, he denied that it was possible to organize socialist production without revolutions occurring in several advanced countries. This second formulation was to become a source of embarrassment to Stalin in his controversy with Trotsky and the cause of some intellectual wrangling. In his preface to *On the Road to October* (1924) he attacked Trotsky's doctrine that the building of socialism in one country was impossible and argued instead that Russia could become socialist but not secure. This second formulation was elaborated in *Problems of Leninism* (1926) but suppressed from all future editions of *Foundations*. Instead, he substituted the idea that the proletariat could and must build a socialist society in Russia, but that it could not be 'completed' until the danger of foreign intervention and counter-revolution had been eliminated.

As he said in a speech in 1924:

Formerly the victory of the revolution in a single country was considered impossible, on the assumption that the combined action of the proletarians of all, or at least a majority of the advanced countries was necessary in order to achieve victory over the bourgeoisie. This point of view no longer corresponds with reality. Now we must start from the possibility of such a victory, because the uneven and spasmodic character of the development of the various capitalist countries in the conditions of imperialism, the development of catastrophic contradictions within imperialism, leading inevitably to wars, the growth of the revolutionary movement in all countries of the world – all these lead not only to the possibility but also to the necessity of the victory of the proletariat in individual countries. The history of the Russian Revolution is definite proof of that.

But he went on to say that

overthrowing the power of the bourgeoisie and establishing the power of the proletariat in a single country does not yet guarantee the complete victory of socialism. After consolidating its power and leading the peasantry after it, the proletariat of the victorious country can and must build up a socialist society.

Though the policy of socialism in one country was adopted by the party in 1925, it was not finally elaborated until 1938 in Stalin's reply to young Ivanov of Kursk. Stalin argued that the building of socialism in one country had been achieved but that its victory could not be complete whilst Russia was surrounded by a hostile world. Hence the international proletariat under the guidance of its Russian guardians had to be, and was, subordinated to the interests of the Soviet Union. The Soviet Union was to be used as a base for the building of socialism, from which imperialism could be overthrown. The first task was to consolidate its own dictatorship whilst attempting to win the support of the proletarians and peasants in Europe and the militant nationalists in the colonial territories.

It has been said that the doctrine of socialism in one country was first devised as a tactic for use against Trotsky. But the doctrine was not really an invention. Rather, it was the product of necessity. World revolution had failed to occur and thus the only reasonable course open to Stalin was to attempt to build socialism in Russia. Alternatively, he could give up altogether or wait patiently for the western proletariat to awake from their comfortable slumber. Moreover, as Deutscher comments, Stalin's doctrine summed up 'a powerful and hitherto inarticulate trend of opinion or emotion' in Russia.[6] It provided a sense of self-sufficiency and, perhaps more important, self-respect to a party and nation that had always regarded themselves as inferior to the West, to which they had looked for both guidance and salvation. Now it could go it alone. As one prominent Russian communist said, 'One Soviet tractor is worth more than ten good foreign communists.'

The drive towards the collectivization of farming and rapid industrialization followed naturally from the emphasis that was placed on the achieving of socialism in one country. Yet collectivization was not really a thought-out result of the doctrine so much as a response to the danger of famine in 1928 and 1929. In 1925 Stalin only expected a small fraction of agriculture to be collectivized and was even, it is said, contemplating a return to small-scale farming. Bukharin could even say 'To the peasants, to all the peasants, we must say: "Enrich yourselves, develop your economy, and have no fear of being dispossessed."' The first five-year plan of 1928 provided for the collectivization of only twenty per cent of farms by 1933. In 1929 Stalin still conceived of the private farmers as playing a predominant role in the agricultural economy. It was the reluctance of the peasants to give up their produce because of the lack of consumer goods, and the consequent threat of famine in the towns, that led to a quickened pace and more repressive

6. Isaac Deutscher, op. cit., p. 292.

measures of collectivization, with disastrous consequences. In 1933 a decree was issued calling for the liquidation of the Kulaks through the confiscation of their property and their removal to forced labour camps.

In 1919 a resolution of the Eighth Party Congress had laid down that:

In encouraging associations of every kind, and also agricultural communes, of middle peasants, the representatives of the Soviet power should not permit the slightest compulsion in founding such bodies ... Those representatives of the Soviet power who allow themselves to apply not merely direct, but even indirect, compulsion in order to attach peasants to communes, should be held strictly accountable and removed from work in the countryside.

Fortunately for Stalin, he was accountable to no one and hardly ever ventured into the countryside. Soon collectivization became a synonym for terror. The peasants were not attracted into the collectives by the vision of more efficient methods and the better standard of living and way of life which they were told would be theirs. Nor were they peacefully integrated by a gradual process as party officials had been proclaiming they would be. Instead, they were coerced at gunpoint or else shot or deported. And far from agricultural production increasing, it decreased – mainly as a result of the slaughter of their animals by the peasants themselves and their refusal to till the land. Nor was industry equipped to provide the machinery necessary to make large-scale farming efficient. The success of the drive towards collectivization was vitiated, if by nothing else, by the paucity of machines and trained instructors.

In *Dizziness with Success* (1930) Stalin blamed over-enthusiastic administrators for the chaos that had been caused by the ill-prepared and forced policy. Whereas a few months previously he had given the order for immediate collectivization, he now claimed that his orders had been misinterpreted. He admitted that only fifty per cent of all farms had been collectivized and that many of these were not viable. Now he argued that 'collective farms cannot be set up by force. To do so would be stupid and reactionary.' Both Marx and Engels had anticipated that the peasants would become proletarianized through large-scale farming, but neither suggested it should be the result of force. Indeed, Engels in *The Peasant Question in France and Germany* had outlined the role of the communist:

Our task in relation to the small peasants will consist, first and foremost, in converting their private production and private ownership into collective production and collective ownership – not, however, by forcible means but by example and by offering social aid for this purpose.

Stalin tried and failed with force before he returned to the precepts of Engels. In 1930 the brake was put on. Only ten per cent more of all farms were collectivized in the next three years so that at the end of the first five-year plan the total was sixty per cent. Besides a reduction in the rate of collectivization there was also a liberalization of the collective régime. The peasants were allowed to share in its profit and own small plots of land while most state farms were wound up and their land given to the collectives.

Besides providing for the collectivization of farming, the first five-year plan called for rapid industrialization. While in 1927 Stalin had expressed his contentment with the rate of economic growth, in 1928 he urged more rapid industrialization and increased capital investment. The underlying aim of the plan was that of 'constructing a socialist society on the basis of the maximum development of productive force and the systematic improvement of the condition of the workers'. No aspect of social and economic life was left unplanned in the drive to establish a strong economy. At the end of 1929 a new labour policy was introduced to aid industrialization. This signalled the end of what Stalin called 'spontaneity' in the labour market and the beginning of the direction of labour. Collective farms were forced to send a quota of men and women to the factories with labour camps provided for recalcitrant peasants.

In 1930 the pace became more fierce with heavy industry being ordered to raise its output by fifty per cent in that year. 'He was now', as Deutscher commented, 'completely possessed by the idea that he could achieve a miraculous transformation of the whole of Russia by a single *tour de force*.'[7] In fact, as he admitted in 1931, industrial output increased by between six and ten per cent. To achieve the plan's objective, prizes were distributed for good work, hours reduced, wages increased and great use made of propaganda and competitive devices. In later periods Stakhanovism was introduced, that is the use of pacemakers for other workers to keep up with, as well as piecework. Equality of wages was now considered to be detrimental to socialist production and wage inequalities were sanctioned.

The second and third plans were more modest and more in the way of an exercise in consolidation. The second plan, too, functioned by paying men according to the amount of work done. Though this was in accordance with the remarks of Marx and Lenin on the transitory stage to socialism, the differentials between the low and high paid were often greater than those that existed in capitalist countries, as Max Eastman indicated in his aptly titled book *The End of Socialism in Russia* (1937). In spite of this, the objective of the third plan, from 1938 to 1942, was to 'complete the construction of a classless socialist society and to accomplish the gradual transition from socialism to communism'. This, of course, was not achieved. With the threat and onset of war the emphasis was placed on the production of military hardware. At least the war could be used as an explanation of the failure to realize the classless, stateless society.

The massive attempt to plan Russia's economy and bring it up to the level of development in the West entailed a great increase in the apparatus and power of the state. Far from withering away it became more and more pervasive, and intervened in every aspect of the individual's life. But Stalin always had rationalizations ready at hand. In 1930 he argued that the state could not wither away until it had

7. ibid., pp. 321–2.

been fully developed. Making the necessary bows in the direction of Marxism, he announced 'we are for the withering away of the state', but he went on to say, 'To keep on developing state power in order to prepare the conditions for the withering away of state power – that is the Marxist formula.' In 1939 he was still prepared to air his belief in the eventual disappearance of the state, but argued that the time was not yet ripe, even though he asserted that Russia was in the process of transition from socialism to communism. Indeed, he argued that when Engels spoke of the withering away of the state he was assuming that socialism had been successful, if not in all countries, then in at least a majority of the most advanced. Thus, so long as Russia remained surrounded by hostile countries, there would need to be a continuation of the policy of building socialism in one country and of developing the power of the state.

In introducing the new Constitution in 1936 Stalin argued that the Soviet state was not one foreseen by Marx, Engels or Lenin, which was probably true enough. It was, he said, of a special type – which few doubted. The state, according to Stalin, however, was not the servant of a class but of society. Instead of the dictatorship of the proletariat, which had in any case long been a lie, a new dictatorship of the workers was set up with a bicameral parliament elected by secret ballot. This was just as much a farce as the dictatorship of the proletariat had even been. The Constitution differed markedly from that of Lenin's in 1918, which had substituted soviets for the state and made no mention of parliament.

To Trotsky the Constitution was another example of the betrayal of the revolution by Stalin. He had already betrayed it by making it a bureaucracy. Now, according to Trotsky, the Constitution represented 'an immense step back from socialist to bourgeois principles'. It created 'the political premises for the birth of a new possessing class' and he described the introduction of universal, equal, and direct suffrage as 'juridically liquidating the dictatorship of the proletariat'. To Trotsky the soviets were the true organs of proletarian democracy and working-class government in that they formed true communities with common interests, not mere territorial groupings of people as was the case with parliamentary democracy. Though he did not deny that the soviets had lost a great deal of their original vitality they were, he believed, potentially the true organs of proletarian democracy.

Yet the difference was marginal. Whatever the appearances, the party, and through it Stalin, ruled. And even the party lost much of its proletarian composition. Congresses of the party were infrequent and supreme power lay with the Politburo and later the Presidium, both pliant instruments of Stalin. He argued that the leadership of the party did not constitute a dictatorship because in addition to the party, there existed organizations like the League of Communist Youth and trade unions. These transmission belts, as they were called, helped the party to maintain contact with the people. More correctly, they helped the party to exercise and maintain control over the people.

(b) The Comintern and the End of World Revolution

Once conceived of as the agency of world revolution, the Comintern had, during Lenin's lifetime, become more of an instrument of Soviet foreign policy than of anything else. Viewed by Lenin as the vanguard of world revolution, the communist parties of the West became, in Trotsky's words, 'the frontier guards' of the Soviet Union. Given that it was the base from which revolution in Europe was to be launched, it was logical enough for Stalin to see the prime duty of communists to be the defence of the Soviet Union. The primacy of the Soviet Union's national interest was made explicit in 1928 when the Comintern's statutes were revised to incorporate Stalin's statement that 'an internationalist is one who unreservedly, unhesitatingly and without conditions, is prepared to defend the Soviet Union because it is the base of the world revolutionary movement'.

The Congress forecast economic crisis in capitalist countries and abandoned the united-front-from-below policy of 1924. Now the communist parties were enjoined to launch their final attack on capitalism. The social democratic parties, or social fascists as they were now called, were to be regarded as enemies no different from the fascists, and all contact with them broken. This 'class against class' policy was completely unrelated to the special conditions of each country and the particular situation of its communist party; it just suited the Soviet Union. It caused the loss of many socialist and communist seats in France, and an increase in the strength of the Right. It led to the demoralization and disorganization of the German labour movement, was a factor in its inability to prevent the rise of Hitler and caused the deaths of thousands of communists. Throughout the world the policy led to the isolation of the communists from the labour movement, which was essentially social democratic in nature. 'The Comintern', as Borkenau vividly put it, 'resembled a lifeless mechanical doll unable to move forwards or backwards, but uttering by means of some hidden gadget, blood-curdling yells at regular intervals.'[8] With the decimation of the German communists by Hitler, the Comintern lost its only party with a mass following and real influence.

The rise of fascism in Italy and Germany caused a change of policy. Stalin made advances to the bourgeois-capitalist governments of France and Britain, and played *God Save the King* for Anthony Eden in the process, obtained a non-aggression pact with France, Poland and the Baltic countries, recognition from the United States, and the Soviet Union joined the League of Nations which Stalin, not without justice, had called the League of Brigands. The home of revolutionary socialism and the supposed initiator of world revolution was trafficking with the capitalist powers and seeking acceptance among them. Of course, there was nothing intrinsically disreputable about this. Marx, Engels, and above all Lenin, had for long instructed communists on

8. F. Borkenau, *European Communism*, London, 1953, p. 68.

159

the need for compromise and deception. Stalin, it could be argued, was doing no more than attempting to protect the only base that socialism possessed from the threat of fascism. It also fitted logically with his policy of building socialism in the Soviet Union. For this to be successful, a period of international stability was desirable if not necessary. Stalin anticipated that this would be forthcoming. He was certainly sceptical about the prospects of international proletarian revolution.

The seventh and last Congress of the Comintern in 1935 laid down the primary duty of the working classes of the world: 'To help with all their might and by all means to strengthen the USSR and to fight against the enemies of the USSR' both in war and peace. This, it went on, would 'coincide fully and inseparably with the interests of the toilers of the whole world in their struggle against the exploiters'. It proclaimed as its policy what Stalin in his diplomacy had been pursuing in practice. The policy now was one of forming popular fronts of socialists, reformist trade unionists, communists and even liberals against fascism. Defence of democracy was the watchword of international communism and unity and united action its slogan. Communists were instructed to put away their radical demands and slogans for fear of them frightening off the middle-class supporters and to be vociferous advocates of the defence of the bourgeois democracies. Accordingly, the Red International of Labour Unions was quietly allowed to lapse. This change of policy went even further to the right than that of 1928 had gone to the left. As Borkenau commented:

It implied a wholesale overthrow of the basic principles of the bourgeoisie. Instead of the Soviet system, eulogy of democracy. Instead of internationalism, nationalism. The revolutionary ideals had failed conspicuously.[9]

Whatever it was in relation to communist and Marxist theory, it was certainly more successful as a policy. It was

9. F. Borkenau, *The Communist International*, p. 387.

especially successful in France where the communist and socialist youth organizations were merged and the two trade union centres amalgamated. Membership of both the communist and socialist parties rose, the communists rising from virtual insignificance to great strength. The united front of the communists and socialists was extended to include the radicals in the Popular Front, and formed a government under Léon Blum. The French Communist Party adopted a 'responsible' attitude and attempted to stop strikes and prevent the occupation of factories. Maurice Thorez, the leader of the party, even proposed the widening of the Front to include all the defenders of France from fascism. Yet Tranamael in Norway refused to accept a communist united front, regarding the Soviet Union as a fascist state, and the right-wing reformist socialist parties of Belgium, Britain, Czechoslovakia, Denmark, Holland, Poland and Sweden refused point-blank to cooperate with the communists.

In Spain, however, a Popular Front coalition came into existence in 1935 when its communist party was one of the smallest in Europe. The attitude of the communists in Spain, however, indicated how far from revolution the communist party had moved, and how far it had become a tool of Soviet foreign policy. It was no joke when Stalin told an American journalist that the idea of world revolution was a 'tragi-comical misunderstanding'. Russian support for the Republic was motivated by concern for Soviet security. The non-revolutionary character of the Spanish communists, the purging of the more extreme left-wing elements and the support given to the Popular Front, were all intended to avoid antagonizing the British and French, whom Stalin needed for an alliance against Hitler and Mussolini. As Gerald Brenan wrote of the Civil War, in Catalonia,

one had a strange and novel situation: on the one side stood the huge compact proletariat of Barcelona with its long revolutionary tradition, and on the other the white-collar workers and *petite bourgeoisie* of the city, organised and armed by the communist party against it.[10]

It was not surprising that El Campesino, a Spanish communist, should write of Russian policy during the Civil War

that the Kremlin does not serve the interests of the peoples of the world, but makes them serve its own interests; that, with a treachery and hypocrisy without parallel, it makes use of the international working class as a mere pawn in its political interests.[11]

In the period 1936–7 the communist party practically eliminated the spontaneous revolution of the anarchists and socialists. But there was perhaps another side to the story than a mere consideration of international policy. At least Rudolf Rocker thought there was:

What the Russian autocrats and their supporters fear most is that the success of libertarian socialism in Spain might prove to their blind followers that the much-vaunted 'necessity of dictatorship' is nothing but one vast fraud which in Russia has led to the despotism of Stalin and is to serve today in Spain to help the counter-revolution to a victory over the revolution of the workers and peasants.[12]

In 1939 Stalin tried to obtain alliances with France and Britain but was not successful. Hence, through the agency of Ribbentrop, the Nazi–Soviet Pact was signed in 1939. Poland was divided between them, the Polish Communist Party having been dissolved by Stalin to facilitate the pact. Stalin could now hardly pose as the enemy of fascism when actually being prepared to share in its spoils. 'Internationalism', George Lichtheim wrote, 'had been sacrificed on the altar of *Realpolitik*, for the only defence offered by the Stalinist régime and its apologists in 1939 was that the interests of the Soviet Union took precedence over all other

10. Gerald Brenan, *The Spanish Labyrinth*, Cambridge, 1960, p. 325.

11. Quoted in Noam Chomsky, *American Power and the New Mandarins*, London, 1969, p. 72.

12. ibid., p. 70.

considerations.'[13] The communist parties in Europe aided Germany in the war until it attacked the Soviet Union in 1941, when they distinguished themselves in the battle. But for them it was a battle to save Russia.

Throughout Stalin's control of the Comintern, it was used to further the fluctuating and often contradictory aims of the Soviet Union and rarely for the purpose of manufacturing world revolution. Indeed, Stalin did his best to prevent the outbreak of revolution. He told the Chinese to trust in Chiang Kai-shek, told the German communists that the social democrats, not Hitler, were their main enemy, instructed the Spanish not to pursue their revolution, instructed the Vietnamese Communist Party to work to remain within the French colonial empire and he agreed to give the British a free hand in eliminating the communists in Greece in return for a free hand in Rumania. Throughout this period Stalin was one of the strongest defenders of the *status quo*, morbidly fearing any revolution he could not control in case it threatened Russia's interests.

Yet, in spite of all the changes of front, the sacrificing of men as well as principle to expediency, the internationalism of the European communists somehow survived. They might have been embarrassed by, and angry at, the compromises but they remained, on the whole, loyal to their idea of Russia – even after the Nazi–Soviet Pact. This is how the Social Democrats should have acted in 1914. The instructions of the International in 1939 might have been misguided, but the loyalty of the communists was admirable. Internationalism, to them, was more important than nationalism, or even common sense. Once Russia had joined the war the idea of world revolution and its vehicle, the Comintern, became a nuisance. It was quietly dissolved in 1943. In 1945 Stalin could say 'today Socialism is possible even under the English monarchy. Revolution is no longer necessary everywhere.'[14]

13. George Lichtheim, op. cit., p. 249.
14. Quoted in Milovan Djilas, *Conservations with Stalin*, p. 104.

(c) Socialism in One Zone and the Cominform

At the end of the war the doctrine of socialism in one country, with its idea of self-sufficiency, gave way to that of socialism in one zone. This became the supreme political objective of the Stalinist régime. Stalin was, no doubt, anxious to fill the power vacuum in central Europe caused by the defeat of its countries in the war. The security of the Soviet Union was paramount in his felt need to have friendly adjacent states. He had, of course, been given permission from Churchill and Roosevelt at Yalta in 1945 for the setting up of governments friendly to the Soviet Union in what was delineated as the Soviet Union's sphere of interest. This required some degree, at least, of communist control exercised from and supervised by the Soviet Union. Yet, at the same time, an overt show of strength or interference on a massive scale might have aroused the opposition of the western powers and provoked their intervention. Hence, Stalin proceeded with unusual caution. What the Hungarian leader Matyas Rakosi called 'salami tactics' were used. There was a slow slice-by-slice movement in eastern Europe towards communist control.

This was, in effect, the realization of a policy which had previously been outlined by Stalin when he had argued that the inevitable world revolution should be prepared by the playing-up of the contradictions that, according to Lenin, existed within the capitalist world. These were the contradictions between bourgeois and proletariat, among the imperialist powers, and between the imperialist powers and their subject nations. In the fight for world revolution the allies of the Soviet Union would be the communist parties in the industrialized countries and the national liberation movements in the colonial and dependent territories. Yet whilst the objective was to establish socialism in as many countries as possible, this should not be attempted unless the communists possessed overwhelming force. The communists were thus instructed to obtain power with the help

164

of all left-wing elements. After their usefulness had been exhausted, they would be eliminated and a Soviet Union socialist system established.

This, broadly speaking, is what happened in eastern Europe. The communist parties cooperated with other parties in national coalitions, popular fronts or coalitions of equals. They moderated their ideology and restructured it to fit the needs and aspirations of each particular country. They were helped, of course, by the prestige that attached to some of them for their service in the resistance, and by their advocacy of nationalistic slogans and the return of lost lands. Thus the Polish Communist Party argued that a communist Poland was the best way of retaining the Oder-Neisse territories, and the German communists believed a communist Germany was the way to regain them for Germany. The next step of the communists was to infiltrate key posts in the government, carry out purges of the leaders of the other parties – and their own – and eventually set up a communist party dictatorship, though the parties went under strange and misleading names, like the Polish United Workers' Party.

Czechoslovakia had a coalition government until 1948 when the communists took over after a coup. In Hungary the Soviet Union actually set up four different parties which governed in a National Liberation Front. But by 1948 the government was in communist hands, and the Communist Hungarian Workers' Party was formed from the two proletarian parties. In East Germany the communist United Socialist Party (SED) was formed as a result of the compulsory fusion of the Communist Party (KPD) and the Social Democratic Party (SPD). Yet even after this there still existed three bourgeois parties until 1948. East Germany was, however, something of a special case. At first the Soviet Union seemed content to set up an anti-fascist democratic system and there is some reason to believe that Stalin was in favour of a reunited Germany and not particularly enthusiastic about the setting up of a separate East German state. Even in 1952 he appeared to be prepared to sacrifice the German Democratic Republic for a united but neutralized Germany.

Whereas Marx and Lenin had anticipated revolution from below, for Stalin it was to be revolution from above, in the wake of the Red Army. The communist parties of the conquered countries were no more than the agents of Stalin and the Red Army; where they refused to play this role they were quickly purged. By one means or another, communist governments were set up in Poland, Hungary, Rumania, Czechoslovakia, Bulgaria, East Germany and Yugoslavia. They adopted the Russian form of government with power vested in communist party organs hiding behind a parliamentary façade. Organizations like the trade unions and the mass media were subordinated to party control and the position of the churches weakened. Soon they concluded 'agreements' with the Soviet Union for the stationing of its forces in their countries and treaties of friendship and alliance were made. There was, however, resistance to the Soviet take-over, from Clementis and Slausky in Czechoslovakia, Gomulka in Poland, Kostor in Bulgaria, Patrascanu in Rumania, and Rajk in Hungary, but they were the exception rather than the rule, and soon desisted or were removed.

Elsewhere in Europe the communist parties had increased in strength particularly in France, Italy (where membership reached the two-million mark) and Finland. At the beginning of the Cold War in 1947 the Communist Information Bureau, Cominform, was formed, partly as a response to the Marshall Plan, in that it was an attempt to integrate the economies of eastern Europe, and partly to tie the satellite countries more closely to the Soviet Union. Only the Russian, eastern European and French and Italian communist parties were represented at the founding conference: the Chinese and Asians were not invited.

At the founding meeting Zhdanov argued that the war had put socialism in a more powerful position in relation to capitalism. As a result of the war, People's Republics had been established in eastern Europe and the crisis in the colonial system exacerbated and had given rise to liberation movements. The world, then, was divided into two hostile camps. The duty of all communists was to unite all anti-fascist, democratic and peace-striving forces against the aggression of the capitalist powers, epitomized by the United States and Britain, and all those who worked for war. Eugene Vargo, who had argued that no crisis of capitalism should be expected, was forced to recant and Zhdanov now stressed the inevitability of war. The French and Italian communist parties were instructed to frustrate the implementation of the Marshall Plan and the Truman Doctrine. Once again, as in 1848 and 1919, the illusion of world revolution came to dominate the international communist movement. Not unnaturally relations between the Soviet Union and the West deteriorated and, as a result, great loyalty and subservience was exacted from Russia's eastern European satellites.

This reliance of what came to be called the People's Democracies on the Soviet Union was explained by apologists of the Soviet Union by saying that they were, with the guidance of the Soviet Union, attempting the transition to socialism. Naturally enough they were, according to the Russians, only in the process of transition. Any recognition that they had already achieved socialism would have obviated the need for Soviet guidance, which in effect meant domination. As with Stalin's policy of socialism in one country so in the Soviet zone; by building socialism a proletariat would be created so that what was to have been the initiator of revolution was to be created by it. The Cominform denounced all attempts to build socialism on any other model than that of Russia. It was General de Gaulle who described the 'Soviet Empire' as the 'largest and last colonial power of the era'. But then, to be fair to the Russians, he had forgotten about the American empire.

9

COMMUNIST REVISIONISM
IN THE 1950s

Not long after the death of Stalin the leaders of the
Soviet Union engaged in what has come to be called a
period of de-Stalinization or revision of Stalinism. The new
view of socialism that they expressed and the role they
envisaged the Soviet Union playing in the world, particularly in relation to the West, became associated with
a growing liberalization in the Soviet régime. The aspiration was expressed in the West that the Soviet Union would
become more democratic, particularly under the impact
of western ideas and influence and the supposedly felt need
of the communist leaders to provide the kind and quantity
of material benefits for their peoples that allegedly existed
in the western liberal democracies.

Revisionism within the Soviet Union is associated with
the name of Khrushchev. He had always been a party worker,
was extremely provincial in outlook and only travelled beyond the borders of the Soviet Union at the age of sixty. But
he was a more flamboyant and extrovert figure than one
normally associates with the Soviet leadership and he made
up for his previous isolation from the world by a series of
well-publicized cavalcades through the countries of the
world. If nothing else, as Deutscher commented, 'For a
nation which had suffered thirty years under the most taci-
turn of tyrants it was a positive relief to be ruled by a
chatterbox for a change.'[1] It was only after his request that
'he be released from his responsibilities' in October 1964
that *Pravda* indicted him by speaking of 'harebrained
schemes; half-baked conclusions and hasty decisions and

1. Isaac Deutscher, *Ironies of History. Essays on Contemporary
Communism*, p. 63.

actions, divorced from reality; bragging and bluster; attraction to rule by fiat; unwillingness to take into account what science and practical experience have already discovered'.

Certainly Khrushchev was prepared to be more pragmatic and adventurous, even dashing, than his predecessor. 'The Khrushchevian style was characterized', as Merle Fainsod wrote, 'by boldness as well as opportunism; above all it was marked by a willingness to experiment and strike out in-new directions without necessarily calculating or anticipating costs and consequences.'[2] The impetus he gave to revisionism in eastern Europe in the mid 1950s was probably not a consequence he anticipated or a cost he had calculated.

(a) Khrushchev: The New Course, World Revolution and Peaceful Coexistence

The new style of leadership, internal management of the economy and attitude to international relations were all set out, albeit superficially, in Khrushchev's secret speech to the Twentieth Congress of the Communist Party of the USSR in 1956. In 1954 he had placed Stalin next to Lenin as the architect of Russia's strength and emphasized the priority of developing heavy industry. However this was no more than a fusillade in the internal struggle for power aimed at Malenkov's campaign for the production of more consumer goods. As early as 1953 Slepov had attacked the cult of personality and a number of old Bolsheviks liquidated by Stalin had been rehabilitated. Now Krushchev distributed Lenin's testament and blamed Stalin for the excesses of the past. He argued that the Trotskyites and Bukharinites had not been enemies of the people, as Stalin has declared, and need not have been annihilated. He catalogued Stalin's mistakes and crimes and yet said that 'Stalin was convinced that all this was necessary for the defence of the interests of the working

2. Merle Fainsod in *Marxism in the Modern World*, ed. Milorad M. Drachkovitch, p. 114.

class against the plotting of the enemies and against the attack of the imperialist camp.'

Of course, Khrushchev had for a long time been a leading member of the party ruled by Stalin. Too much criticism of Stalin's era would also have led to a questioning of the role of those who also held power. As Isaac Deutscher wrote:

We readily believe in the defendant's guilt, but we wonder whether the prosecutor has not gone too far in self-exculpation. We even feel a sneaking suspicion that in order to exonerate himself he may have painted, here and there, the defendant's character just a shade too black.[3]

All the failures and mistakes were laid at Stalin's feet, the successes and achievements at the feet of the masses, the party or Leninism.

Nevertheless, changes were made. The attack on the cult of personality and terrorism implied that personal despotism should end and a return be made, to some extent at least, to intra-party democracy. Yet no open debate or conflicts of opinion have materialized, or at least they have not been made public. Even the resolutions at the Twentieth Congress were all passed unanimously, in the Stalinist tradition. Though some debate seems to have been tolerated in the Central Committee the differences of opinion that exist are still kept a secret from the party. On the other hand, one-man leadership was replaced by collective leadership, the rule of law was reasserted and the powers of the state security police reduced. In place of the emphasis on heavy industry, Khrushchev promised to make more consumer goods available. 'And what sort of communist society is it', he had said in 1954, 'that has no sausage?'

A relaxation of the rigid régime imposed on the collective farms and better prices for their products was promised. For the industrial worker he held out the promise of increased wages, shorter hours, release from the Stakhanovite system and the substitution of time rates for piece rates. Wages were to become more egalitarian than they had been under

3. Isaac Deutscher, op. cit., p. 12.

Stalin. There was also to be improved housing and pensions and more freedom for intellectuals. Authority was to be decentralized in the economy and factory managers given more power in a move towards planning from below. It all sounded like the programme of a welfarist social democratic party seeking electoral support. And like such a programme, he offered all things to all men.

In 1961 it was announced that 'the present generation of Soviet people will live under communism'. This was to be achieved in twenty years and meant no more than that there would be an abundance of goods, each family would have its own flat and all public utilities would be free. The 1961 Party Programme, in defining the task of 'building communism' in terms of improvements in the quantity and quality of goods rather than in terms of structural change marked the end, as Richard Lowenthal pointed out, of the imposition of a permanent revolution from above on Soviet society.[4] It announced that agencies of self-government would gradually replace the state organs. Authority would be transferred to trade unions, sports societies and soviets. The supposed aim was to develop mass participation as the state gradually withered away. Yet this sounded more like syndicalism, or more correctly guild socialism, than communism. Whatever it was, neighbourhood assemblies meted out punishment and People's Guards enforced order. But they, and all other organizations, were still guided by, and subject to, the control of the party; the artistic community, especially, had to be loyal to the party line.

The Party's policy, according to Khrushchev,

expresses the interests of society as a whole and consequently of each separate individual as well ... As an orchestra conductor sees to it that all the instruments sound harmonious and in proportion, so in social and political life does the Party direct the efforts of all the people toward the achievements of a single goal.

4. Richard Lowenthal, *The Revolution Withers Away, Problems of Communism*, Vol. 1, 1965, p. 15.

Hence the theory of the dictatorship of the proletariat was replaced by the concept of an all-people's state; the party of the proletariat became the party of the people. The rule of a despotic leader was repudiated and bows made in the direction of greater individual freedom, but never for a moment was the control exercised by the party weakened.

Khrushchev was followed by the rule of conservative oligarchies who, while not wishing to return to the practices of the Stalinist period, wished nevertheless to hold back the liberalization process introduced by Khrushchev and which threatened the power of the party bureaucracy. An indication of the de-liberalization process was the heavy sentences passed upon Andrei Sinyavsky and Yuli Daniel. There have been, however, continuing signs of unrest in the Soviet Union in the 1960s and the fear of it spreading may well have been one of the motivating factors contributing towards the Soviet invasion of Czechoslovakia in 1968.

Perhaps more important than the internal changes in the Soviet Union was the more pragmatic approach to international relations introduced by Khrushchev. He announced in 1956 that war was no longer inevitable and that Russia sought peace and better relations with all countries. In the early 1950s he had declared that nuclear war would mean the end of capitalism but this, like his then emphasis on investment in heavy industry, was probably more connected with internal Soviet politics, and, especially, Malenkov's earlier announcement that nuclear war would mean the end of all civilization. Khrushchev now argued that socialism could be achieved by other means than revolution, that even parliaments could serve as institutions of genuine democracy for the working class, that it was possible, indeed essential, to cooperate with social democrats, and that separate paths to socialism were both possible and permissible. It was no longer necessary, then, to apishly copy the Soviet model as Stalin had insisted. 'Creative Marxism in action' was now defined as adjustment to 'the peculiarities and specific features of each country'.

Against the doctrine of Lenin and Stalin that war was

inevitable between the capitalist powers and the Soviet Union, Khrushchev said in 1956:

As long as imperialism exists, the economic base that gives rise to wars will also remain. That is why we must display the greatest vigilance. As long as capitalism survives in the world, reactionary forces that represent the interests of the capitalist monopolies will continue their drive toward military gambles and aggression and may try to unleash war. But war is not a fatalistic inevitability. Today there are mighty social and political forces possessing formidable means to prevent the imperialists from unleashing war, and, if they try to start it, to give a smashing rebuff to the aggressors and frustrate their adventurist plans. For this it is necessary for all anti-war forces to be vigilant and mobilised; they must act as a united front and not relax their efforts in the struggle for peace. The more actively people defend peace, the greater the guarantee that there will be no war.

This is the basis of the doctrine of peaceful coexistence and was an attempt, and a not unsuccessful one, to present the Soviet Union as peaceloving and accommodating. Khrushchev was concerned to ease international tensions and end the Cold War. Similarly the Twentieth Congress of the Party in 1956 accepted the doctrine of neutralism, thought to be impossible by Stalin, and the existence of a third world and peace zone of non-aligned countries independent of the warring camps of the West and East.

Khrushchev pointed out to the Rumanian Communist Party in 1960 that Lenin's propositions on imperialism were still in force. 'But it should not be forgotten', he added, 'that Lenin's propositions on imperialism were advanced and developed tens of years ago, when the world did not know many things that are now decisive for historical development, for the entire international situation.' What this meant was that the Soviet Union was now strong and the number of socialist countries had increased. Ultimate victory could be accomplished through the peaceful battle of ideas, though help would be given to liberation movements in colonial countries. Moreover, in 1963 he had said that 'If

G

someone says that war is necessary for revolution, one must reply that in a war the working class die most of all.'

The assertion that war was not inevitable did not mean that Khrushchev had either given up hopes for a world communist order or accepted the existing balance of power between the Soviet Union and the West. It meant only that war should not be considered to be inevitable if it threatened the destruction of civilization. Certainly, he had told the West: 'We will bury you,' the United States: 'Your grandchildren will live under communism' and had proclaimed in Austria: 'Life is short, and I want to see the Red Flag fly over the whole world in my lifetime.' Again, he announced in 1957 that 'society develops in accordance with its laws, and now the era has come when capitalism must make way for socialism as a higher social system than capitalism'. Hence, although he was a revisionist, he did not renounce the goal of world communism.

The emphasis that Khrushchev placed upon the peaceful transition to socialism and coexistence between the communists and the West led him to be characterized by the Chinese communists as a revisionist. In the eyes of the Chinese communist leaders, as Merle Fainsod has observed, 'Khrushchevism became a term of contempt, the symbol of a peculiarly degenerate form of revisionism that sacrifices the revolutionary élan of Leninism to serve the bourgeoisified interests of a chauvinist great power masquerading as a communist state.'[5] To the Chinese, Khrushchev was a 'hen in the backyard of the working-class movement, among the dung heaps'.

Certainly Khrushchev, like Stalin, put the interests of the Soviet Union above all others. The interests of the Soviet Union took priority at all times over those of other communist countries or that apparent entity called the international communist movement. Soviet primacy within the communist bloc was reasserted. While announcing that it would be wrong for the Russians 'to eat ham every day while

5. Merle Fainsod, in Milorad M. Drachkovitch (ed.), op. cit., p. 133.

the rest look on and lick their chops' and that they would all 'enter the communist world together' it was, nevertheless, to be in the 'same historical epoch', not at the same time. Thus the Soviet Union was given considerable room for manoeuvre in leading and dominating the rest of the bloc. But then it was still the major guardian of the communist revolution.

Soviet interests were also of paramount concern to Khrushchev in his dealings with the world communist and revolutionary movements. He wooed the anti-colonial, anti-imperialist and nationalist leaders in the Third World and offered them aid and trade in an attempt to weaken their ties with the West and to get them to adopt a policy of positive neutrality. He also dabbled with the security of Berlin, threatened the United States from Cuba, and intervened in Egypt and the Congo. Yet he agreed to an armistice in Korea in 1953, helped to end the war in Indo-China in 1954, persuaded the Chinese not to attack Formosa, and signed a declaration of friendship with Yugoslavia in 1955 and a treaty with Austria on neutrality. He also gave aid to the Nassers and the Nehrus who were imprisoning communists, refused military aid to China, denied it nuclear weapons in case the Chinese involved the Soviet Union in war, refused to back China in its fight with India and called for a cessation of the conflict while continuing to give India aid. He signed the nuclear test-ban treaty with the United States and Britain, established the 'hot line' between Moscow and Washington and withdrew Soviet troops from Austria and Finland.

There were, of course, obvious advantages to be had by an accommodation with the West. It meant that the Soviet Union could concentrate less on the manufacture of armaments and more on industry, and especially consumer goods. Indeed, there seems little doubt that Khrushchev's more conciliatory posture towards the capitalist countries and his evident willingness and ability to adopt the phraseology of the man of peace and goodwill had their origin in internal Soviet politicking, and especially the growing and insistent demand for consumer goods. As he said in 1964, 'If we should promise people nothing better than only revolution, they would scratch their heads and say: "Is it not better to have good goulash?"' In reality, the special and selfish interest of the Soviet Union transcended the shared Marxist–Leninism of the communist world. Khrushchev's actions and declared policy implied, indeed often explicitly stated, an acceptance of the international *status quo*. This was a strange idea, to say the least, to be in the head of a Marxist-Leninist. It meant, apart from the deviations from Marxist orthodoxy in its theoretical respects, that Khrushchev might have to take action to slow down the revolutionary initiative of the rest of the world so as not to strain Russian resources or cause the loss of the trust of the West in Russia. In these circumstances it was easy for him to be portrayed as the betrayer of the revolution. He could always escape by reasserting the peaceful evolutionary victory of communism on a world scale but this did not look so good coming from the leader of the first revolutionary socialist state. It looked too much like what it was, a rationalization of great-power status.

Though the doctrine of peaceful communist revolution has been played down since Khrushchev's fall, still, in 1967, the Central Committee of the Communist Party of the Soviet Union accepted the 'possibility of using, in the transition to socialism, diverse – peaceful and non-peaceful – forms of struggle, depending on the concrete relationships of class forces in this or that country . . .'

(b) Revisionism within the Communist Bloc

The break with Stalinism and the de-Stalinization drive launched by Khrushchev had a more profound impact upon the east European communist countries than it had upon the Soviet Union. Besides the confusion that Khrushchev's repudiation of Stalinism occasioned there was also a ferment of revisionism. There had been riots by students and workers in East Germany in 1953, and there were riots in Poland in 1956 and an attempted insurrection in Hungary in the same year. While the Soviet leaders blamed Stalin for the excesses, barbarities and failures of the past, the east European communists were apt to put the blame on the political and economic system that had bred and accommodated Stalin. The myth of Soviet infallibility had been exploded. It was the Stalinist model of a centralized state, rule by a single party, society controlled by a bureaucracy and police terror, the absence of a market system and the concentration of power in the hands of a few men immune from all popular control that was a cause of complaint. Against the control and discipline exercised by the party in all areas of life, the revisionists asserted the primacy of their own moral judgements.

'No one', wrote the Pole, Leszek Kolakowski in 1957, 'is exempt from the moral duty to fight against a system or rule, a doctrine or social conditions which he considers to be vile and inhuman, by resorting to the argument that he considers them historically necessary.' Khrushchev's disclosures about Stalin opened the floodgates that had dammed up the frustrations of the past and released torrents of criticisms that were stilled by the intervention of Soviet tanks. Whereas Salin had used the secret police to prevent criticism and revolt, the demise of the secret police meant that Khrushchev and his lackeys in the 'People's Democracies' had to use the army.

But it was not just the communist system that was considered by the revisionists to be at fault. In Russia reforms of the system were introduced from above. In Poland, Hungary and East Germany they were, in the main, the result of the anti-Stalinism of the masses. But there was, in addition, a different set of circumstances existing in the east European satellites than in the Soviet Union. To begin with, communist rule was associated with Russian conquest and domination. There were strong nationalist sentiments in existence. Again, communism had not long been introduced, let alone consolidated. Many features of capitalism were still in existence. There were anti-communist forces and ideas as well as a bourgeoisie and capitalist traders.

Yet in the main the continued existence of a socialist society was accepted. Generally, the revisionists demanded that within the communist commonwealth all nations and communist parties should be equal, that the idea of separate roads to socialism should be officially accepted and, therefore, the Soviet policy of imposing the Russian variety of Marxism on the bloc be repudiated. They wanted the communist parties to become more democratic, more power to be given to parliament so that it could act as a check on the party and that there should, indeed, be a multi-party system with the corollary of a free press and elections, and the removal of constraints on cultural activity. Nevertheless, it was only rarely suggested that these parties should be other than socialist parties. In the agricultural and economic spheres they demanded that collectivization should cease to be forced and become more gradual, that the emphasis that had been placed on heavy industry should end and that more attention be given to the production of consumer goods and food. They advocated economic decentralization, the restoration of a free market in certain sectors of the economy, the institution of profit-sharing and workers' democracy.

However, the revolt, if it can be properly called that, was a revolt of party intellectuals aimed at party bureaucrats – a criticism, in fact, of the gap between the theory and the practice of socialism. In a sense the critique of the party intellectuals directed towards the party machine implied a commitment and return to the moral and humanist elements of Marxism. It was not, therefore, contained to an attack on Stalinism but was extended to Leninism, especially the Leninism of *What is to be Done?* To most the goal of communism was still important, but so also were the means towards it. Though many anticipated that the political and economic reforms that they advocated would leave socialism intact and triumphant, many, nevertheless, came very close to, and some adopted, the philosophy of democratic socialism. Only in Hungary was there a determined attempt to dismantle the communist state.

After the Twentieth Congress of the CPSU, Budapest took to arms. At first the revolt was aimed at reinvigorating the revolution, but after the intervention of Soviet tanks it became anti-communist. The government of Imre Nagy announced the abolition of the one-party state and the inclusion of non-communists like Anna Kéthly, Béla Kovács and Zoltán Tildy in the government. The government withdrew from the Warsaw Pact and started working towards an Austrian-style neutrality. Soviet tanks intervened again. In a last message to the people Nagy announced 'This fight is the fight for freedom by the Hungarian people against the Russian intervention.' But it was an unequal and lost fight. János Kádár was brought to power by the Soviets in November 1956 and Imre Nagy executed. Yet the Workers' Councils set up in October 1956 functioned for over a month after the end of the bitter street fighting. They negotiated with the Kádár régime and put forward demands for worker–management relations to exclude the communist party. The Central Workers' Council of Budapest went further still and demanded that the workers be allowed to 'build our social and economic system independently, in the Hungarian way'.

The revisionists elsewhere were helped in asserting their independence of Moscow and in attempting to trace their own path to their definition of socialism, by the Sino-Soviet dispute. This, no doubt, caused Khrushchev to be more lenient towards what he must have considered dangerous movements, especially as the east European states were still prepared to follow and support him in his dispute with the Chinese. Yet Khrushchev himself had accepted the notion of separate roads to socialism in the June 1955 Khrushchev–Tito Declaration at Belgrade and in his speech to the Twentieth Congress of the CPSU in 1956. By 1957 Moscow was characterizing revisionism as the main danger to international communism and revisionist tendencies were curbed or eliminated. Separate paths to socialism was one thing, excessive liberalization and a weakening of the internal coherence and stability of the bloc another.

(i) EAST GERMANY

From its foundation in 1949 to 1952 the German Democratic Republic (DDR) was subjected to a forced class struggle which included discrimination against bourgeois students and the confiscation of the ration cards of the middle class. In 1952 Walter Ulbricht announced a period of socialist construction and the establishment of a 'People's Democracy'. This was followed by the collectivization of agriculture and the socialization of industry and commerce. The peasants were intimidated and the bourgeoisie coerced by police terror. The result was social dislocation and economic chaos. Ulbricht appealed to the Soviet Union for help and was advised to stop the process of socialization. Instead, he responded by issuing a decree increasing work norms by ten per cent. The Soviet leaders then ordered the introduction of the New Course. The expropriation campaign was stopped, many businesses were returned to their former owners and the campaign against the church dropped. The increased work norms remained, however, and a general strike and popular uprising followed in June 1953, only to be put down by Soviet military intervention. After the uprising of the workers the New Course was extended. Consumer goods production was increased, greater legal security was promised, parliament was revived, the severity of political sentences diminished, greater freedom given to artists and intellectuals, credits given to private firms, political indoctrination in educational establishments reduced and travel facilities between the two Germanies made easier.

At the same time as the New Course was introduced, two officials of the SED, Wilhelm Zaisser and Rudolf Herrnstadt, formulated a more liberal programme of political reform. This included the removal of Ulbricht and the introduction of an economic programme virtually indistinguishable from capitalism. Both men were arrested, and details of their programme never became available in the West. Yet other state and party functionaries joined in the orgy of criticism and programme formulation. Of these, Fritz Behrens and Arne Benary questioned the efficiency of central planning and advocated workers' management on the Yugoslav model. They argued that now the class enemy had been suppressed the time was ripe for revaluing the role of heavy industry in the economy and for a decentralization of economic decision-making. To increase the productivity of labour Benary advocated that more autonomy be given to enterprises to organize work and distribute profits and, by implication, that the leading role of the party be relinquished. Benary recanted in 1958 and called himself a revisionist. The Director of the Institute for Agricultural Economics, Kurt Vieweg, advocated the dissolution of unprofitable collective farms, state support for family farms and the gradual run-down of the state machine tractor stations. He, however, fled to the West in 1957, only to be arrested on his return.

More dramatic and radical was the programme of opposition drafted by an academic of the Humbolt University, Wolfgang Harich. Harich's Testament, as it came to be called, was an attempt to apply Hungarian and Polish ideas of a national road to socialism to Germany. Harich wanted the DDR liberalized as a democratic-collectivist rival to West Germany. The régime, he argued, should therefore place more emphasis than it had in the past on the production of consumer goods, introduce workers' councils to manage industry, profit-sharing and eliminate the collective farms. Moreover, he urged the introduction of intellectual and religious freedom and the creation of a parliamentary coalition with, however, the SED retaining overall control.

Harich regarded his programme as the beginning of a transitional stage towards German reunification. Extremely eclectic in his approach, he wanted Marxist–Leninism 'enhanced' by the thoughts of Trotsky, Bukharin, Luxemburg, Kautsky, Fritz Sternberg and other social democratic theorists, as well as by the incorporation of Yugoslav, Polish

and Chinese experience. He put his proposals to the leaders
of the SED and the Soviet ambassador and distributed his
testament in the West. As a reward he was imprisoned and
eventually released in 1964. 'Men', Machiavelli has written,
'commit the error of not knowing when to limit their hopes.'

The ferment of ideas and the apparent freedom of debate
and criticism did not last for long. Ulbricht had always
been, and remains, a Stalinist. He had no liking for the
New Course in any of its multifarious manifestations. It was
not long before the party reasserted its control and the
rigidity of its doctrine. Ironically, Ulbricht used the leeway
given by the Twentieth Congress of the Communist Party
of the Soviet Union to prevent de-Stalinization and increase
the pace of socialization. He was prepared to go along with
the rest of the bloc in condemning Stalin and pay lip-service
to the idea of liberalization but not to translate his words
into deeds. Ulbricht was lucky. The 23 October revolt in
Hungary enabled him to restrain the growing demands for
reform in East Germany by arguing that the prior need
now was to prevent the spread of counter-revolution. With
the aid of the well-proven technique of police terror, the
opposition was eliminated.

After 1956 all opposition among the intellectuals and
within the party was effectively wiped out. The workers
had been bribed by economic concessions and did not, in
any case, see the need to come to the aid of those who had sat
on the byelines during the June days of 1953. The complete ascendancy of Ulbricht was indicated by the accomplishing of complete collectivization in ten weeks in 1960,
though many peasants left for West Germany and the food
supply slumped. The Berlin wall was built the following
year. Though strange and macabre as this last act was, and
heavily criticized as it has been in the West, there was some
justification for it. West German agents are now acknowledged to have been operating in the DDR to recruit
labour and provide fake ration cards to disrupt the food
supply. There had also been a number of international
events, like the U 2 spy plane incident and the abortive US

invasion of the Bay of Pigs, that appeared to denote a more aggressive attitude on the part of the West. Furthermore communist allegations about the activities of the American Central Intelligence Agency (CIA) are given some substance by the acceptance by the CIA of responsibility for the downfall of the government of Guatemala and of Mossedegh of Iran.

(ii) POLAND

Long before the so-called thaw of the mid 1950s Wladyslaw Gomulka had, in 1945, spoken of the Polish road to socialism when he outlined his conception of a people's democracy without the dictatorship of the proletariat, collectivization or the other features of the Soviet model. In 1947 he had talked of a 'Polish Marxism more closely tied to our Polish realities' and, in 1948, went so far as to assert that 'the independence of Poland is the primary concern to which all else is subordinate'. This was heresy and Stalin, unfortunately for Gomulka, was still alive. Accused of 'rightist-nationalist deviation', Gomulka was imprisoned.

On his return to power in 1956, he still adopted basically the same position and insisted on the sovereignty and independence of his government. He was not in this asserting that Poland would renounce either socialism or the Soviet Union, only that it would find its own way to its own brand of socialism. 'What is constant in socialism', he said, 'boils down to the abolition of the exploitation of man by man. The roads of achieving this goal can be and are different.'

Gomulka was helped in asserting his independence of Moscow by the deep-rooted hostility of the Poles towards the Soviet Union. Even amongst the communists there were many who remembered with distaste the dissolution of the Polish Communist Party by Moscow in 1938 so as to facilitate the Nazi–Soviet Pact and the subsequent invasion and partition of Poland by Germany and Russia. Gomulka came to power 'on the crest of an anti-Soviet, revisionist, at least potentially anti-communist, and Polish nationalist popular wave, acceded to despite Soviet opposition, by a Polish communist leadership who (correctly) felt him the only alternative to the collapse of the PZPR and thereafter (also correctly) of Soviet military intervention'.[6]

The Polish challenge to Marxist orthodoxy and Soviet hegemony and the demand of the revisionists for democratic freedoms can be seen in the following quotations from *Po Prostu*, a weekly student newspaper that soon became a national best-seller. Echoing Bernstein it said in 1956:

for the communist the goal is not only communism, but also the movement towards it.

Again:

We think that Marxism should be subjected to the same methods of scientific verification as any other field of thought ... We must never cease to confront it with facts, revising and developing it wherever necessary.

And, more important:

Two ideas of Rosa Luxemburg are of special interest for us today. One is the idea that a degeneration of the socialist revolution becomes inevitable when in its process law, Liberty, and democratic guarantees are destroyed or severely restricted.

The other is that it is harmful to propose as the model for the revolutionary strategy and tactics of the international working class the experience of the first victorious proletarian revolution which took place under the specific conditions of a backward and isolated country.

Both these ideas are valid and tremendously important for our present situation. Today we formulate them both by saying that socialism cannot be built without democracy ... and we talk about specific national roads to socialism.

The thaw came to Poland later than to other countries but it also lasted longer. The specific Polish road to socialism was maintained to a greater degree than elsewhere, mainly because of Polish support given to the Russians in international affairs but also because the leadership was

6. Hans Jakob Stehle, 'Polish Communism', in *Communism in Europe: Continuity, Change and the Sino-Soviet Dispute*, ed. William E. Griffith, Vol. I, p. 101.

more moderate in its liberation and contained any excessive enthusiasm for change.

As early as 1944 Gomulka had said:

For collectivized agriculture one needs, besides a technical-industrial base, which Poland does not have, one more vital factor: the consent of the peasants themselves. To institute any changes in the manner in which agriculture is conducted against the will of the peasants is unthinkable, for no government can maintain itself in Poland without the support of the peasant masses.

And in spite of the forced collectivization in the Soviet Union and East Germany, he stood by this formula in the years in which he was in power. Indeed, between 1956 and 1957 there was a large-scale spontaneous collapse of the collective farms. Though he always spoke, in the late 1950s, of the final goal in agriculture being 'voluntary collectivization' he never mentioned it in two important speeches on agriculture in 1962 and 1963. Along with a number in his party, Gomulka had apparently lost all enthusiasm for collectivization. Instead, agricultural policy was firmly based on the private farmers who accounted for over eighty per cent of land ownership and who were helped by the state to lease and buy land.

Industry and the economy were also liberalized. Decision-making was decentralized, enterprise given more independence and emphasis placed upon profitability. Professor Oskar Lange announced in 1957: 'I think we will finally come to the point where the profitability of the enterprise will be the basic measure of effectiveness.' This did not mean the entire dismantling of the apparatus of central planning but it certainly became less important than previously and certainly less so than in the Soviet Union. But whilst there were many announcements in favour of gearing production towards the satisfaction of consumer demand, in practice the emphasis continued to be placed on investment.

The workers, too, came in for benefits under the liberalization programme. In 1959 a Conference of Workers' Self-administration was set up with the right to supervise and control all the activities of the enterprise, subject, however, to the one-man direction remaining undisturbed. Though a large step towards industrial democracy, the workers had no more than advisory functions and, like the joint consultative committees in Britain, the workers' councils fell into disuse.

Poland was more significant than the other Soviet bloc countries for the amount of political freedom that was tolerated. There were free discussions in parliament, laws instead of pre-1956 government by decree, and the draft laws of the government were frequently rejected and more often criticized by the opposition that was allowed to exist. In addition increased opportunities for travel to the West and access to western books, films and music was available and Poland even received cultural aid and agricultural credits from the United States.

(iii) TITOISM

Much more distinctive and enduring than the reforms introduced in the other communist countries of Europe in the 1950s was the version of Marxist socialism introduced by Tito in Yugoslavia. Tito was helped in this by the fact that the Yugoslav revolution was the only indigenous one in eastern Europe and he was determined from the beginning that Yugoslavia would go its own way. Tito had made his position clear in a speech in 1945 on the question of Trieste: 'We seek', he said, 'also a just end; we demand that everyone shall be master in his own house; we do not want to pay for others; we do not want to be used as a bribe in international bargaining; we do not want to get involved in any policy of spheres of interest.'

Tito was the first leader of a communist state to challenge the authority and leadership of the Soviet Union, the first indication of a weakening of the monolithic solidarity of the communist world. Tito outmanoeuvred Stalin in his attempt to build up a pro-Soviet faction in Yugoslavia and accepted Marshall Aid from the United States, thus causing the break with the Soviet Union. Tito became the 'worst enemy of the working class', 'a tool and willing puppet of imperialism' and Yugoslavia, according to a 1948 Cominform resolution, was following 'the wrong line', being 'adventurous and non-Marxist'.

In fact, the peculiarly Yugoslav form of socialism and flirtation with the West was forced upon the country by Soviet policies. In a fit of pique because Tito refused to play the lackey to Stalin, the Soviet Union imposed an economic blockade, became more hostile towards it than it was towards the West and appeared, for a time, to be preparing for an invasion. Not surprisingly, Tito turned to the West for economic, military and political aid. Since the war it has received over $2.8 billion from the United States alone.

Though the Yugoslav road to socialism has been highly regarded in the West, initially it was no more than a vigorous assertion of self-determination and national pride. Stalin had once used the slogan of different roads to socialism to disarm the latent nationalism of the eastern bloc countries. Now Tito used the slogan against Stalin. Though at one time he had been a dogmatic supporter of Stalin, especially in relation to his Spanish policy, Titoism was denounced by Stalin as a heresy. 'I shall shake my little finger', he is reported to have said, 'and there will be no Tito.'

The theory of Yugoslavia's special brand of socialism, called Titoism, grew inevitably out of its disagreements with the Soviet Union. This led to criticism of the Soviet system aimed at unifying Yugoslav opinion behind Tito and of providing an ideological rationale for the dispute. What existed in Russia was bad and Yugoslavia, then, had to show that it was in some way different. Its theory of socialism began as no more than a series of rationalizations for Yugoslav differences with Moscow. Moreover, the alleged dissimilarities were more apparent than real. They were quietly and conveniently forgotten when relations were normalized in the mid 1950s.

Yugoslav criticism of the Soviet Union took the form of an assertion that socialism there had degenerated into a bureaucracy controlling a powerful imperialist state. Stalin's personal dictatorship was condemned, Soviet communism characterized as being spoilt by bureaucratism and great-power chauvinism; as a state-capitalist despotism ruled by a caste of near-fascist bureaucrats. This caste, the Yugoslavs argued, had become a new ruling class which had done immeasurable harm to the development of world communism and, furthermore, had held back economic development in the Soviet Union.

Milovan Djilas argued in 1949 that when the Soviet Union was the only socialist state, communists had a special duty towards it, but that now other states had emerged, absolute equality between the communist parties and non-interference in internal affairs of each country became essential. The notion of the leading role of the Soviet Union had to be dropped because of its implication of Soviet dominance and its right to infringe national independence. This, essentially, was the beginning of the concept of polycentralism enunciated by Togliatti. When the rapprochement with the Soviet Union was in full swing in the mid 1950s, Djilas went so far as to advocate the abolition of the political monopoly of the Yugoslav Communist Party, more freedom of discussion within the party, the elimination of its professional bureaucracy and its relegation to an association for disseminating ideas. The result was the loss of all his party offices. But in 1955 Vice-president Edvard Kardelj argued that social democratic reform was an equally good road to socialism in certain circumstances as communist revolution. Djilas went further still and became converted to social democracy. True socialism, he argued, could not be achieved without the freedom of organized opposition. This time he was imprisoned.

If Soviet communism had degenerated into a bureaucratic state, the state in Yugoslavia, the Yugoslavs argued, was withering away. This was being achieved by the decentralization of administration and economic decision-making and the institution of workers' control. For Tito the state had to wither away even before the accomplishment of full industrialization. Hence income inequalities were reduced, privileges abolished, some degree of artistic freedom allowed, the collectives allowed – for a time – to collapse and a free market permitted to operate. Instead of being state property, the means of production became the 'higher' forms of social property and factories were given over to workers' collectives. These were given free scope to operate under market conditions with the state acting as the regulator. Its plans did not prescribe compulsory tasks in regard to profits, prices and quality as they did in the other communist countries, but rather they were left to the operation of supply and demand. 'Herein', said Tito, 'lies our road to socialism, and it is the only right road.' Yet this attempt from 1952 to 1954, called the period of 'high Titoism', to establish grass-roots participation through communes and workers' councils did not entail the end of the central control exercised by the party. Indeed, it became even more essential for it to exercise control and it became more powerful. Even the much vaunted workers' control works only within well-defined limits. The director of the company often manipulates the workers, especially if he can work with the enterprise's party organization. On the other hand, no employee can be sacked without the approval of the workers' council and their natural distaste for redundancies has meant that Yugoslavian enterprises often suffer from a surfeit of labour.

With the reconciliation with the Soviet Union in 1953 Tito toned down his liberalization measures, abandoned his policy of non-alignment, gave support to Soviet foreign policy and stopped stressing the international validity of Yugoslav socialism. He now argued that the withering away of the party would be a long process and could not be accomplished until the last class enemy had been eliminated and socialist consciousness become normal and all-pervasive. Until this unlikely event transpired, the party and the state would require strengthening.

10

THE WARM-HEARTED PRAGMATISTS– SOCIAL DEMOCRACY FROM 1918 TO THE 1950s

In 1904 the Congress of the Second International adopted a resolution condemning

in the most decisive fashion revisionist efforts to change the victorious tactics we have hitherto followed based on the class struggle, in such a way that instead of conquering political power by defeating our opponents, a policy of coming to terms with the existing order is followed. The result of such revisionist tactics would be that instead of being a party which works for the most rapid transformation possible of existing bourgeois society into the socialist order, i.e. revolutionary in the best sense of the word, the party would become one which is content with reforming bourgeois society.

By 1918 most of the social democratic parties of the world had became parties 'content with reforming bourgeois society'. Except for their left wings, which turned to Lenin, became communist parties and joined the Third International, the formerly Marxist social democratic parties of Europe settled down to a search for votes in the market place of the bourgeois political systems; they became domesticated. They became the staunchest defenders of democracy – indeed, they introduced it in Germany in 1919 and in Austria – and of liberty. They watered down the revolutionary content of their programmes and became pragmatic and empiricist, in theory and practice.

(a) The British Labour Party

Unlike the continental social democratic parties, the British Labour Party was still not a socialist party at the end of the

First World War and had never paid any great attention to ideology. As continental socialist observers have frequently pointed out, it has always lacked a systematic and coherent theory of socialism. Following the tradition of the Fabians, its conception of the socialist society was no more than a humanization of the present system. Hugh Gaitskell, the leader of the party from 1955 to 1963, could say in 1955 for example that he 'became a socialist because [he] hated poverty and squalor', and the same could be said of many of the other leaders of the party. Few came to socialism and the Labour Party via an economic analysis of capitalism, let alone Marxist economics. Just as the pioneers of the Labour Party had been influenced by Dickens, Carlyle, Ruskin and the Bible so the members of the modern Labour Party have been influenced by Shaw, H. G. Wells, R. H. Tawney and Harold Laski.

And unlike the socialist parties of Europe the Labour Party never attempted to stand aside from the political system but instead made strenuous efforts to become an accepted and respectable part of it. And it succeeded. By 1922 it had become the official opposition. 'His Majesty's Loyal Opposition', it formed minority governments in 1924 and 1929, entered the war coalition in 1940, formed majority governments in 1945, 1951, 1964, and 1966. It has always been an 'integrative' political party concerned with something called the 'national interest' or the 'community' rather than the exclusive interests of a class. Even the left wing of the party has sought change constitutionally and its present-day leader, Michael Foot, has been referred to as a typical Whig in the concern he expresses for the sanctity of parliament. Certainly, many of its members have been democrats first and socialists second. As Gaitskell wrote in his *Amplification of Aims* (1960), the party

seeks to obtain and hold power only through free democratic institutions whose existence it has resolved always to strengthen and defend from threats from any quarter.

Class dictatorship was not only alien to the thought of the

party; it was also something its members were pledged to resist. And though the party has been identified in the public mind with the advocacy of the interests of the working class the party has, through its leaders and its policy statements, explicitly rejected this. *Labour and the New Social Order* (1918), which committed the party, for the first time, to a socialist programme, also explicitly rejected the idea that the programme was a class programme. Again, *Labour and the Nation* (1927) claimed that the party spoke 'not as the agent of this class or that, but as the political organ created to express the needs and voice the aspirations of all those who share in Labour which is the lot of mankind'. This has been a recurrent theme in party pronouncements and literature though there have always been those like Maxton, Tawney and Laski who, in the 1930s, expressed doubts as to the feasibility of socialism being introduced without force.

Socialism to the Labour Party has always been a concept that, to say the least, was ambiguous. So ambiguous, in fact, that Herbert Morrison could arrogantly assert that 'Socialism is what the Labour Government does', and G. D. H. Cole, in a description that has been endorsed by many, including Gaitskell, could put it no higher than a 'broad human movement on behalf of the bottom dog'.[1]

Yet it was not until 1918, with the adoption of its new constitution and the programme enshrined in *Labour and the New Social Order*, that the party became a socialist party. The now famous Clause Four of the party objects, drafted by Sidney Webb, committed the party

To secure for the producers by hand and brain the full fruits of their industry, and the most equitable distribution thereof that may be possible, upon the basis of the common ownership of the means of production and the best obtainable system of popular administration and control of each industry or service.

Not until 1929 did the party add to its objectives the common ownership of distribution and exchange.

1. G. D. H. Cole, *A Short History of the British Working-Class Movement*, London, 1948, Vol. III, p. 22.

Labour and the New Social Order asserted that the party wanted to build a new social order 'based not on fighting but on fraternity – not on the competitive struggle for the means of bare life, but on a deliberately planned cooperation in production and distribution for the benefit of all who participate by hand and brain'. This document, the first attempt at a synthesizing of the disparate ideas of the party, remained the basis of the party's policy until the 1950s and contained four major principles. First was the principle of the National Minimum, emanating from the Fabians. This included full employment, a minimum wage and working conditions, a forty-eight hour week maximum, a health service and increased educational opportunities. Secondly, the programme called for the democratic control of industry by means of the immediate nationalization of mines, railways and electric power and the extension of the powers of local authorities into the fields of housing, town planning, parks and libraries and the provision of certain services. Thirdly, the programme called for a revolution in national finance whereby the social services listed above would be paid for by the introduction of a steeply graduated income tax and a capital levy. Finally, the surplus wealth of the community should, it argued, be used for the common good. It should be used for the sick, for expanding educational opportunities, for research and for the 'promotion of music, literature, and fine art, which have been under capitalism so greatly neglected, and upon which, so the Labour Party holds, any real development of civilization depends'. *Labour and the New Social Order* was, as Ralph Miliband has commented, 'an explicit affirmation by the Labour Party of its belief that piecemeal collectivism, within a predominantly capitalist society, was the key to more welfare, higher efficiency and greater social justice'.[2]

But it was also, as Sam Beer has pointed out, 'the acceptance of a theory of society, a system of beliefs about how the main social forces actually operated and how they could be

2. Ralph Miliband, *Parliamentary Socialism: A Study in the Politics of Labour*, p. 62.

brought to operate differently'.[3] Capitalism was to be blamed for the evils that afflicted society and the remedy, as Attlee said in 1937, was public ownership. It was the system that had to be changed and a 'new civilization' created.

Right up to the revisionist controversy of the 1950s, and still after it to many, nationalization was synonymous with socialism, though it was wedded to the idea of planning in the early 1930s. It was argued that nationalization would enable the state more effectively to control and plan the economy, to redistribute income and wealth more equitably, to increase the pay and improve the working conditions of the workers, to substitute cooperation and fellowship for selfishness and give the workers more influence in the running of their industries. Thus the nationalization shopping-list got gradually larger. To the railways, mines and electric power listed in 1918 were added coal, land, transport, power, the Bank of England and insurance in the manifesto *Labour and the Nation* of 1928. However, most of these proposals were justified in 1945, not on the grounds that they would create a better and more just society but on the grounds that they would be more efficiently run if owned by the state.

Few of the proposals of *Labour and the New Social Order* could be implemented in the first two minority Labour governments. What contributions were made by these governments were in the field of foreign affairs. The Soviet Union was recognized in 1924 and military expenditure reduced. But then the government was restricted in its freedom of action by its need for Liberal support in parliament. Nevertheless, it failed miserably during the years from 1929 to 1931 to develop anything approaching a comprehensive policy for dealing with the economic crisis that could have been presented to parliament and, assuming the defeat of the government, to the electorate.

1945 was different. For the first time a Labour government had a majority, and a large one, and it quickly implemented most of the legislative programme outlined in *Let*

3. Samuel H. Beer, *Modern British Politics*, London, 1965, p. 128.

Us Face the Future (1945). It nationalized the Bank of England, coal, railways, canals and road haulage, the cable and wireless companies, the airlines, gas and iron and steel. The school-leaving age was raised to fifteen, a free national health service and a system of social security introduced and independence given to India, Burma and Ceylon. At the same time there was general austerity and wage restraint, charges were introduced for dentures and spectacles in 1950, Britain joined the North Atlantic Treaty Organization aimed at containing communist influence in Europe, pursued an anti-communist foreign policy and increased its expenditure on armaments. The national minimum was still a long way off and the party later moved away from the universal provision of social and health services to their selective provision.

Labour Believes in Britain (1949) added no more than sugar, cement, water supply, meat wholesaling, sections of the chemical industry and industrial insurance to its nationalization list and *Labour and the New Society* (1950) proposed nothing except steel (nationalized in 1951). From this point on there was a retreat from the advocacy of nationalization, though for party reasons sections of the chemical and machine tool industry were added in 1955. Yet *Labour and the New Society* emphasized that public control could be exercised by investment decisions, the Monopolies Commission, the Development Councils and government location of industry. Control rather than ownership was stressed. The document dealt with the various fiscal and monetary controls that a Labour government would have at its disposal for controlling private industry. This was taken further in *Industry and Society* (1957) which outlined alternative types of common ownership. It advocated the payment of death duties in the form of shares and land rather than cash, as advocated by Gaitskell in *Socialism and Nationalization* (1956), and the formation of a National Superannuation Fund which would invest pension contributions in the shares of private companies. Nothing could have been more gradual than this approach to public ownership, or better designed to bolster capitalism. In addition there was the notion of 'competitive public enterprise' floated in *Labour Believes in Britain* – the state taking over the direct control of private firms in certain industries so as to set a competitive example to the rest of the industry. Efficiency rather than socialism was important.

This efficiency-conscious trend was further manifested in the 1959 election manifesto. Whilst it pledged the party to the re-nationalization of steel and road haulage, de-nationalized by the Conservatives and re-nationalized by Labour in 1966, and the municipalization of private housing that was rent-controlled prior to 1956, it also said that 'where an industry is shown, after thorough inquiry, to be failing the nation we reserve the right to take all or any part of it into public ownership if this is necessary'.

(b) Germany

Before 1914 the German SPD had been strong on Marxist slogans and revolutionary phraseology. But after the 'bloodless revolution' of 1918 when power fell into their hands the party leaders had little if any idea of how is should be used. 'The SPD had got so used to struggling for minor improvements that it was in no psychological position to take up the reins of government.'[4] They were, as William Allen White had said of the American Progressive Party, 'all dressed up, with nowhere to go'. An SPD provisional government was set up with the majority socialist Friedrich Ebert as Chancellor. Men with 'pressed minds and crumpled suits', they showed themselves during the period in which they held power to be almost completely devoid of ideas, except that they did not wish to proceed to the building of socialism so much as creating a political democracy. But then Philipp Scheidemann had warned a conference of the party in 1917

4. David Childs, *From Schumacher to Brandt: The Story of German Socialism 1945–1965*, p. 10.

not to imagine that 'that which will come after the war will be a pure socialist economic order'. Whatever he may have meant by 'pure' it certainly was not socialist.

The controlling Majority Socialists wanted the state left intact. Accordingly they left the civil service, the judiciary and the federal structure exactly as they had found it. They wanted to absolve themselves from thinking and acting by holding elections for a Constituent Assembly. Having castigated and worked for the overthrow of capitalism for years, now when they had the power to implement their *Weltanschauung* they recoiled in the absence of the approval of a popular vote, though they did introduce legislation for trade union recognition and an eight-hour working day. The Independent Socialists, on the other hand, formed in 1917 by SPD opponents of the war, pressed for power to be vested in the newly formed Workers' and Soldiers' Councils established on the model of the Russian soviets. They argued, furthermore, that the provisional government should go ahead with social and economic reforms so that a socialist society could be established before the convening of a Constituent Assembly. Only the small revolutionary left, led by Karl Liebknecht and Rosa Luxemburg, wanted power to be wielded by a dictatorship, though even these were divided on the form the dictatorship should take.

Given the nature of the political, social and economic chaos of Germany immediately after the war, it would not have seemed unreasonable for the SPD leaders to have started on the road to socialism, if only under the guise of social reconstruction. Had they done so, then the Constituent Assembly might conceivably have proved to be more socialist than in fact it was. Given the revolutionary sloganizing of the past, it is difficult to escape the conclusion that the leaders of the SPD did not proceed to the building of a 'workers' state' because they did not know how to start, were timid, were afraid of the responsibility of power and wanted it thrust, as quickly as they could manage it, into the hands of a properly elected assembly.

But to be a little more charitable to the SPD leaders,

they were inhibited from implementing nationalization by their lack of coherent plans. All they possessed were pious intentions. They had always refused to discuss the details of the future socialist state on the ground that the revolution would decide. Now that they were the beneficiaries of a revolution, they found that it supplied no answers. They were also inhibited in their actions by their fear of the likely response of the allied powers to nationalization proposals and were hesitant to take over broken-down industries because their inevitably poor performance, initially at least, might discredit socialism in the eyes of the electorate. As Otto Braun said in 1918:

For socialisation generally no time could be more unfortunate than the present. Germany is starving, raw materials are lacking, machines are defective. Any upheaval may discredit socialism for years.

Perhaps, after all, what they were concerned about was not the creation of a socialist society but the preservation of their own and their party's position in society; that they were concerned lest any precipitate revolutionary action on their part endanger the position of the social democratic movement. As it happened, their timidity and ineffectualness, except in putting down the left revolutionaries, led to the erosion and eventual decimation of their organization. Even after the Kapp putsch had been put down, they still refused to form an all-socialist government and went, instead, into coalition with the Catholic Centre, with Hermann Müller as Chancellor.

The elections the Majority Socialists considered more important than socialism were held in 1919, and resulted in the Majority Socialists receiving nearly forty per cent of the votes and the formation of a socialist government with Ebert as President and Scheidemann as Chancellor. This government set up the Weimar Republic on liberal democratic lines. The Constitution of the Republic, their endorsement and defence of it against the Left and the Right, manifested

the perpetual reformist socialist belief in the essential good-
ness and rationality of man. Like the Fabians in Britain,
the SPD leaders believed that, given the chance to choose
freely, the electorate would reject capitalism and vote for
socialist men and measures. In fact, a non-socialist government was formed in 1920. Perhaps they should have heeded
what Proudhon had written in 1861, when he wrote that
'the most backward thing in existence, the most retrograde
element in every country, is the mass – is what you call
democracy'. But then socialists were included in the cabinet
in 1920 and in most subsequent cabinets in the 1920s, on
the grounds that it was necessary in order to defend the Republic.

The socialists' fear of alliance with the bourgeoisie and
distaste for socialists who entered bourgeois governments
had somehow evaporated. Yet their more amenable attitude
to their bourgeois rivals did not achieve anything in the way
of socialist reforms and, indeed, their Reichstag representation fell from 165 to 100 in 1924. The SPD was also becoming more cautious in its policy pronouncements. The
Goerlitz Programme of 1921, for example, promised no
more than the nationalization of land and natural resources
and control over the means of production. However, the
Heidelberg Programme of 1925 was more radical, in that it
harked back to the 1891 Erfurt Programme in its analysis
of capitalism and its reiteration of the Marxist view of concentration, pauperization and the need for an international
struggle of the proletariat. 'The aim of the working class',
it proclaimed, 'can only be achieved by transforming private
capitalist property of the means of production into public
property.' Yet this programme also laid great stress on the
need for immediate reforms.

By 1928 the SPD had again become the strongest party in
the Reichstag with 153 members, and held the key positions
in the cabinet. The socialists were, however, unable to
achieve anything of importance in the way of social and
economic reform because of the anti-socialist attitude of
their coalition supporters. 'The Social Democrats were

content to be Republicans.'[5] The government fell in 1930 and the SPD was banned by Hitler in 1933. The Nazis were strong but the socialists, when united, were stronger. What they lacked, along with Stalin, was an appreciation of the character of National Socialism and, more important, the will to fight it. The strongest and most powerful socialist movement in the world lost out without so much as a pretence of opposition. The trade unions marched with the Nazis on May Day 1933.

(c) Some Other Socialist Parties

The socialists became electorally important in France at the end of the First World War, but mainly because they had become one of the 'teams' competing for office. Even the minority group, led by Marx's grandson Jean Longuet, was in no sense revolutionary. They blamed the Germans for the war, saw the Russian revolution not as the starting point for European revolution but as making for a negotiated peace. Longuet and his followers remained loyal to the idea of parliamentary democracy and still anticipated the peaceful conquest of political power via the ballot box. What evils they believed to exist – imperialism, secret diplomacy, militarism (which they believed had brought about the war) – were to be dealt with not by a proletarian revolution but by more democratic control. Even the formerly revolutionary CGT made major concessions to reformism in its post-war programme of 1918. Among other things, it called for the eight-hour day, the recognition of trade union bargaining rights for public employees and old age pensions. The destruction of capitalism and wage slavery was a thing of the past.

In 1919 the parliamentary strength of the SFIO fell from 104 deputies to 68, and the following year the party split at the Tours Congress over acceptance of the 21 Points of the

5. G. D. H. Cole, *History of Socialist Thought*, Vol. IV, Part 2, p. 653.

Comintern. The majority created the Communist Party, taking over the party machine, while the minority refounded the Socialist Party, which included Longuet, Guesde, Marcel Sembet, Pierre Renandel and Vincent Auriol who were joined by Fossard, the former general secretary of the Communist Party, in 1924. The party, however, lost a great deal of its traditional working-class support to the communists, though it gained many petit bourgeois votes from the Radicals.

In 1921 the party reaffirmed its 1905 Charter and its programme called for extensive socialization. In 1922 it rejected the communist call for a united front and allied itself with the Radicals at the local level in elections. As a result it increased its number of deputies to 103, compared to the 27 of the Communist Party. After the election the party supported but did not join the Édouard Herriot Radical Cabinet, and supported the Radical cabinets from 1932 until 1936. The socialists consistently refused to participate with or ally themselves to the CP but the increasing fascist menace led to the formation of the Popular Front between socialists, radicals and communists to fight the 1936 elections. The Popular Front fought the elections on a programme which included collective security, the limitation of armaments, international sanctions to be imposed on aggressors, laws against fascist leagues, a national unemployment fund, a reduction in working hours and tax reform. The election resulted in the socialists becoming the largest single party and a government with Léon Blum as Prime Minister with communist support.

The first socialist government in France however, did not introduce socialism. Indeed, it could hardly do so as its radical allies were strongly opposed to socialistic measures. What it did achieve was the Matignon Agreement, whereby employers agreed to increase wages and give trade union bargaining rights. Laws were passed providing for a forty-hour week, paid holidays, the virtual nationalization of the Bank of France, increased public works expenditure and an extension of the school-leaving age. However, the government fell in 1937 and the socialists thereafter supported and participated in Radical governments on the grounds that in doing so they were helping to preserve the Republic.

When the Second World War broke out, the socialists voted their support of the government and were represented in the war ministry, but they were outlawed when France was defeated. In 1946 the party, which had 135 representatives in the National Assembly, adopted a declaration of principle which included the statement that:

The goal of the Socialist Party (SFIO) is to free the human person of all the servitudes by which it is oppressed, and, consequently, to assure to man, woman and child, in a society founded upon equality and fraternity, the free exercise of their rights and of their natural faculties.

It went on to say that:

The distinctive character of the Socialist Party is to cause human liberation to depend upon the abolition of the régime of capitalist property.

It claimed to be revolutionary, the party of the class struggle aiming to abolish classes. In spite of this affirmation of revolutionary faith it was a party of government for most of the time of the Fourth Republic, pledged to defend it against all attacks, including those of the communists. They participated in a coalition government and Félix Gomin became President in 1946, and Vincent Auriol in 1947. It shared the values of democracy, tolerance and the welfare state with the Christian Democrats, Radicals and Conservatives. It became in effect a reformist party retaining nationalization in principle but not in practice. And in spite, or because, of this its percentage of the votes cast fell consistently. This led to splits in the 1950s and the formation of the United Socialist Party (PSU).

The Swedish Socialist Party has been most successful of all in terms of its achievement of political power. It participated in a liberal coalition in 1917, and formed minority governments in 1920, 1921, 1924 and 1932, and has been the majority government since 1945. The party has continued to maintain its traditional moderate, constitutional approach and, indeed, it was the author of the resolutions at the International condemning Bolshevism and affirming the values of democracy and liberty. The Swedes have not been as obsessed as the other social democratic parties with nationalization and its 1960 manifesto said that

... Social Democracy supports the demand for public ownership or public control of natural resources and enterprises, to the extent that it is necessary to safeguard important public interests.

Socialism to the Swedish Social Democratic Party has meant a welfare state and economic planning.

In Holland, Denmark, Switzerland, Austria, Belgium and Italy, the socialist parties joined coalition governments after the second world war but most were in opposition by the 1950s. Not until the 1960s did they emerge again as governing forces. In Italy, for example, the two socialist parties were parties in the Centre Left Coalition and in 1964 the first socialist President was elected. In Australia and New Zealand, on the other hand, the Labour Parties have had a greater share of power, but neither can be termed socialist in the sense in which the term is used in Europe.

In the United States the development of socialism is still awaited. Though the American Socialist Party, on the initiative of Hillquit, tried to link itself with other progressive groups in the 1920s, it continued to lose support, especially in the 1930s when Norman Thomas advocated the setting up of a Labour Party rather than support Roosevelt's New Deal policies. In fact, no one heard what the ASP said and cared less about what it did, even though Norman Thomas ran in every presidential campaign from 1928 to 1948. He received fewer votes in 1936 than he had in 1932. Americans obviously preferred the New Deal to socialism. Nor did the 1950s bring success. Darlington Hooper, the socialist presidential candidate in 1952, received only 20,000. From this date on, the party gave up serious campaigning and put up no candidates, turning instead to educational activities as manifested by books like Michael Harrington's *The Other America*. 'The plain truth is', Cole wrote, 'that at no point after 1914 did Socialism amount in the United States to a movement of any real significance.'[6]

(d) The Labour and Socialist International and the Socialist International

Immediately after the end of the First World War Arthur Henderson sent out invitations for the reconvening of the Second International. His intention was that representatives of world socialism should meet simultaneously with the Peace Conference of the Allied Powers so as to be able to convey to it the ideas of the International on the forms of the peace settlement and international relations.

The International met in Berne in February 1919, though there were many refusals from those associated with communist parties and from those unwilling to sit down with the Germans. After disposing of the war guilt of the Germans, the conference turned to the question of parliamentary democracy versus the revolutionary dictatorship of the proletariat. Though the conference hailed the revolutions that had destroyed the reactionary régimes in Russia, Austria, Hungary and Germany, it nevertheless emphasized the inseparability of democracy and socialism and declared itself to be firmly adhered to the principles of democracy. 'A reorganized society', it declared, 'more and more permeated with socialism cannot be realised, much less permanently established, unless it rests upon triumphs of Democracy and is rooted in the principles of liberty.' It went on to declare that the traditional liberal democratic rights of free assembly, freedom of speech and press and universal suffrage provide the working class with the means of carrying on the class struggle. Thus the social democrats wanted

6. ibid., p. 743.

to break with Lenin just as much as he wanted to disassociate himself and his followers from them.

By the time the Geneva Congress met in 1920 a number of parties had left the organization so that it became dominated by the British and the Germans. The Congress passed evolutionary reformist resolutions inspired by the British Labour Party. The 'historic mission' of socialism was proclaimed to be the carrying of democracy to completion and the Congress strongly condemned the tendency in some countries and groups to convert industrial strikes into political revolution. It declared itself in favour of 'ownership and control by the community' of essential industries and services but emphasized that socialism was to be introduced gradually, capitalism was not to be disturbed and compensation paid to the owners of industries that were to be nationalized was to be fair.

The Third International opposed the new International of the reformist social democrats, and as an attempt to build a bridge between them, the Vienna or $2\frac{1}{2}$ International was set up in 1921, composed of the minority and left groups like the Independent Labour Party. It argued that there was room both for a reformist and revolutionary policy, but its attempts at unity failed even though in 1923 the Labour and Socialist International (LSI) as the reformist organization came to be called, held a uniting Congress in Hamburg in 1923, when it merged with the $2\frac{1}{2}$ International.

Once the dispute between the reformists and revolutionaries had been settled (by their going their own separate ways), the LSI became preoccupied with the growth of unemployment, fascism and the threat of war. On the unemployment issue it opposed wage cuts and proposed instead that there should be a reduction in hours, the introduction of a five-day week, unemployment pay and increased state expenditure on public works. The LSI and its constituent parties attempted to work within capitalism, not to destroy it. The depression of the 1920s and early 1930s did not, they argued, foreshadow the doom of capitalism. Rather, capitalism was experiencing a crisis described as a

'phase of the capitalist trade cycle'. Accordingly they advocated palliatives to moderate immediate evils.

In international affairs the LSI worked for international
recognition of the Soviet Union, repeated the declaration of
the pre-war International on the causes of war and criticized
the inadequacy of the League of Nations in preserving
peace. Nevertheless, it attempted to work within the League
to promote disarmament and the acceptance of arbitration
in international disputes and advocated the imposition of
sanctions on Italy in 1935. While the Third International
attempted to bring down imperialism by subversive activities in colonial territories, the LSI, on the other hand,
adopted a gradualist approach of working towards limited
self-government for the colonies and an improvement in the
living conditions of the indigenous population.

The LSI was undermined by the destruction of many
social democratic parties in the 1930s and the outbreak of
the Second World War completed its demise. At the end of
the war only the British, Swedish and Swiss social democrats
were left in anything like their pre-war position. During
the war, however, there had been frequent meetings of
exiled European social democrats who had attempted to map
out the future of democratic socialism. At the end of the
war informal contacts continued, ostensibly to exchange
information and to attempt to work out a common policy on
post-war reconstruction. In fact, the conferences that were
held were more concerned about the spread of communism
in Europe. Hence those social democratic parties that had
tainted themselves by cooperating with the communists
were expelled, and the organization adhered to and supported NATO.

However, it was not until 1951 that the new Socialist
International (SI) was set up which adopted the document
entitled *Aims and Tasks of Democratic Socialism*. This declared that nationalization was not an end in itself but a
means towards the satisfaction of human needs and that
socialist planning 'does not presuppose public ownership of
all the means of production'. The SI continued the work of

the LSI in that it worked for an extension of democratic liberties and condemned their suppression by all forms of dictatorship. As the Oslo Declaration of 1962 proclaimed:

To us, both freedom and equality are precious and essential to human happiness. They are the twin pillars upon which the ideal of human brotherhood rests.

Accordingly, the task the SI set itself was the education of governments in the desirability and necessity of eliminating poverty and especially the need to eradicate the disparity in the material prosperity of the rich and poor nations.

The Frankfurt Declaration of 1951 had asserted that socialists work for a world of peace and had announced that 'Democratic Socialism regards the establishment of the United Nations as an important step towards an international community'. The Oslo Declaration went further and asserted that

The ultimate objective of the parties of the Socialist International is nothing less than world government. As a first step towards it, they seek to strengthen the United Nations so that it may become more and more effective as an instrument for maintaining peace.

Certainly, socialists had been active in getting the United Nations established. Attlee was present at the drawing up of its Charter, Paul Henri Spaak, the Belgian socialist, was the first President of the General Assembly and Trygve Lie, the Norwegian socialist, its first General Secretary. And just as the LSI had sought to strengthen the power of the League of Nations, so the SI has sought to strengthen that of the UN. Gaitskell in 1962 proposed, among other things, that it should set up a disarmament agency to obtain and supervise disarmament, the establishment of a permanent police force and the admittance of China. In 1960 the SI gave firm support for the strengthening of the UN, condemned apartheid in South Africa, called for majority African rule in Rhodesia and the convening of a peace conference to end the war in Vietnam.

PART THREE

INTRODUCTION

One of the remarkable features of the resurgence of Marxism in the last few decades is that it has found new life and supporters in what are politically, economically, socially and culturally the most backward areas of the world. What was devised as a doctrine for the proletariat of the advanced countries has, paradoxically, become the new religion of the peasants of many of the underdeveloped countries. This may be accounted for by the felt need of the population as a whole, in the absence of a bourgeoisie, for a great collective effort on their part to advance their countries economically. It is, of course, the intelligentsia that has been the motivating force behind modernization in these countries. That they have chosen Marxism as their intellectual hand-baggage may be due to the appeal it makes to their imagination, in that it provides a vision of a clearly identified goal, a picture of a fully developed society. Or perhaps it is, as Adam Ulam commented in *The Unfinished Revolution*, that Marxism is 'the *natural* ideology of underdeveloped societies in today's world' in that the peasants experience instinctively the feeling that Marxism formulates in theoretical language. Whatever the reasons for the increased fashionableness of Marxism, there can be no doubt that it has become and is becoming a political force in areas that its originators would have deemed highly unlikely.

The Yugoslav break with the Soviet Union was the first sign of the demise of Soviet authority in the communist world. A far more important challenge to its leadership of the World Communist Movement was that represented by Mao and China. The Soviet Union, and with it Europe, could no longer be unreservedly considered as the centre of communist power. Marxist–Leninism passed into new hands and, as a consequence, underwent profound changes.

11

CHINA AND REVOLUTIONARY NATIONALISM

Just as the Russians were losing their revolutionary fervour, settling down to the management of their extended empire and playing the role of a great power in international politics, so in 1949 the Chinese achieved their own revolution. The revolution owed little to Soviet help – indeed it was often retarded by the contradictory and muddled advice given by Stalin and the Comintern – and still less to orthodox Marxism, or even to Soviet communism. And, unlike the Russian revolution, but like the Vietnamese, it was the culmination of long years of arduous struggle, and, moreover, of guerrilla warfare rather than proletarian advance. And, as with the revolutionary movements in the rest of Asia, nationalism rather than socialism was to the forefront, anti-imperialism more than anti-capitalism was the slogan used to rally the masses.

(a) Maoism

Much of the character of the revolution and the subsequent character and growth of the Chinese People's Republic is owed to Mao Tse-tung. He is represented, not least by himself and his Chinese sycophants, as the all-wise, all-seeing leader and philosopher of the revolution and the state, whose theories are offered as infallible guides to the aspiring revolutionaries of the Third World. Like most deifications, this suffers from a trace of exaggeration, to put it mildly. Yet at the same time Mao had undisputedly been the major formative influence, both on the course of the revolution and the development of the state.

Mao became a Marxist in 1920, though he had been committed to revolution long before this. Soon after his conversion to his somewhat naïve conception of Marxism, he became a Leninist in that he accepted the need for an élite party to destroy the existing order of society. Thus, he participated in the founding of the Chinese Communist Party in 1921. He did not create it, as he now claims, and for a short time he attempted to organize and agitate among the workers in the manner laid down by Marx and Lenin. In 1925, however, he went on a sojourn into the Hunan countryside. From this date can be traced the beginning of the revolutionary theory that is claimed to be distinctively Chinese and Maoist.

Marx emphasized the importance of the proletariat in the revolution, Lenin the role of the party. Mao, on the other hand, stressed the revolutionary role of the peasantry and the importance of mobilizing the masses and emphasized the importance of the revolutionary will of the people. For Mao the revolutionary movement was a popular, not a proletarian, movement. Marx laid great stress on objective conditions, Mao (like Lenin) on subjective factors. He stressed the importance of guerrilla warfare and its tactics rather than on insurrection, the organizing of a labour movement and a political party. For Marx the revolution was social; for Mao it was a political and military struggle.

Anti-imperialism was more important to Mao than anti-capitalism. Of course, this is not surprising. There was little in the way of capitalism to object to, and there were many foreign imperialist adventurers carving up China. Indeed, it would not be too much of a distortion of his doctrines to present Mao as a militant nationalist more than anything else. Though infused with some Marxist ideas and a desire to free the energy and abilities of the Chinese from the constraints of tradition in line with his estimation of the value of men's will, he nevertheless appealed to all and sundry to support the fight against the Japanese imperialists. He appealed to Chiang Kai-shek and often invoked the memory of China's great past and its heroes like Genghis Khan.

Mao has always been, as Stuart Schram has written, 'determined that [his] "new China", [his] "people's China", should resume her rightful place among the nations – the first place'.[1]

In spite of the rather grandiose claims made for him by the Chinese, Mao is not a brilliant philosopher; indeed he is a rather poor one. Much of what is offered as being distinctive has been said before and in a more concise and comprehensible fashion, and what is new is often no more than a platitude dressed up as a profound insight. His image is of 'speaking through barely comprehensible oracles'.[2] What is unique in Maoism is the marriage of some aspects of Marxism to Chinese conditions and peculiarities and the synthesizing of a plethora of ideas, Marxist, nationalist and populist, into a fairly coherent doctrine. Yet criticism of Mao as a theorist should not lead us to detract from, or ignore, his importance in other areas. Criticism is necessary, if for no other reason, because of the claims of originality and greatness made on his behalf and to which he lends a willing hand, especially in the re-writing of his books to incorporate the lessons of hindsight. A philosopher he may not be, a great revolutionary leader he no doubt is.

(b) Revolutionary Theory, Guerrilla Warfare and the People's Democratic Dictatorship

The traditional communist view of a revolution was that it would start with a rising in the cities and ripple outwards to the countryside. It would also be relatively short. Mao reversed this and the Russian example by starting in the countryside and moving into the cities from rural bases in a long war. In his *Report of an Investigation into the Peasant Movement in Hunan* (1927) he emphasized the role that the peasants would play in the revolution, and particu-

1. Stuart R. Schram, *Mao Tse-tung*, p. 16.
2. Stuart R. Schram, 'The Man and His Doctrine', *Problems of Communism*, Vol. XV, No. 5, 1966, p. 2.

larly the role of the poor peasants. 'Without the poor peasants there can be no revolution. To reject them is to reject
the revolution.' Certainly the proletariat of the cities was
small in number and did not give any significant help to the
revolution but instead passively waited for the take-over.

Mao's stress on the revolutionary role of the peasants has
often been presented as a significant departure from both
Marxism and Leninism. Certainly, Mao accorded to them a
greater role in the revolution than Marx, Lenin or any other
Marxist theorist. Yet Marx had, in 1877, pointed out that
Russia could start moving towards socialism without going
through capitalism and had repeated this assertion in his
correspondence with Vera Zasulich. Lenin and Stalin had
also emphasized the importance of the peasants in backward and colonial countries, though they had qualified this
by insisting that the peasant revolts should not become isolated from the cities and that the cities should assume
leadership of the revolution. Mao too, in 1928, argued that
the peasant revolution should be led by the proletariat, but
which to him meant the disaffected intellectuals that made
up the communist party. And just as Lenin had pre-dated
Mao on the importance of the peasants, so also he had pre-
dated him on the revolutionary importance of the poor
peasants. Nor was Mao the first Chinese communist to
recognize their importance, or even attempt to organize
them. He was, however, the most persistent and consistent
advocate of peasant revolution and its most effective
organizer.

What is unique in Mao's thought is the idea of guerrilla
war waged from rural bases. The central feature of his doctrine, and upon which all else was based, was the idea of a
long war rather than a quick and successful insurrection.
Given the nature of his own support and the forces arrayed
against him, this was no more than a rationalization of
necessity. Mao adopted a strategy of total war, of attempting
to gain control of the population in a given area, of eliminating all opposition in the area and then persuading and co-
ercing the peasants to support the revolution.

The particularly unique part of the Maoist formulation is the concept of the rural base area. In *The Struggle in Ching-Kang Mountains* (1928) Mao enumerated the prerequisites for the establishment of rural bases. These were that there should be a strong mass basis; first-rate party organization; a strong Red Army; favourable military terrain; and economic self-sufficiency. But though Mao's concept of a rural base area is a unique contribution to the Marxist-Leninist strategy of revolution, he had little alternative than to attempt victory in the countryside first. As he and his fellow co-authors wrote in *The Chinese Revolution and the C.C.P.* (1939), as 'powerful imperialism and its reactionary allies in China have occupied China's key cities for a long time' the communists 'must build the backward villages into advanced, consolidated base areas'. Nevertheless, as he wrote in *Why Can China's Red Political Power Exist?* (1928):

The phenomenon that within a country one or several small areas under Red political power should exist for a long time amid the encirclement of White political power is one that has never been found elsewhere in the world.

By 1928 sixteen principles of guerrilla warfare had been elaborated. The general idea was that, once having consolidated their rural strongholds, the communists would gradually expand them. When the enemy advanced, the guerrillas would retreat; when he camped they would harass, when he tired they would attack; when he retreated they would pursue. There was also the stratagem of luring the enemy deep into the rural base and then encircling and annihilating him. In taking the offensive, the guerrillas would always ensure that they had military superiority; they would never fight decisive battles unless confident of victory and never fight a decisive engagement on which the future of the revolution would depend. As Mao said in 1938 'even a gambler needs money to gamble with, and if he stakes all on a single throw of the dice and loses it through bad luck, he will not be able to gamble again'.

In *A Single Spark can Start a Prairie Fire* (1930) Mao claimed: 'The tactics we have derived from the struggle in the past three years are indeed different from any other tactics, ancient or modern, Chinese or foreign.' Though these tactics have been presented as innovatory, Marx had written along similar lines when outlining the important rules of insurrection. He had then instructed his followers never to play with insurrection but to see it through, to concentrate a great superiority of force at the decisive moment, to pursue the insurrection with determination and take the offensive, to attempt to take the enemy by surprise and attempt daily, if small, successes. Besides, the rather cautious tactics of Mao were no more than what common sense dictated. As Mao explained, the base area bore the same relation to an army as did the buttocks to a person. If deprived of either, one could never rest and recuperate, but would be obliged to run around until exhausted.

Like Che Guevara and Régis Debray after him, Mao wrote a great deal about such things as how to obtain and sustain peasant support, stay alive and fight. In this he exhibited the skill of a tactician rather than that of a theorist. And even these were not particularly original. Most of Mao's tactical principles can be found in the military writings of Sun Tzu, writing in 500 B.C. It is no surprise then to find his tactics being denounced in 1931 by Ch'in Pang-hsien and Chou En-lai as guerrillaism. But then Mao could not retort that, as Lenin had said in *Partisan Warfare* (1906), 'Marxism does not tie the movement to any particular combat method.'

While in the late 1920s and early 1930s Mao used Lenin's idea of a democratic dictatorship of workers and peasants as the basis of the state to be created by the revolution, in the late 1930s he included the national bourgeoisie in the dictatorship. In 1939 he used the term 'joint dictatorship' to denote the dictatorship of several revolutionary classes and in *New Democracy* (1940) wrote that the Chinese revolution aimed at creating 'a state under the joint dictatorship of all revolutionary classes'. What was classed as 'revolutionary' in this formulation was militant nationalism or, more precisely, anti-imperialism. In fact, the formulation was similar to the mid-1930s idea of the Comintern for a united front against fascism.

Even after the Communist Party had obtained power in 1949 the state was still described by Mao as the People's Democratic Dictatorship, and there were in fact non-communists in the government. The title was retained when the socialist revolution was proclaimed in 1953 and when the first five-year plan was announced. In his definition of the 'people' Mao goes beyond classical Marxism, and Leninism too. In this it can be rightfully claimed that he introduced novelty. But then, as Arthur Cohen has observed, 'Mao's definition of "people" is, of course, reducible to the simple question: who is a friend and who is an enemy of the C.C.P.?'[3] As few are prepared to be openly hostile to the régime and as Mao, in any case, has a strong populist streak rather than a narrow class consciousness, there would appear to be some substance in the definition of the Chinese government as one of four classes – the proletariat, the peasants, the petty bourgeoisie and the national bourgeoisie, albeit under the leadership of the proletariat. Though allowed formal political rights, the bourgeoisie are in reality the puppets of the Communist Party, as indeed are the other classes, including the proletariat.

The widening of the dictatorship, and the explicit rejection of the title of dictatorship of the proletariat was, and remains, inevitable if the appearance is to bear any relation to reality. Mao would not willingly dispute with, or dispose of, those who like himself are concerned with re-establishing the greatness of China. Nor is the proletariat significant enough in number to be a credible base for a dictatorship. Another possible reason for Mao's widening of the dictatorship, which has nothing to do with making it fit political facts, is Mao's belief, dating from his guerrilla days and sustained since, that it is possible to educate the

3. Arthur A. Cohen, *The Communism of Mao Tse-tung*, p. 83.

bourgeoisie through 'thought reform' to communism. It is not, therefore, according to Mao, necessary to eliminate the bourgeoisie elements in China; it is sufficient to remould their minds. 'The Chinese leaders in this sense seem to view the capitalist's brain', wrote Arthur Cohen, 'as Pavlov viewed his dog's.'[4]

Marx, Lenin, and the rest of the pleiad of Marxist theorists believed it to be necessary for the proletariat to smash the bourgeoisie during the transition to socialism, though, as we have seen, Lenin came to accept its utility to the revolution. Mao believed the transition to socialism could be peaceful. For Mao the transition to socialism could take place with the continued existence of the national bourgeoisie. Thus in the early period of the new republic there was a peaceful transformation of capitalist enterprises into state-run enterprises. After 1949 the enterprises were left in the hands of their capitalist owners, though they worked on government orders, sold their products to the state and received a government commission. In 1952 a further step towards state control was taken when public-private enterprises administered jointly by representatives of the capitalists and the government were established.

In *Our Economic Policy* (1934) Mao had written that

so long as private enterprises do not transgress the legal limits set by our government, we shall not only refrain from prohibiting them, but shall promote and encourage them.

And, as we have noted, private enterprises were allowed to exist alongside the socialist sector during the period defined as 'New Democracy' from 1949 to 1953. In the latter year private industry and commerce were earmarked for the transformation to socialism. Hence the era of the toleration of private enterprise was to be, *ex post facto*, short-term. The period of New Democracy was now presented as the period in which the transition to socialism would take place,

4. ibid., p. 129.

though this was not what was meant by the term when it was originally coined.

In 1953 China claimed to have begun building socialism. A campaign was launched to organize the Communist Party and the masses against merchants. This was a campaign waged in psychological terms to prepare for the gradual take-over of all private industry by the state and which was finally accomplished in 1956. In the 1960s a military-style discipline was introduced into the economy.

After coming to power Mao initiated a campaign to consolidate Communist Party control in the countryside by means of public trials and executions of 'class enemies'. The success of this paved the way for the equally successful introduction of large-scale collectivization in 1955–6. Unlike the forced and brutal collectivization drive begun by Stalin, that of the Chinese was accomplished without bloodshed, though not without resentment on the part of the peasants. More radical and singularly unsuccessful was the people's commune programme of 1958–9, a part of the so-called 'Great Leap Forward' aimed at promoting China's industrial advance so as to overtake the productive capacity of the western powers, especially Britain, but also of the Soviet Union. The absence of machines led Mao to mobilize and galvanize the masses into increased productivity in accordance with his view of the primacy of subjective factors. Mao has a great and unbounded belief in the ability of men's will. It is, for him, the most important factor in social change. No doubt because of his guerrilla experiences. he regards the revolutionary will of the people as a force capable of shaping the material environment. This, of course, was very similar to Lenin's belief in the efficacy of the conscious revolutionary vanguard portrayed in *What is to be Done?*

In the people's commune distribution was according to need, wages paid according to work, the town government integrated with the commune and differences between town and country, as well as between mental and manual labour and workers and peasants, eliminated. A pattern of communal living in barracks and mess halls was introduced, a militia established and an austere military-style régime imposed, with the inmates being awakened by bugle call and marched to work with songs. Described by Khrushchev as 'primitive communism', the communes certainly had a pedigree that went back to the utopian precursors of Marx and as far back as Plato. Even the Chinese Communist Party leaders described them as utopian. Not unnaturally they aroused a great amount of resentment on the part of the peasants and caused them a lot of discomfort. Admission of failure came in 1958, and the blame, as usual, fell not upon the instigators of the scheme but upon the local party workers. The leaders were still infallible.

Lenin had argued that whilst antagonism would disappear in a socialist society contradictions would not. There would, for example, be contradictions between productive forces and the relations of productions. These, he argued, were necessary in a socialist society if it was not to stagnate. Hence there was nothing original in Mao's almost identical statement in 1957. However, his notion in *On the Problem of the Correct Handling of Contradictions Among the People* that there were still contradictions among the 'people' under socialism was new. But then to Mao the 'people' included the bourgeoisie. 'In our country', he wrote, 'the contradiction between the working class and the national bourgeoisie is a contradiction among the people.'

What was even more novel – but only because it was the first public admission by a communist leader of the obvious – was the idea that there could be contradictions between the Communist Party and the people, though Liu Shao-chi had, in 1941, pointed out the contradiction between the leaders and the led in the Communist Party. To Lenin and Stalin the communist party was the vanguard of the masses. Like Rousseau's general will, the policy of the communist party expressed what the proletariat would want and accept if they had the same level of consciousness. It certainly could not deviate from the interest of the masses. Now Mao argued that the interests of the party and the people could diverge.

This was the basis of the Hundred Flowers campaign, the brief period of free speech and toleration of strikes and criticism, not just of party members but also of the party. The campaign was claimed to be a method of resolving the contradictions between the people and the Communist Party. Various schools of thought were tolerated and allowed the freedom of debate and a more liberal attitude towards intellectuals was put into effect in 1956. In 1957 this was further applied to the party. Like John Stuart Mill in his essay *On Liberty*, Mao seemed to conceive of truth as emerging from a battleground of competing opinions. In fact, even his terminology during this period is reminiscent of Mill. Criticism was to make the Marxists re-examine their ideas instead of accepting them as dogma. 'Correct ideas', Mao said, 'if pampered in hothouses without exposure to the elements or immunization against disease, will not win out against wrong ones.' Yet he always believed that Marxism, as the incarnation of truth, would survive.

However, this more liberal régime did not last long. Though by far the most radical attempt at de-Stalinization and repudiation of the rule of the monolithic party, its curtailment was defended on the grounds that the increased freedom that had been granted was being exploited by counter-revolutionaries. This, as we have seen many times, in Stalin's Russia as well as Husak's Czechoslovakia, is the easy get-out for a communist leadership in trouble. Counter-revolutionaries play the same role in communist mythology as do the communists in western mythology.

But there was more to the so-called Hundred Flowers campaign than a desire to ensure that the party was kept in touch with the people. It was a device used by Mao to increase his control over the party apparatus, though he had, as we have indicated, been a believer since his student days in the value of spontaneity and the creative energy of the masses. 'For half a century', Stuart Schram has written, 'Mao has been torn by the conflict between an ideal of spontaneity and the will to improve the discipline necessary for effective action. This contradiction obviously still persists in the

China of the Red Guards.'[5] The Great Proletarian Revolution of the late 1960s in which gangs of Red Guards went on the rampage against the entire party apparatus was, however, certainly an attempt by Mao to subordinate the party to his will.

In 1965 Mao had spoken of there being some in the party who were taking the capitalist road. The Great Proletarian Revolution was an affirmation that the supremacy of the Communist Party was no longer to be taken for granted. This meant no more than that it had become less responsive to his will than he deemed desirable. On his instructions and with his willing consent, the party at all levels was terrorized by bands of juvenile hooligans called Red Guards. Party members were criticized, ridiculed and humiliated publicly, and the opposition to his rule that had been gathering strength in the early 1960s crushed. A new political force was created in opposition to that of the Communist Party, composed of the People's Liberation Army, new revolutionary activists and old and trusted party members. These formed Revolutionary Committees which took over, for a time, the administration of the provinces and cities. In effect, what Mao attempted and achieved was the setting up of himself above the party. This was made explicit in the draft constitution of 1968 which laid down the citizen's cardinal virtue as loyalty to the leader.

(c) World Revolution and the Sino-Soviet Dispute

Khrushchev had exhibited the Soviet fear of nuclear war which he believed would destroy civilization and the 'centres of culture'. Mao, on the other hand, did not exhibit the same fear or distaste of nuclear war. His notion of the ability of men's will to overcome objective factors was used to assert that it could even overcome the nuclear armoury of the West. He used the concept of a 'paper tiger' to instil

5. Stuart R. Schram, *The Political Thought of Mao Tse-tung*, p. 23.

optimism and confidence in the masses and encourage their revolutionary determination.

All reactionaries [he said in 1946] are paper tigers. In appearance they are frightening, but in reality they don't amount to much. From the long-term point of view, it is the people who really have great strength, and not the reactionaries.

Moreover, as he wrote in *On the Correct Handling of Contradictions Among the People,*

The First World War was followed by the birth of the Soviet Union with a population of 200m.; the Second World War led to the emergence of a Socialist Camp with a population of 900m. In the event of a Third World War, it is certain that several millions more would turn to socialism.

Stalin talked in much the same bravado manner before the Soviet Union possessed the H-bomb. It was left to Khrushchev to point out in 1962 that if 'certain people say that the imperialists are paper tigers they should not forget that those tigers have atomic teeth'. Mao, of course, could afford to be a little more blasé, given that in the event of nuclear war more Chinese are likely to survive than Russians or Americans. Yet in response to China's inability to dislodge the Nationalists from Formosa and the presence of the United States there, he admitted that some paper tigers had, after all, turned out to be real tigers.

Mao gives full encouragement and a modicum of aid to revolutionary wars, especially against the United States, on the assumption that it will not use its nuclear strength in such conflicts. He argues that the revolutionaries should work for small 'breakthroughs' in the United States position and develop these into a broad international front aimed at driving the USA from the underdeveloped countries. Mao sees the underdeveloped countries as being more ripe for revolution than the advanced countries. The ex-guerrilla fighter comes out in statements like 'Power grows out of the barrel of a gun' and 'State power, independence, freedom, and equality can be won by armed force alone. This has been, and is, the universal law of class struggle.' He places a high value on wars of liberation. To him the under-developed and colonial countries become the foci for the assault on capitalism. And just as the revolution in an in-dividual country starts in the countryside and moves to the cities, so Asia, Africa and Latin America represent the rural parts of the world. Revolutions there will move out to-wards the advanced countries. The cities of the world will be encircled by the rural areas of the world. In A. J. Toyn-bee's terms, the Chinese have transferred the revolutionary mission from the 'internal proletariat' of the West to its 'external proletariat' in the underdeveloped countries.

Revolutionary liberations would also, of course, serve China's national interests in making its borders more secure against the United States, providing it with a number of dependent client states and enhancing China's prestige in the world. As Schram notes, 'China's glory is at least as im-portant to [Mao] as world revolution.'[6] Only if there are revolutions in the countries of the Third World can the Chinese break the diplomatic and economic blockade of the West and the Soviet Union, though President Nixon's desire for re-election in 1972 seems to have helped. In weakening the USA and the Soviet Union through revolu-tion in countries where they have an influence then the Chinese are also increasing their own relative strength. But though national self-interest and delusions of grandeur obviously play some part in the Chinese promotion of revo-lutionary wars of liberation, the Chinese could argue, as do the Russians, that what is in China's interest is also in the interest of world socialism. China, after all, is the only country that knows the true way to socialism now that Russia has degenerated into revisionism.

Unlike the more cautious and pragmatic Russians, Mao does not accept that support for revolutionary movements necessarily entails the threat of nuclear war. He argues that the imperialists would be constrained from starting such a war by the weight of opposition in their own countries and

6. ibid., p. 30.

that their morale would be eroded by their inability to control the revolutionary movements. There may well be some substance of truth in this optimistic analysis. The morale of the United States administration has certainly suffered from its patent inability to control the Viet Cong. But it could also be argued that the actual success of revolutionary movements on a large scale would precipitate desperate measures on the part of the USA. There have, indeed, been influential calls from official quarters for an atom bomb to be dropped on Vietnam. Besides, the increased diplomatic activity of the Chinese and their more conciliatory posture towards the West might indicate a recognition on their part that revolutionary movements have not been as successful as they had hoped for, and that they are now more prepared to accept the *status quo*.

Besides advocating and helping revolutionary movements, the Chinese claim that their model of revolution is applicable to all underdeveloped countries. We have already seen that Mao claimed his revolutionary tactics to be unique. The 'way of Mao Tse-tung' is now considered appropriate for export.

Thus just as the Chinese people have done [he wrote in 1951] all or at least some of the colonial peoples of the East can hold big or small base areas and maintain revolutionary régimes for an extended period, carry on protracted revolutionary war to encircle the cities from the countryside, and proceed gradually to take over the cities and win nationwide victory in their respective countries.

Not only is the Chinese form of revolution considered by them to be most appropriate to backward countries, but so also is the Chinese model of a people's democratic dictatorship. In 1940 Mao wrote that although the Soviet model of the dictatorship of the proletariat was appropriate for advanced countries, it was not suitable for colonial and semicolonial countries. He argued that the form of state for these countries 'can *only* be . . . the new democracy republic. This is the form for a given historical period and therefore a transitional form; but an *unalterable and necessary form.*' It is further claimed by the Chinese that their method of gradually buying out the capitalists is one that should be followed by the underdeveloped countries.

Marxism for Mao is internationalist but it 'must take on a national form before it can be applied'. Thus, 'if a Chinese communist, who is part of the great Chinese people, bound to his people by his very flesh and blood, talks of Marxism apart from Chinese peculiarities, this Marxism is merely an empty abstraction.'

The importance attached to world revolution by the Chinese leaders has not prevented them from cultivating relations with the capitalist countries. They do, however, distinguish between the anti-Chinese powers, notably the United States, but also until recently the Soviet Union, and the non-communist countries in what is called the 'intermediate zone'. This means they are considered to be friendly to China. France, for example, fell into this category for a time. India, too, was considered to be friendly and Mao both woos the non-aligned but bourgeois governments of Africa and Asia, and plans their downfall.

Mao's insistence on the greatness of China, its special road to socialism, and on supporting revolutionary movements has brought him into conflict with the leaders of the Soviet Union, though there have been other causes of dispute. Of these the determination of Mao that the Chinese Communist Party would be independent of Moscow and determine its own policies and his refusal to allow China to be a mere instrument of Soviet foreign policy have been most important. Mao also resented the exploitation of China by Russia through its joint-stock companies, and he had been incensed during the civil war at the financial support given by Stalin to Chiang Kai-shek. Stalin certainly had a rather dubious conception of the Chinese communists: he called them 'radish communists – red on the outside and white on the inside'.

The Sino-Soviet dispute became public only in 1958, though there had been a weakening of their friendly relations before then. Against Khruschev the Chinese hurled the epithet 'revisionist'. They viewed with distaste his attempts to seek a détente with the West and argued that he was sacrificing the revolutionary movements of the Third World and using the communist parties of the West as diplomatic tools rather than as a means of sharpening the class struggle. They were further incensed by Khrushchev's flirtation with the West, the summit conferences, the test-ban treaty, his mockery of the people's communes, his favouring of India in its border dispute with China, his withdrawal of economic aid to China and his refusal to provide the H-bomb. The Chinese repudiated the idea that socialism could result from parliamentarianism. The use of parliamentary means was limited. The communist revolution still required the destruction of the old social and political order. In 1962 they described the parliamentary road to socialism as 'parliamentary cretinism' and asserted that history offered no example of peaceful revolution.

Even Khrushchev's attempts to defuse the conflict were of no avail. At bottom, what the Chinese wanted was equal leadership of the world communist movement, at least. The Russians wanted them excommunicated from it. Mao now claims to be the leader of the international communist movement. Until this, or at least equality with the Soviet leadership, is accepted, there is no likelihood of a real and lasting reconciliation. 'Maoism', as Merle Fainsod has written,

may be viewed as a reaction to Khrushchevism. It registers the plight of an underdeveloped and ambitious communist country which is motivated by an urgent desire to achieve great power status quickly and which sees the key to future strength in assuming the leadership of the world revolutionary movement and in forcing the pace of revolutionary change wherever it can find pliable instruments.[7]

Mao then is more properly regarded as a militant nationalist than an eminent Marxist philosopher, and

7. Merle Fainsod, in *Marxism in the Modern World*, ed. Milorad M. Drachkovitch, p. 134.

his emphasis has always been populist rather than proletarian. An example of this is the relations, known as the
mass line, that are supposed to exist between the Communist
Party and the people. As he directed in 1943:

> All correct leadership is necessarily from the masses, to the
> masses. This means: take the ideas of the masses (scattered and
> unsystematic ideas) and concentrate them (through study then
> through into concentrated and systematic ideas) then go to the
> masses and propagate and explain these ideas until the masses
> embrace them as their own, hold fast to them and translate
> them into action, and test the correctness of these ideas in such
> action.

At the same time the Communist Party has been made
into a powerful instrument of political power. Rigid discipline has been imposed on the party and the people with
dedication and obedience exacted and reinforced by periodic purges, the extraction of confessions and the processing
of people by thought reform. Though the purges have not,
so far as is known, been as barbaric as those instituted by
Stalin, Mao's rule is as arbitrary and, except for the brief
periods when dissent was allowed, more severe in its repression of dissent and potential sources of opposition. The
masses have been subjected to indoctrination and 'education' on a mass scale in order that they may be purified and
to ensure that they do not become corrupted by the humanism of the West and, latterly, of the Soviet Union. Family
life has been disparaged and disrupted, as has the individual
and the western emphasis on individual happiness. A puri-
tan morality has been enforced with regard to dress and
behaviour.

Nor is Mao content, as was Stalin, with passive obedience.
He wants and demands active adulation and participation
in his harebrained schemes. The party is probably more
totalitarian than its Soviet equivalent and Mao represented
as a god-like figure to a greater extent than Stalin was. Even
the *Thoughts of Chairman Mao* are claimed to have magical
qualities.

12

ASIAN COMMUNISM

Though China is undoubtedly the major communist power in Asia and has rightly attracted most attention from both scholars and the public it should not be allowed to obscure the fact that elsewhere in Asia there are communist states and other countries with powerful communist movements. Not unnaturally the Asian communists often take their lead from China. Frequently, however, they ignore the blandishments of the Chinese leaders preferring to find their own way to their revolution.

As in China communism in Asia is both a method for obtaining power and of holding onto it once it has been gained. Like the Chinese communists those operating in the rest of Asia exhibit a commitment to violence, both internally in terms of class struggle and externally in the rejection of the doctrine of peaceful coexistence with the Western World. Of course regimes like those in North Vietnam and North Korea were the product of violence and are still engaged with their southern neighbours in what they see as a war of liberation while the communists in Indonesia have not exactly been treated with respect by their opponents. Only in Ceylon, India and Japan are the communists tolerated as part of the political process. Elsewhere they are illegal and are consequently forced, whether they choose to or not, to operate as clandestine groups committed to the armed overthrow of their respective governments. And yet, perhaps, the commitment to violence of the communists in Asia is no more than a reflection of Asian political culture in which democratic values have had little if any place.

(a) North Vietnam

To the south of China is the communist state of North Vietnam, the first communist state to be established in south-east Asia. Although the régime only came into existence officially in 1954 it had possessed a large and active communist party for a number of years. Indeed, in 1929 there were three rival communist organizations which, with the persuasive help of Ho Chi Minh, joined forces in 1930 to form the Vietnam Communist Party. The aims of the new party were listed in ten points. Among these were the overthrow of imperialism, the feudal system and the reactionary bourgeoisie in Vietnam; the winning of independence for Indochina; the forming of a government of workers, peasants and soldiers; the nationalization of the banks, etc. and for these to be put under the control of a proletarian government; the sharing out of agricultural estates to the poor peasants; the introduction of an eight-hour working day; the introduction of democratic liberties; and education for all.

The same year the party changed its name to the Indochinese Communist Party. This was dissolved in 1945 in order to facilitate the formation of a national united front aimed at ejecting the French. Yet, at the same time as the party had been apparently dissolved, it was, in effect, replaced by the Association of Marxist Studies led by Truong Chinh, and the Cominform claimed in 1950 that the party had a membership of 500,000. It was no surprise then when the party officially reappeared in late 1950 calling itself the Vietnamese Workers' Party, a name once again changed in 1951 to its present designation of the Dang Lao-Dong Party. Its 1951 Programme asserted that

the fundamental tasks of the Vietnamese revolution are as follows: to drive out the imperialist aggressors, to win independence and unify the nation, to abolish the colonial régime, to obliterate feudal and semi-feudal vestiges, to give land to the peasants, to develop popular democracy as a basis for Socialism.[1]

1. Quoted by Jean Lacouture, *Ho Chi Minh*, p. 160.

Led by Ho Chi Minh, the Communist Party was the most important and active centre of resistance to the French. As with Mao in China, so with Ho in Vietnam. The 'Saint-Just of the twentieth century', as he has been called, exploited nationalist sentiments and peasant grievances to further the armed struggle that would lead to the creation of a communist state. The revolution began, as Hoang Van Chi has written, 'with nationalism and ended with communism'.[2] Indeed, Ho had admitted that it was patriotism, not communism, that led him to believe in, and support, Lenin and the Third International. Only much later did he come to believe that only communism was capable of emancipating the workers and the oppressed.

At first communism was but a means; later it became an end in itself. Thus in 1919 Ho had drawn up and dispatched an eight-point programme to the Peace Conference calling for the emancipation of his country. At this time he was not yet a socialist, still less a communist. His programme was, like Castro's *History Will Absolve Me*, extremely moderate and liberal. It called, for example, for the introduction of a free press and for Vietnamese representation in the French parliament. Even in 1945 he was still advocating negotiation with the French for independence for Vietnam and wanted it to be given willingly. Again, the proclamation of independence in 1945 was inspired more by the American Declaration of Independence than the works of Marx or Lenin, while his 1946 Constitution enshrined the principles of democracy with no mention of the communist nature of the state. This was, perhaps, not surprising. After all, Mao was not yet in control of China; the United States, to whom Ho looked for support against the French, had observers in Hanoi and the French were relatively firmly entrenched in the rest of the country.

Certainly, it is difficult to determine just how far Ho's commitment to communism went. There can be little doubt

2. Hoang Van Chi, *From Colonialism to Communism: A Case History of North Vietnam*, p. 29.

about his moderation in dealing with first the French and later the Americans, and less doubt still about his pragmatic approach to the problems of Vietnam and the objective of achieving independence. As Jean Lacouture observed, 'Passionate concern for his country animates Ho above all else, just as it animates Giap and most of the hard-core militants.'[3]

What is true is that what attracted him to communism in the first place was not communist ideology, but the concern expressed by the communists for the colonial peoples. As he said in 1960, when he joined the extreme, and eventually the communist, section of the French Socialist Party in 1920, he did not know what a party was or what socialism or communism meant. And he became a Leninist and a supporter of the Third International after reading some of Lenin's works on nationalities and imperialism. As he said at the Tours Congress of 1920:

I don't understand a thing about strategy, tactics, and all the other big words you use, but I understand very well one simple thing: The Third International concerns itself a great deal with the colonial question. Its delegates promise to help the oppressed colonial peoples to regain their liberty and independence. The adherents of the Second International have not said a word about the fate of the colonial areas.[4]

Soon after this Ho was sent to Moscow as a delegate from the French party and then to China and a number of Asian countries as an emissary of the Comintern. After founding the new party in Vietnam in 1930, he left for more international work but returned in 1940, staying to direct the struggle for independence. Under his leadership the party grew from a small sect to a position where it was able to seize and maintain control over the liberation movement in North Vietnam, and direct the struggle in Cambodia and Laos.

3. Jean Lacouture, op. cit.
4. Quoted in Bernard B. Fall, *The Two Viet-Nams: A Political and Military Analysis*, p. 90.

Yet, although Ho has become something of a legend in the West – particularly in the late 1960s – among students, he was not a great theorist. His writings amount to little more than collected speeches, a play and a volume of verse. Probably most important are his pamphlet, *Black Race* (1924) criticizing European and United States racial policies, and *Le procès de la colonisation française* (1926). He has had no real or lasting influence on Marxism–Leninism. But then he never aspired to do so. Unlike Mao, Ho has been content to be a doer rather than a pseudo-philosopher. As Joseph Ducroux, the French communist and Comintern agent in Singapore who met Ho in 1931, reported: 'He devoted little time to doctrinal wranglings. He was first and foremost a militant, an organizer ...'[5] This remained true until his death in 1969.

In 1945 Ho officially proclaimed the formation of the Democratic Republic of North Vietnam with himself as President, even though his forces occupied only a small part of Tonkin. The following year he gave the order for an offensive against the French. In this the communists were helped by the nationalists. Until 1949 the resistance movement (the Viet Minh as it was called) was a coalition of forces that were often at odds with each other but who managed to subsume their ideological differences under the common objective of getting rid of the foreigners. But, as in other countries in similar circumstances, the communists were not content for long to take a back seat in the drive for national liberation. After the success of the revolution in China, the Vietnamese communists gradually assumed open control of the movement in steering it to success.

Communist hegemony of the liberation movement was, in any case, aided by the fact that the nationalists relied upon the communist countries for support. It was natural, therefore, for the bulk of the material aid to be channelled to the communists. Again, as elsewhere, the communists were better organized, had a more disciplined membership

5. Quoted in Jean Lacouture, op. cit.

and were able to attract both the middle-class idealists and the underprivileged peasants. In many ways more important was the ability of Ho to change his political image with changing circumstances. At one and the same time he managed to pose as a liberal, a nationalist liberator, a communist and an advocate of the underdog.

Though in 1950 both the Soviet Union and China gave official recognition to the North Vietnam Communist government, the communists still only controlled the countryside with the French fairly firmly entrenched in the towns. It was not until 1954, as a result of the Geneva Conference, that independence was given to Vietnam. By the end of the war the Communist Party was the unchallenged leader of the liberation movement and yet, in spite of the well-known communist military victory at Dien Bien Phu, Vietnam was divided into a North, under communist control, and a South under President Ngo Dinh Diem. Surprise has been expressed in many quarters at the apparent ready acquiescence of the communists in the division of their country, although pressure from the Soviet Union was probably instrumental.

After the division of the country Ho continued with the policy of establishing front organizations and of allowing non-communists in his government. Thus a former servant of the Emperor, Phan Ke Toai, was deputy premier until 1963. Of course, Ho had to pursue a moderate policy in order to placate opinion in the South, as the Geneva Conference had laid down that there would be elections there in 1956 to determine whether or not the country should be reunited. The communists had great hope of winning the election, which probably goes a long way to explain Diem's refusal to hold them.

From 1954 onwards the communists consolidated their power in the North and after 1956 made more strenuous efforts to bring down the régime in the South. This was to be expected, but there was also an additional incentive for the North to incorporate the South. The North has always been a food-deficit area and has always relied upon South

Vietnam for food supplies. The undoubted failure of Ho's agrarian reform provided an added impetus for the capture of the South.

At first Ho had believed that the South would crumble of its own accord and that the North would be left to pick up and assemble the pieces. He had the aces of the promised election and the Geneva agreement that prohibited foreign interference in the affairs of Vietnam, to sustain his hopes. However, the sympathy which the United States had once extended to the Viet Minh when it was fighting the French evaporated in the heat of the Cold War. North Vietnam's designs on the South were now seen not as a worthy nationalist cause but as an attempt to expand communist influence. The result was increasing United States involvement in support of the government of the South, first with aid, then advisers, and finally full-scale military intervention. Instead of waiting for what he once thought of as inevitable, Ho was forced in 1959 to proclaim the 'people's war'. There was no open declaration of war with the South, but aid and assistance was given by North Vietnam to the guerrillas operating in the South, many of whom were in fact regular North Vietnamese units. The result has been the devastation of large parts of North Vietnam by the excessive, though apparently ineffective, military might of the United States. The first communist state in south-east Asia has become a laboratory where the United States tests its newest weapons in a conflict that appears to be never-ending.

In the North the Chinese tax system was introduced in the early 1950s, aimed at eliminating the wealthy. Taxes were deliberately set high so as to bring about the ruin of the bourgeoisie. Conceived as the first step towards the establishment of the dictatorship of the proletariat, the result was the gradual elimination of landlords. The new tax system was followed in 1953 by a reign of terror, referred to as the 'Political Struggle', aimed at eliminating all landlords, traders and 'opposition elements'. The campaign slogan was 'Give the masses a free hand to fight reactionaries.' And, as the people were always right, there was little the party could do when the campaign got out of hand. Many party officials were accused of being reactionaries and consequently tortured. The whole thing was given some veracity by the holding of 'trials' of alleged traitors who conveniently 'confessed' to belonging to clandestine organizations. As it happened, those who were tried tended to be the biggest landowners, as well as a number of Roman Catholic clergy.

The political struggle strengthened the authority of the party and prepared the way for the land reform which marked the transition to a communist-type society. The landlords had their land confiscated and it was distributed to the peasants, but only in the form of collective property under the control of the cooperatives. In 1960 Ho said that the state farm was the basis of future agricultural cooperatives. In this he seemed to be following the pattern laid down by the Soviet Union rather than that of China. Yet he added that the state farms would process agricultural production and supply industry with raw materials. Other Vietnamese communist leaders said that the farms would have industrial functions, develop their own militias and be based on some form of communal living. This latter provision was not spelt out, though it seemed to indicate a move towards emulating the Chinese communes. In 1964 cooperative farms accounted for ninety-five per cent of all lowland agriculture (and included eight-seven per cent of all rural families) with about fifty-nine state farms run by the People's Army.

In 1956 the régime admitted that mistakes had been made in the course of the 'Political Struggle' and the ensuing land reform. Hence, the programme of 'Rectification of Errors' was introduced. The party admitted, among other things, that it had failed to unite the middle-level peasants and form alliances with the rich peasants. Moreover, they had failed to treat landlords who had supported the resistance differently from the way they had treated the other landlords. Too many people had been executed and too much

I

use had been made of torture. Ho Viet Thang, the Minister in charge of the land reform, was dismissed, as was Truong Chinh, the general secretary of the party. What happened, in effect, was that the now reinstated party members carried out their own purge of those who had denounced them. Terror, on a smaller scale, continued.

The 'Rectification of Errors' campaign also entailed a relative degree of freedom for intellectuals. No doubt there was more than coincidence in the fact that it followed Mao's 'Hundred Flowers Campaign'. And, like Mao's experiment with liberalization, the Vietnam experiment was short-lived. It lasted a brief three months and was put down soon after the Hungarian uprising. Soon after the régime introduced 'Thought Reform' on the Chinese model, and 'Reform by Manual Labour' with intellectuals being forced to do manual work.

The war against France had left what industry North Vietnam possessed in disrepair. After 1954 the government started a massive industrialization campaign. Help was provided initially by China, but it soon became apparent that China was unable to provide either the skilled technicians or the sophisticated machinery necessary for economic recovery and progress. As a result greater reliance was placed on the Soviet Union and the Eastern bloc countries.

At first the communists had taken a decision to do no more than repair the war damage but, with the failure to increase food production and an ever-expanding population, the decision was taken to force the pace of industrialization. Private traders were gradually eliminated and a totally planned economy realized by 1956. In 1960 Vo Nguyen asserted that 'economic construction has become the central task of the party'.

North Vietnam cannot really be understood unless it is put into the context of being between, and wanting to please, the two major communist powers of China and the Soviet Union. At least its leaders have assiduously tried not to offend them. Thus, in 1958, according to Tran Quyuh, Vietnam accepted that the socialist camp was headed by the Soviet Union, although at the same time vociferous support was given to China and its policy, especially in respect of Taiwan. Yugoslav revisionism was attacked, but in most cases the Vietnamese were content with words and took no action that would displease either of the major communist powers. At the height of the Sino-Soviet dispute it praised China but also urged unity. It has rarely taken sides in the dispute and has often spoken of the Soviet Union as the 'centre of the socialist camp', while referring to China's 'big achievement in building socialism'. China is near and a potential threat to the security of North Vietnam. The Soviet Union is far away, but is responsible for most of the economic aid entering Vietnam. Indeed, it is possible that massive Soviet aid was conditional on North Vietnam's support for Russia in its dispute with China in 1960.

In many ways the policies of North Vietnam have been designed not so much as to accord with its own circumstances as to what is expected of it by the two communist giants. Not surprisingly, the Vietnamese have developed the art of verbal ambiguity to the full. In words they try to please both; in practice they pursue, as far as possible, their own interests.

In international affairs North Vietnam, in the person of the Premier Pham Van Don, gave support in 1959 to Khrushchev's idea of a nuclear-free zone in the Far East. They went further still and advocated a peace zone. Yet their words did not always accord with their actions. They trained and armed the Pathet Lao and provided troops and representatives in the 'neutral' government of Laos, and exercised great influence in Cambodia. And, whilst going along with Khrushchev on peaceful coexistence in 1959, they played it down after 1960 when the split between the Soviet Union and China widened. At one and the same time they demand peace and justify the war in the South as being necessary to preserve the peace against the imperialist designs of the United States.

239

(b) North Korea

The only other communist state in Asia, North Korea, has, like North Vietnam, been engaged in a long struggle to unify the country. Occupied by the Japanese at the beginning of the twentieth century and liberated by the allies after the Second World War, Korea was divided into a North under the protection of the Soviet Union and a South supported by the United States.

A Korean communist party had been formed in 1925 but the present Korean Workers' Party (KWP) dates from 1949. Led by Kim Il-sung, North Korea has become economically and militarily one of the strongest of Asian states. Kim had led an anti-Japanese guerrilla force in Manchuria before the Second World War but fled to Siberia in 1941 where he is alleged to have become an officer in the Red Army. Though this is now disputed, what is certain is that he returned to North Korea with the Red Army in 1948 and shortly seized power in Pyongyang. Though relatively young for a leader of a state (he was in his early thirties), he was aided in his capture of power by his undoubted ability and cunning and, not least, his adroit Machiavellian tactics. Moreover, he was helped by the fact that the 'older domestic communists', like Pak Hon-yong, stayed in the South for too long and had discredited themselves by endorsing the nationalist Syngman Ree as President of the Peoples' Republic. When they eventually returned North Kim was firmly entrenched in power. They returned in time to be purged. Since then Kim has consolidated his power by frequent purges of his critics.

The day after the announcement of the new Republic in 1948 Kim, 'capable of commanding the heavens and the earth', as a laudatory biography claims,[6] set the main objectives of his régime as being national unification, the building of a national independent economy, and the strengthen-

6. Bong, Baik, *Kim Il-sung Biography*, 3 vols., Tokyo, 1969 and 1970.

ing of its military power. These objectives have been constantly reiterated throughout the life of the régime and are still being pursued. 'Indeed, the history of North Korea's first two decades can be viewed primarily in terms of an unremitting quest to achieve these basic objectives.'[7]

In terms of national reunification Kim refused to allow the United Nations to supervise elections in 1948 and instead formed a 'Fatherland United Democratic Front' 'to emancipate South Korea from the enslavement of American imperialism and attain the peaceful unification and complete independence of the fatherland'. However, he possessed a rather strange conception of 'peaceful unification'. In 1950 he declared war on the South in an attempt to unify the country by force. No doubt confronted with a South that, as a result of American assistance, was politically stable and economically prosperous he had little choice but to embark upon the adventure, particularly as he wanted to retain the legitimacy of his own régime.

He was labelled as the 'aggressor' by the United Nations, and the war ended in a stalemate. But this did not end the North's drive for unification. At the Fifth Congress of the KWP in 1970 Kim asserted:

The oppressed and exploited popular masses can win freedom and emancipation only through their own revolutionary struggle. Therefore, the South Korean revolution should, in all circumstances, be carried out by the South Korean people on their own initiative. But the people in the northern half, being of the same nation, have the obligation and responsibility to support and actively encourage the South Korean people in their revolutionary struggle.[8]

Indeed, in the same speech he asserted that:

To reunite the divided fatherland is a great national duty of all the Korean people at the present stage. It is our most urgent

7. B. C. Koh, 'North Korea: Profile of a Garrison State', *Problems of Communism*, Vol. XVIII, No. 1, Jan.–Feb. 1969, p. 21.
8. Quoted in Joungwon A. Kim, 'Pyongyang's Search for Legitimacy', *Problems of Communism*, Vol. XX, No. 1–2, Jan.–April 1971, p. 38.

task, and we cannot forget it even for a moment. The policy of our party for the unification of our fatherland is already known widely throughout the world.[9]

Given that he appeared to believe that the South was en-slaved by the 'American imperialist aggressor and their lackeys', this was a laudable objective. But then Kim has always claimed to be the leader of the whole country and suffered a great deal of discomfort, to put it no higher, at his lack of success in the South.

Thus Kim has spent a great proportion of North Korea's national income on armaments, some estimates putting it as high as thirty per cent. His slogan of 'Let Us Turn the Entire Country into a Fortress' and Koh's description of North Korea as a 'garrison state' emphasizes this.[10] Nor has he been content to stockpile military hardware or accept the 1950 stalemate. Instead he has engaged in a number of plots against the government in the South and provocations of the United States. In 1968, for example, North Korean commandos attempted a raid on the presidential residence of Park Chung Hee in Seoul and North Korean gunboats captured the United States 'spy ship' *Pueblo*.

Kim's second objective of building an independent national economy has also been vigorously pursued. When faced with the failure of his war of liberation of the South in 1950 he turned back to concentrate on industrializing North Korea and attempted to emulate Mao's 'Great Leap Forward' by introducing his own 'Flying Horses Movement' in 1968. This was aimed at mobilizing mass support for rapid industrialization though, unlike the similar campaign in China, great emphasis was also placed on developing tech-nical expertise. As in Russia during Stalin's early years, the emphasis was placed on the development of heavy industry and the elaboration of detailed economic plans. Though the plan's targets have not always been hit the North Koreans have, nevertheless, been relatively successful in building up

9. ibid.
10. B. C. Koh, op. cit.

their industry. Of course they have been helped in this enterprise by the legacy of the Japanese industrial base, a plentiful supply of natural resources and economic and technical assistance from the communist bloc. The Stalin-like authoritarian and totalitarian government system has also played a not inconsiderable part in North Korea's industrialization. Now nearly fifty per cent of the population is employed in industry and the collectivization of agriculture had been completed by 1958.

But for Kim an independent national economy also means one that is independent of the two major communist powers. At first North Korea was little more than a satellite of the Soviet Union but this did not last for long. Kim soon established himself in undisputed control of his country, despite several attempts of the Russians to undermine him. Since then he has pursued a careful course of independence of both China and the Soviet Union, though at times he has veered towards one or the other. In practice he adopts a posture of being a friendly ally of both and, in 1961, signed mutual defence treaties with them both.

In international communist affairs Kim has steered his country towards a policy of neutrality between the two major powers and he has constantly emphasized his policy of non-interference of communist states in each others' affairs. Indeed, he seems obsessed by the desire for independence. In 1966 he stressed the policy of the KWP was to 'build an independent national economy on the principle of self-reliance'. And, in August that year, the party organ *Nodong Sin* in an article entitled 'Let Us Defend Independence' said:

No matter how good the guiding theory of the party of a certain country may be, it cannot be applied to all parties, because the requirements and situation of revolution differ in all countries ... a single centre can never give unified guidance in the world revolutionary movement.

The same year Kim attacked both the 'modern revisionists'

of the Soviet Union and the 'Left opportunism' and 'dogmatism' of China.

Nor has Kim been content with words. There was no North Korean ambassador in China in 1966 and he refused to send delegates to the Ninth Congress of the CCP in 1969. However, in 1970 Chou En-lai said in the course of a visit to North Korea in 'the future, we will, as always, support and assist each other and fight shoulder to shoulder'. The Soviet Union also followed suit with promise of support.

Much of the animosity that Kim has directed towards the two major communist states can probably be explained by his undoubted desire to present himself as the communist revolutionary leader of the world. He has made great efforts to woo the leaders of the communist and nationalist movement in the Third World and both he and his friends have gone to great lengths to project an almost supernatural image. It is possible too that he sees himself as supplanting Mao as the leader of the world revolutionary movement. Certainly he has not hidden his belief in the need for violent revolution. 'The greatest lesson of the historic anti-Japanese movement,' he asserted in 1969, 'is that the highest form of struggle for freedom is revolutionary violence.' Yet this 'hero of the twentieth century' as he has been called, has a long way to go before he can claim to be in the same class as Mao, either as a theorist or revolutionary leader.

(c) The Communist Parties

(i) JAPAN

The Japanese Communist party (CJP) is the largest non-governing communist party outside western Europe, claiming a membership of over 300,000 in 1970. A legal part of the Japanese political system with a strong and influential following among students, it has not, however, been conspicuously successful in electoral terms. Though founded in 1922 it was, until 1945, an illegal organization with an unbounded loyalty to Moscow. During the inter-war period it was more of a group of conspiratorial theorists than a mass political party and it swam against the mainstream of the nationalist tide that swamped Japanese political life.

Standing outside the political system and subjected to frequent police repression, its leaders believed, in the Leninist tradition, that the party should preserve itself as an elite group. And, like Lenin in the early 1900s, they believed after 1932 that Japan had first to have its bourgeois-democratic revolution before they could proceed to the proletarian-socialist revolution.

At the end of the war in 1945 the C J P was reconstituted as a legal political organization and actively cooperated with the allies in democratizing the country. Naturally enough the party saw this as a means of hastening the long-awaited bourgeois-democratic revolution and, therefore, of the much longer awaited socialist revolution. It did not seem to occur to them as it had done to Trotsky and Mao, albeit in different ways, that the era of bourgeois-democracy could either be telescoped into or bypassed by the socialist revolution.

As a result of its cooperation with the allies in the reconstruction of Japan's economic life and the establishment of a democratic political system the C J P, as one would have expected, saw itself as an integral part of the new system. It became more moderate and conciliatory in its policies and strategy and even coined the bizarre phrase 'a lovable communist party'. Who found it lovable, apart from its members, is difficult to ascertain. Its more conciliatory posture brought it closer ties with neither the unions nor the Socialist party. And the failure of the party to extend its influence in these areas was due to no lack of effort or willingness to compromise on principles. Nor was it any more successful in gathering votes. It is true that it received ten per cent of the votes cast in the general election of 1949 and sent thirty-five members to the House of Representatives, but the percentage of the vote had declined by 1963 to four per cent and its seats to five.

The C J P's lack of electoral success was partly attributable to its decision in 1950 to reject the 'peaceful path to power' of Sanzo Noska, now the party's chairman, and instead to espouse direct action and a more militant philosophy. It also launched a full-scale attack on United States imperialism, which it saw as the prop of capitalism in Japan. Perhaps more important as an explanation of its declining popularity was that it was viewed by many as a puppet party pulled by strings that stretched to Moscow or Peking. Certainly both the Soviet Union and China exerted a great deal of pressure on the CJP to become more militant.

By the mid 1950s, after the beginning of deStalinization in the USSR, the party had discarded its conspiratorial strategy and attempted to play down its militant uncompromising image. It had certainly earned the party little except resentment and unpopularity. Instead it presented a new programme more attuned to the newly affluent and democratic nature of Japan. At its Eighth Congress in 1961 it affirmed that Japan was a highly developed capitalist country, though one that was dependent for its stability on the United States. Accordingly there was no longer any need for a bourgeois-democratic revolution; it had already occurred. There was however the obstacle the socialist revolution presented by the close relationship that existed between Japan and the United States. Hence the CJP has directed most of its attention towards the need for a break in this servile relationship and in attacking United States imperialism. As a resolution of its Eleventh Congress in 1970 stated:

Japan continues to be a semi-occupied, semi-independent country chained to the US imperialist policy of war and aggression. It is, and as the party programme puts it, a country which is 'virtually dependent, being semi-occupied by American Imperialism'.[11]

If the bourgeois-democratic revolution had taken place, as the party affirmed it had, then the next step was, or

11. Quoted by Paul F. Langer, 'The New Posture of the CJP', *Problems of Communism*, Vol. XX, No. 1–2, Jan.–April 1971, p. 18.

should be, the proletarian-socialist revolution. Yet whilst the C J P had retained its commitment to international revolution in the mid 1950s and did not rule it out in the 1960s, it still believed, like the Italian communist party, that the socialist revolution could be carried through, in Japan, by peaceful means. It could revolutionize society in a socialist way by transforming the existing power structure. The revolution was to be started by the formation of a united national democratic front led by the C J P to challenge United States imperialism.

Like the other Asian communist parties, whether in power or not, the C J P was beset by a crisis of identity, and a crisis of identity occasioned by the split between the Soviet Union and China. Loyalty was due to both but hardly reconcilable. The former was revisionist but also realist and its ideas fitted well with the domestic political environment inhabited by the C J P. On the other hand the Chinese were *the* revolutionaries and, after all, was not Marxism a revolutionary theory above all else? Moreover, the C J P operates within an Asian political system in which revolution was espoused by those parties in power and was the only reasonable path to power available to most of the others.

Before 1965 the party was strongly pro-Chinese, mainly because the pro-Chinese faction was in the ascendency in the party. Indeed a pro-Soviet group led by Yoshio Shiga was forced out of the party in 1964 for supporting the nuclear test ban treaty. Since 1965 the C J P, like North Vietnam and North Korea, has attempted to tread the delicate path of independence between the two communist antagonists and expelled its pro-China group, including Nishizawa Ryuji, in 1966.

The move against China in 1966 was partly the result of general distaste for the abortive coup of the Indonesia communist party in 1965. The Indonesian communists were accused by secretary general Kenji Miyamoto of 'left-wing adventurism' and condemned for slavishly following the Chinese line. In any case, Chinese tactics were hardly appropriate to a mass party in an advanced economic and political

system. Instead the CJP allied itself with the North Vietnamese and Koreans in calling for united action on the part
of the Soviet Union and China in Vietnam, but which the
Chinese opposed. More important to the CJP than the
quarrels within the communist camp was the forming
of a 'united front of the peoples of the world for world
peace and national independence against American imperialism'.

Thus the tenth Congress in 1966 clearly affirmed the
autonomy of the CJP and pledged the party, like the North
Koreans, to fight both 'revisionism' and 'dogmatism'. Now,
since the Eleventh Congress of 1970, the party asserts its independence of both the Soviet Union and China. It argues
that the cause of communist disunity is to be found in 'great-
power chauvinism,' that both of the big communist powers
are really concerned with establishing domination over all
other communist parties. The Japanese communists, on the
other hand, claim to have created a programme which
'creatively adapts Marxist–Leninist theory to the realities
of Japan'. If the results of the 1969 general election are any
guide then they have had a certain measure of success, their
percentage of the vote having increased to nearly seven per
cent.

(ii) THE INDONESIAN COMMUNIST PARTY

Founded in 1920, the Communist Party of Indonesia (P K I)
was, until 1965, the second largest communist party in
Asia with an alleged membership of 3 million. Until 1926
it operated as a legal organization but that year it attempted
a revolution in Java and Sumatra and was almost completely
destroyed by the Dutch by 1927.

After Indonesia had declared its independence of Holland
in 1945 a revolutionary struggle began in which the communists participated and for which they were accorded
legality. By 1948, however, the communists had become dis-
enchanted with the new Republic, arguing that it had sold
out to the West, and they initiated their own anti-Republic
revolution aiming to capture the state and dislodge the

Dutch. The result was that most of the party leaders were killed and the party became, once more, an illegal organization.

Not unnaturally, the communists date the revolutionary struggle as being from 1945 to 1948, though the Dutch were not finally expelled until 1950, when the party achieved legality. The years from 1945 to 1948 are referred to by the communist party as the period of the 'people's revolution'. It was, they argue, a period in which the revolution was making headway against the forces of imperialism by such means as taking over foreign property. But the revolution ended abruptly for the communists in 1948 when their own attempt to achieve power was forestalled.

The P K I emerged after 1950 with a greatly enhanced prestige because of the part it had played in the nationalist movement. Yet it immediately asserted that the momentum of the 'people's revolution' had to be regained. For the P K I the revolution was an unfinished revolution; it had to continue the bourgeois-democratic revolution started in 1945 and which would lead, inexorably, to the proletarian socialist revolution.

And indeed, until 1965 the P K I behaved in an extremely moderate and conciliatory manner. Though the party leader and leading theoretician, Dipa Nusantara Aidit, was apt to mouth Maoist slogans, he was careful not to upset the nationalist currents which were so strong in Indonesia and more careful still in keeping his party within the bounds of parliamentarianism. The 1959 programme and constitution of the P K I affirmed its preference for the peaceful parliamentary road to socialism, though it added that it doubted that this could be achieved without violence. When, in 1960, a Presidential decree laid down that all political parties had to subscribe to peaceful means of advancing their objectives the P K I was quick to comply and altered its programme and constitution accordingly.

In 1960 Aidit had argued that Indonesia was a 'national-democratic' regime and that, therefore, no real steps towards socialism were possible. First the national-democratic, or bourgeois-democratic, revolution had to be completed. Only then could the party go on to establish a people's democracy. Thus for Aidit, and many of his co-leaders, the revolution was to be a gradual one, and he constantly emphasized the need to unify all social classes behind demands for social reform. Aidit believed that the party could go forward, without the necessity for armed struggle, in pushing forward the national democratic revolution into the socialist revolution. 'At present,' he said, 'in our national democratic revolution, we are siding with [the national capitalists] and fighting a common battle of expelling foreign economic domination from this soil.'[12]

In 1959 he had endorsed the Guided Democracy of President Sukarno, he called for political cooperation between the Moslems, Nationalists and Communists in 1960–61, and, in 1962, went further still and advocated the formation of a coalition government. He preferred, he said, nationalists who opposed imperialism (Sukarno) to revisionists (Khrushchev) who warmly embraced it. He and Lukman Njono were soon rewarded with cabinet posts though neither had any real power. Certainly this policy of cooperation had been advocated by the party in the early 1950s when it was supposedly militant. Both in 1953 and 1955 the party put forward the idea of the people's democracy by which they meant, at that time, a national coalition of all revolutionary classes. And all revolutionary classes were defined as those who would help the cause of nationalism and economic development. The PKI professed to be content with pursuing limited objectives in a non-communist government.

This was spelt out more explicitly in the programme and constitution of 1962. It called for the establishment of a 'people's democratic state' based upon the masses. It was to be an alliance of the peasants and the workers; a government led by the working class but expressing the power of the

12. Quoted by Jusus van der Kroef, 'The Vocabulary of Indonesian Communism', *Problems of Communism*, Vol. XIV, No. 3, May–June 1965, p. 4.

people aiming at national independence and the introduction of democratic reforms. The latter included a guarantee of democratic rights, the elimination of unemployment, and the redistribution of land to the peasants. Socialist reforms would follow as the government established itself. The 'democracy of a new type', as it was called, would obtain the support of the intellectuals, the urban petty bourgeoisie, patriotic elements and the national bourgeoisie.

In 1965 the P K I appears to have changed its line. President Sukarno had been weakening his ties with the Soviet Union and strengthening those with China for a number of years. He sided with the P K I against the army over the issue of arms to the masses and dissolved the parties of the P K I's rivals. Indeed, in May 1965 he referred to Aidit as the 'fortress of Indonesia' and said that he embraced the P K I. Yet in September 1965 there was an attempted coup, with six generals murdered, for which the P K I has been generally blamed. Certainly Sukarno's health was deteriorating and it is possible that the P K I was afraid that the cordial relations they had enjoyed with Sukarno would not be repeated by his successor and that the leftward trend of the government would be reversed. Accordingly, the argument goes, the communists attempted a takeover before it was too late.

Though most commentators attribute the coup to the P K I, it is possible that certain elements in the army were responsible. They had already quarrelled with Sukarno over arms to the masses, disliked his flirtation with the P K I and the latter's influence in government, limited though it was, and resented the cutting off of the Soviet Union's military aid because of Sukarno's ties with China. No doubt they too were fearful of a left-wing successor to Sukarno just as the P K I were alleged to fear a right-wing successor. Again, for a party staging a coup, the P K I appears to have been totally unprepared. As Ruth McVey has pointed out, the

Communist Party's response to the coup was completely dysfunctional: party leadership was virtually missing, and the

P K I cadres neither backed the affair with massive demonstrations of the 'people's will' nor endeavoured to keep their skirts clean, but rather varied in their reactions from nervous withdrawal to opportunistic enthusiasm.[13]

Moreover, Sukarno appears to have been unaware of the intended coup, even though he had good relations with the PKI and could arguably be said to have favoured a move against his increasingly powerful army. In fact, most of the leaders of the coup were supporters of General Suharto, and shortly afterwards he had effective control of the country.

Whoever was responsible, there is no doubt that the P K I lost. Its leaders were killed or fled into exile, its organization was destroyed and many of its members murdered – some estimates putting the deaths as high as a million. In 1966 it became, yet again, an illegal organization with a membership reduced to around 100,000. It did not, however, disappear altogether. Several underground organizations were formed like the one led by Sudisman in Djakarta, destroyed in 1967, and others in East Java, destroyed in 1968.

As a result of the coup and its aftermath the remaining leaders reassessed the programme and strategy of the party. Jusuf Adjitorop asserted in 1966 that the failure of the coup had discredited the idea of a peaceful road to socialism. Instead he outlined three tasks for the P K I. These were to reconstruct the party on a working-class basis aiming at organizing the masses, the workers and the peasants; to renounce coups and lead a long armed struggle in alliance with the peasants; and to form a united front of all those opposed to Suharto.

But this was not enough; the old party leadership had also to be criticized. Thus the Politburo of the party issued a statement attacking Aidit and his comrades for collaborating with the national bourgeoisie and Sukarno. They were criticized for ignoring the class struggle in Indonesia and paying too much attention to the international struggle. The statement advocated a revolutionary united front led

13. Ruth T. McVey, 'P K I Fortunes at Low Tide', *Problems of Communism*, Vol. XX, No. 1–2, Jan.–April 1971, p. 27.

by the communists working for an agrarian revolution and a people's democratic regime.

Thus the P K I today is more militant and Maoist than it has been for years. As Adjitorop said in 1966, 'One criterion for determing whether or not a working-class party is firmly siding with Marxism–Leninism is its attitude to the C C P.' The Soviet Union, after all, was after 'world domination'. Whereas in the mid 1960s the P K I attacked the Soviet Union for being revisionist whilst itself was pursuing an essentially revisionist policy in domestic politics, it is now firmly and unambiguously in the Maoist camp internationally and in its strategy for Indonesia. Yet its more militant line and its emphasis on armed struggle is natural enough, given the illegality of the party, the repression of communists by the Suharto regime and the recent failure of peaceful means. And though the party looks weak, disorganized and disoriented, one has to remember that it has risen from defeat more than once in the past.

I3

CUBA AND CASTROISM

The first communist revolution occurred in Russia, China spearheaded the communist advance in Asia and now the first successful communist revolution in Latin America occurred in that most unlikely country, Cuba. And just as the two other revolutions had been stamped with the personality of a charismatic leader, so also the Cuban revolution was to be fashioned by Fidel Castro.

'Castroism', Theodore Draper has written, 'is a leader in search of a movement, a movement in search of power, and power in search of an ideology.'[1] Certainly the Castro-led revolution in Cuba owed little to traditional revolutionary theory and still less to Marxism. Both Castro and his followers seem to take a great delight in professing their ignorance of the writings of Mao on guerrilla theory and of Marxism in general. But then such disclaimers make them look more theoretically original and there is nothing in Castro's actions to suggest that he is not vain. The revolution owed little to a social and economic analysis of Cuba and was not class-oriented; its proletarian ideology and anti-imperialism followed the conquest of power rather than serving as a motive and rallying cry for revolution. The revolution had little in the way of an ideology or nationalistic basis but began as a movement of protest by a small group of disaffected idealistic liberals against the corruption of the Batista régime. The defeat of Batista was the main objective; all else followed in response to internal and international circumstances, a gradual, almost imperceptible, accommodation to the objective conditions of power.

It was only during his incarceration on the Isle of Pines

1. Theodore Draper, in *Marxism in the Modern World*, ed. Milorad M. Drachkovitch, p. 219.

from late 1953 to mid 1955, after the abortive Moncado rising, that Castro attempted to define his conception of his movement. It was during this period that he wrote in its present form *History Will Absolve Me*. Even this over-famous document is more a catalogue of the evils of the Batista régime and of the brutality of the army towards the captured revolutionaries than a programme for the future. What positive proposals are espoused amount to no more than a list of the often-quoted liberal cures for the evils of the régime. 'It contains', as Jean-Paul Sartre has observed, 'vague ideas for social reform but it has no ideological structure.'[2] It is hardly a rousing call to revolution.

What it promised was the restoration of the 1940 Consti-tution and a 'government of popular election', the restric-tion of large holdings of land, an increase in the number of small holdings, a thirty per cent share of profits to em-ployees, fifty-five per cent of sugar production to the planters and the nationalization of the United States' electric and telephone companies. Cuba, Castro argued, was to become the 'bulwark of liberty' and the problems of land, industrial-ization, housing, education, unemployment and health dealt with.

History Will Absolve Me represents a moderate constitu-tional programme of action. Castro was always cautious in his statements and constantly invoked the return of the 1940 Constitution as his guiding objective. Of course, Castro later announced that had it, and he, been more revolutionary, then the revolutionary movement would not have obtained the breadth of support that it did. Yet this retrospective attempt to present himself as a consistent revolutionary and a consummate Machiavellian – a communist revolu-tionary when all around him thought him to be a nice liberal forced into armed combat by the repressive nature of the régime – does not exactly square with the facts.

Castro had run for election as a candidate of the liberal

2. Quoted by K. S. Karol, introduction to *History Will Absolve Me*.

Ortodoxo party in 1952 and still belonged to it when he wrote *History Will Absolve Me*. In a message to a gathering of militants of the party in 1955 he still claimed to be an Ortodoxo, faithful to the ideals of Chibas, and he invited the support of all who wished to see the re-establishment of political democracy. He claimed, further, that his 26 July Movement, formed in Mexico in 1955, was of Ortodoxo faith and would become a political party on the democratic model after the fall of Batista. Free enterprise too was to be allowed. And though he resigned from the party in 1956, he insisted that it was organizational, not political, separation. Even after the success of the revolution he visited the grave of Chibas and declared that his movement 'was the continuation of the work of Chibas, the harvest of the seed that he planted'.

Castro was primarily concerned with the overthrow of Batista and to achieve this he sought to unite all in the struggle. For this reason he refused to endorse radical agrarian reform for fear of alienating the landlords and foreign interests. *The Manifesto of the Sierra Maestra* (July 1957) signed by Castro, Felipe Pazos and Raúl Chibas, the brother of Eduardo Chibas, was really no more than a plea for a unification of all anti-Batista forces. It claimed that the rebels were fighting because they had been denied the right of free elections and democratic government and it advocated the restoration of all liberal-bourgeois values. Castro probably thought no further ahead than the downfall of Batista and, when he did, lacked the imagination to construct a vision of the new society.

Whether or not Castro was sincere in his statements when he made them, the liberal democracy he had promised did not materialize after the revolution. In 1961 he publicly announced his attachment to Marxism: 'I am a Marxist–Leninist and shall be until the day I die.' To be fair to Castro, it could plausibly be argued that this was a conversion, even though he would have us believe that he had always been a Marxist but possessed the qualities of a confidence trickster. There can be no doubt that open rivalry and conflict existed between the communists and Castro until 1959. In 1953 the Communist Party had repudiated his military tactics and he had, in 1959, characterized communism – along with Peronism and fascism – as totalitarian. Some form of alliance with the Communist Party was formed in 1958, though there were many anti-communists in Castro's movement and many democratic communists in the Communist Party. Not until after the revolution was fusion finally achieved, when the Popular Socialist Party was absorbed into the ruling party in December 1961.

Many argue that Castro was a communist all along but hid his belief so as to aid the revolution, others that he knew nothing of Marxism but searched for an ideology with which to clothe his assumption of power and was helped towards communism by the hostility of the United States and the friendly attitude of the Soviet Union. Whichever, if either, is true, the democratic sentiments of the earlier period were soon forgotten when he was in power. His only attempt to provide an ideology of his own – humanism – failed after a few months. But what really matters is that Cuba became the first outpost of communism in Latin America and that Fidel Castro assumed the role of the leader of Latin American revolution.

(a) Revolutionary Tactics and Latin America

What is regarded as uniquely important in the Cuban revolution is the tactics that were employed to achieve power. Castro's success was not based upon his espousal of liberal ideas – they were advocated by many who were often more radical – but upon his military tactics. First was his emphasis on armed struggle. However, his was not the only group to engage in armed combat. There was Rafael Garcia Barncena's Movimiento Nacionaliste Revolucionario and Aureliano Sanchez Araligo's Triple A. But whereas these aimed at the régime's power base and tried to obtain the cooperation of the army and assassinate Batista, Castro attacked the army, from Oriente in 1953 and Mexico in 1956. 'Power is seized and held in the capital,' he said, 'but the road that leads the exploited to it must pass through the countryside.'

The second major feature of Castro's tactics was his conception of guerrilla warfare built up from a guerrilla *foco* which was extremely mobile and gradually expanded its operations and support to the point where it could destroy the enemy. Though this is now represented as a significant contribution to revolutionary theory it was, as Theodore Draper has pointed out, 'an *ex post facto* rationalization of an improvised response to events beyond Castro's control'.[3] Castro and his followers were forced into the countryside and guerrilla warfare by their lack of success in fomenting insurrection and general strikes. In the early period of revolutionary activity Castro anticipated that the campaign would be short. There would be military operations, sabotage and a general strike, followed by a popular uprising. As late as 1958 he said the 'strategy of the decisive blow is based on the revolutionary general strike, assisted by armed action'. Nor did he believe in 1957 and early 1958 that guerrilla war would be successful. It became necessary when all other stratagems had failed. Fortunately for Castro, it was successful. Yet even here a note of reservation must be entered. What defeated Batista in 1959 was not so much the military tactics and genius of Castro as the crumbling morale of Batista's army and the hostility of the people.

Ernesto Che Guevara and Régis Debray have used the Cuban experience to construct theories of revolution and guerrilla war which are now offered to Latin American revolutionaries as the road to power. Guevara had turned to a study of Marx and Lenin after the CIA-backed invasion of Guatemala in 1954. Guatemala was, as his wife wrote, that which finally convinced him of the necessity for armed struggle and for taking the initiative against imperialism'.

3. Theodore Draper, in Milorad M. Drachkovitch (ed.), op. cit., p. 205.

Guevara's guerrilla theory consists of the setting up of a *foco*, the emphasis on survival at all costs during its initial period, and concentration on increasing the morale of the guerrillas and winning the support of the peasants until the point is reached where it becomes an army able to confront the enemy. In *Guerrilla Warfare* (1961) he insists that revolutionaries do not need to wait for objective conditions to be ripe in order to make a revolution, that popular forces can defeat an army and that rural areas are the best battlefields. Nevertheless, he is careful not to deny that the guerrilla can only operate as the advanced party of the masses and must have popular support. He must know his terrain and only engage in successful actions using the strategy of 'strike and get out'. Psychological warfare must be waged against the enemy by means of constant strikes, encirclement and harrassment. Much of the book is taken up with the tactics of mobility and surprise, the use of mines, the tactics for difficult terrain and the appropriate weapons for different circumstances. He goes on to define the guerrilla's social role as a 'crusader', exhibiting a strong moral code and self-discipline and always being ready to help the peasants. This he does by starting in the liberated areas the process of indoctrination, of establishing justice and distributing land. Not content with this, Guevara goes on to list the qualities necessary for a guerrilla and his needs, even to the extent of describing the most effective knapsack, the use of propaganda, the training of recruits and the role of women. Guevara was shot in Bolivia in 1967. He started out as a Marxist but, as Kenneth Minogue has written, 'he bucked the theory to make a revolution, reconstructed the theory to fit the revolution he had made, and then proceeded to demonstrate by his actions in Bolivia the inadequacy of his own theory'.[4]

Like Guevara, Debray argues in *Revolution in the Revolution* that Latin America is ripe for revolution. His schematized model of the Cuban revolution is offered as a third

4. Kenneth Minogue, 'Che Guevara', in *The New Left*, ed. Maurice Cranston, p. 30.

way to socialism different from that adopted in Russia and China. This third way is achieved by 'means of the more or less slow building up, through guerrilla warfare carried out in suitably chosen rural zones, of a *mobile strategic force*, nucleus of a people's army and of a future socialist state'. The guerrilla force is clandestine, independent of the civilian population and passes through three stages of development: absolute nomadism; the development of supply lines, arms depots, mail service, and relief forces in a liberated zone; and the stage of revolutionary offensive. He dismisses the conceptions of armed self-defence as practised in Bolivia and Columbia, armed propaganda as used against the French in Vietnam and the rural guerrilla base of Mao.

More important to socialist theory is the relation of the Communist Party to the guerrilla *foco*. Debray argues that the Cuban revolution has made a 'decisive contribution to international revolutionary experience and to Marxism–Leninism'. Whereas classical Marxist–Leninism would subordinate the armed wing to the political wing, Debray argues that Cuba has indicated the need for the unification of military and political leadership, in one person if possible. '*Under certain conditions*', he wrote, '*the political and the military are not separate, but form one organic whole, consisting of the people's army, whose nucleus is the guerrilla army. The vanguard party can exist in the form of the guerrilla foco itself. The guerrilla force is the party in embryo.*' This, for Debray, is the 'staggering novelty introduced by the Cuban revolution'.

It is the guerrilla *foco* that is the 'motor that moves the masses'. From it a political leadership emerges that politicizes the masses and defeats the armed power of the state. The military element is not, and should not be, subordinate to a separate political element. As Castro argued, those who want to make the revolution have the right and duty to constitute themselves the vanguard.

Debray hardly refers to socialism and does not offer a social or economic analysis of Latin America but blithely assumes that the disparate countries of the continent are all equally ripe for revolution on the Cuban model as presented by Debray, even though he admits that the revolutionary struggle encounters specific conditions on each continent, in each country.

Castro, too, has offered his model for export. He assumed the leadership of Latin American communism in 1963 and lectured the communists on the correct road to power. Like Guevara and Debray, he argued that objective conditions for revolution existed in Latin America and that only revolutionary will was lacking. Yet, unlike Debray and Guevara, he has often modified his pronouncements to take account of special conditions as he did, for example, before the Chilean elections in 1964.

Cuban tactics were adopted in Venezuela and Guatemala, though the former dropped them in 1969. Luis de la Puente's attempt to establish a *foco* in Peru in 1965 failed, as did Guevara's expedition to Bolivia in 1967. Of course, Guevara and his band could no longer pose, as Castro had done, as the defenders of democratic ideals and therefore hope to gain the allegiance of the bourgeoisie. They were – and had to be – explicitly Marxist revolutionaries, if for no other reason than that they were backed by Castro. Moreover, while the United States had largely stood aside in Castro's confrontation with Batista, this time it stood firmly against Guevara. Guevara could not obtain a Bolivian of note to fight with him and he alienated the local communist party and the peasants. Though Castroite splinter groups were formed in most of the countries with communist parties, most of the leaders of the parties, and especially in Argentina, Brazil and Chile, preferred the old-style electioneering. Luis Corvalán, the Chilean communist leader, was particularly opposed to the Cuban model, though he admitted in 1963 that the violent road might be admissible in certain circumstances. He was at the time concerned about the Chilean elections and hence concerned to emphasize democratic procedures and repudiate armed adventurism. 'In upholding the peaceful way, our Party', he announced, 'aims at solving the tasks of the revolution without civil war or armed uprising.' Though the elections were a failure for the Communist Party and Castro again reiterated the necessity of armed struggle in Chile, the Marxist Salvador Allende was elected President of the Republic in 1970, and has embarked upon a massive nationalization programme.

(b) The Cuban State

When fighting in the rural areas, Castro had repeatedly proclaimed his allegiance to democratic principles and the constitution of 1940. Now Cuba has a government structure that has been built from the leader downwards. Power is concentrated in the Communist Party, within the party in its Central Committee and within the Central Committee in the leader. Castro did however suggest in 1970 that some outside body should supervise the activities of the party, but this appears to be no more than a gesture.

In July 1960 all United States property was taken over. Later the same year all large private enterprises were nationalized. Not until 1968 was all private enterprise nationalized. All state enterprises operate under plans laid down by the centre and monetary incentives to production have been gradually eliminated, though this to some extent is less a matter of ideology than of necessity, given the lack of consumer goods. The Central Planning Commission determines the overall plan, enterprises are not allowed financial independence and all profits from enterprises and receipts from state farms are paid into the national budget.

In the early years of the régime the major emphasis in economic policy was on creating a base for economic development but with the balance of payments problem caused by this the emphasis was shifted to agriculture. The government laid down that the régime would specialize in sugar and cattle, and gear industry and investment to these products. Indeed, the achievement of a ten-million-ton target of sugar production in 1970 became, in Castro's words, a 'point of honour for the Revolution'.

In the field of agriculture the first agrarian reform (1959) confiscated holdings in excess of 1,000 acres. Part of this was given to renters and the remainder cultivated by state farms. The second agrarian reform (1963) confiscated holdings in excess of 165 acres. This still left a fairly substantial private sector in agriculture (thirty-five per cent in 1965) able to provide food for private consumption and for sale on the free market.

What has characterized the agricultural sector more than anything else in the last few years has been the military-style discipline imposed on the workers. Agricultural workers, proletarians and students have been mobilized on a large scale to till the ground and get in the crops. Although one of the motives behind this has been an attempt to mould the minds of the young to accept new work habits, the idea of service to the community and duty to the revolution, manifested by the school goes to the Countryside Programme in which pupils and students lived in barracks and worked for nothing, it also had a more practical rationale. Agricultural production has been reduced, not so much as a result of a scarcity of labour as by absenteeism and an unwillingness to work on the part of the peasants now that the threat of starvation has been eliminated. The success of the Castro régime in achieving this has, ironically, forced it to adopt military-style regimentation and discipline in order to increase production.

While the economic policies have not always been successful and the régime had recourse to moral persuasion and the massive mobilization of the population in an attempt to achieve its targets, it has also some dramatic achievements to its credit. There has been a massive educational campaign to eradicate illiteracy, which slumped from 23·6 per cent of the population in 1961 to 3·9 per cent at the end of the campaign. Medical attention is now free and vastly extended with newly qualified doctors spending two years in rural areas. Telephones, water, gas and electricity are free

263

and public transport inexpensive. Except in Havana, household rents have been abolished and the occupants of new flats receive free furniture. All those under sixteen are also fed, clothed and educated by the state. Thus many of the specific economic and social promises made by Castro in *History Will Absolve Me* have been fulfilled and the waste, corruption and social degradation of the Batista régime eradicated. Though Castro appears to be genuinely popular with the Cubans, the liberal political reforms are still awaited.

14

AFRICAN SOCIALISM

In Africa socialism is growing in significance and is espoused by an increasing number of political leaders. It is, however, a very amorphous doctrine, a pot-pourri of ideas rather than a coherent theory, and it differs from country to country. Julius Nyerere's socialism, for example, is more of an affirmation and statement of human values and a condemnation of capitalism than a clearly thought out theory. Moreover, as Jitendra Mahon has pointed out, few African leaders have 'resisted the temptation of insinuating "Socialism" into their political rhetoric, even while their actual policies are strikingly similar to those pursued by countries like Nigeria and the Ivory Coast, whose leaders are unabashed both in espousing and following "free enterprise" '.[1]

Yet some categories can be formulated. There are small groups of communists in Algeria, the Cameroons, Guinea, Mali and Senegal, but who are in the main fighting, unsuccessfully, to import a doctrine that is regarded by most as alien and inappropriate to Africa. African Marxists are influential in Ghana, Guinea and Mali where the state régimes are monolithic and authoritarian. At the same time they accept economic aid from both the East and West, and affect a non-aligned posture in international relations. What might be termed pragmatic socialists are predominant in the United Arab Republic, Tunisia, Senegal, Dahomey and Tanzania. In those countries the emphasis is placed on Africanism and the African past and a more tolerant attitude adopted towards private enterprise. Finally, democratic socialism, as it is understood in the West, is least

1. Jitendra Mahon, 'Varieties of African Socialism', in *The Socialist Register,* ed. Ralph Miliband and John Saville, London, 1966, p. 220.

important of all, though it was at one time espoused by Jomo Kenyatta and Chabi Mama of Dahomey. It is no surprise therefore to find that the Dakar conference of 1962 failed to provide a definition of African Socialism. In Africa, as in many other places, socialism is often no more than a convenient rhetoric with which to hide the basis of political power and stimulate the masses into greater economic productivity.

Yet in spite of the bewildering proliferation of ideas and programmes enunciated by African leaders from time to time, certain basic themes can be discerned. First there is the attempt on the part of African leaders to find a common identity and mark off African socialism from both the democratic socialism of the West and the communism of the East. This search for a distinctive doctrine that will unite the continent is manifested, for example, in such writings as Kwame Nkrumah's *African Personality* and Leopold Senghor's *Negritude*. It is also made clear in a white paper issued by the government of Kenya in 1965 which said:

In the phrase 'African Socialism', the word African is not introduced to describe a continent to which a foreign ideology is to be transplanted. It is meant to convey the African roots of a system that is itself African in its characteristics.

The termination of the fight against colonialism has left a vacuum which the leaders have tried to fill by creating an African consciousness; a consciousness that has certainly been successfully developed among the Negroes of the United States if not those of Africa.

In a real sense socialism in Africa is an outgrowth of nationalism and a reaction against imperialism. Having rid Africa of the political domination of the European powers, the African leaders now wish to end the economic exploitation of their countries and their dependence upon the former colonial powers. The Ghanaian Convention People's Party, for instance, was originally inspired by anti-colonialism rather than socialism. But the reaction to Europeanization goes farther than hostility towards political and economic domination. Tom Mboya, and many like him, objected to western conceptions of socialism being imported and saw it as now being necessary to fight against what he calls 'intellectual imperialism'.

Thus the search for a specifically African socialism and, more important, the legitimization of the concept, has entailed a search for socialist roots in traditional African society. Nearly all African leaders argue that these are to be found in the traditional African society with its belief, as Tom Mboya put it, that they were all 'sons of the soil'. It is argued that in this society there was communal ownership of land, equality, a low degree of stratification, co-operative social relationships, community consciousness and responsibility, and an absence of acquisitive instincts and individualism. Thus for President Tsiranana of Malagasy, their socialism would be based on the 're-awakening of our ancestral socialist traditions'. This was echoed by Kenyatta in his introduction to the election manifesto of the Kenya African National Union in 1963 when he said:

Our nation must grow organically from what is indigenous; whilst adapting that which is suitable from other cultures from East and West, we must give our people pride and self-respect, building upon all that is good and valid in our traditional society.

What is good and valid in traditional society for Tanzania's Nyerere is the extended family: 'The foundation, and the objective, of African socialism is the extended family.' For him socialism is a way of transposing the concept of the extended family to that of the nation. Thus Tanzania has concentrated more on the construction of village schemes than the more grandiose industrial projects of her neighbours.

Nyerere, like Mboya, Nkrumah and Senghor, insists on the superiority of traditional African socialism. Mboya is willing to go abroad for loans and technical aid but not for ideals or ideologies. Senghor, too, repudiates capitalism for its emphasis on materialism and selfishness. Indeed, they want to purge African society of the corruption of western values. 'Of all the crimes of colonialism', Nyerere said in his inaugural speech as President of the new republic in 1962,

there is no worse than the attempt to make us believe we had no independent culture of our own: or that what we did have was worthless – something of which we should be ashamed instead of a source of pride.

So far as Nyerere, Mboya and Nkrumah are concerned, it was the colonists who introduced exploitation, classes and idlers, none of which were to be found in tradititonal society. Hence the African leaders have no need for the terminology of class war or revolution or for more than one political party. The self-imposed task of the African leaders, as Nkrumah outlined in *Consciencism* is to return to the past and adapt its values to modern conditions. The first step is that of re-education to former attitudes of mind that existed in a society where the individual took care of the community and the community the individual.

But whilst these leaders extol the virtues of traditional society, they are, in the drive towards modernization, engaged in breaking up the organizations of traditional society. Even in Tanzania, the epitome of the approach aimed at restoring traditional values, the Rural Settlement Commission is physically relocating the villages and breaking up what remains of traditional society. And in Zanzibar, nominally a part of Tanzania, the revolutionary government under Sheikh Abeid Karume has erected a rigid authoritarian régime, reallocated 12,000 acres of land to the peasants, nationalized most industries, introduced free but compulsory medical care, interfered in social and family life and introduced forced marriages across the races.

African socialism is also associated with, and a means towards, economic development. For many leaders socialism is indeed synonymous with modernization. In Ghana the adoption of socialism was the result of a policy decision of the Convention People's Party that it was the most effective means of promoting economic development. Given that the major motive force for development is most often, if not exclusively, the state, this is not surprising. There are not, of course, many indigenous entrepreneurs. Governments are more often than not responsible for planning and the accumulation and provision of capital. The governments in many cases were forced to take over the economy when the Europeans left or face chaos.

Yet, even so, the forms of economic development differ. Ghana under Nkrumah was committed to state ownership and the development of an industrial society and used the mechanism of central planning to achieve this. The state-owned sector includes electricity, water, hydro-electric projects, all administered by an Industrial Development Corporation. The state also participates in private industry as well as regulating the extensive cooperative movement. Nyerere, on the other hand, has placed greater emphasis on the cooperative movement (for which he has received Israeli help), village projects, self-help and land reform. Cooperatives have been extended to almost every sector of the economy, albeit controlled at the centre. In the villages plans are prepared for their development and then coordinated at area, regional and national level. Both the cooperative movement and the village projects allow a great degree of mass participation and the enthusiasm for them is evident. Harking back to the past, Nyerere has said that 'in Africa, land was always recognized as belonging to the community', and he went on to say the government 'must go back to the traditional African custom of landholding'. Thus in 1963 all freeholds were abolished. This was designed to eliminate the European landowners and ensure that the new leaseholds would develop in conformity with national policy.

Socialism in Africa is also a slogan with which to mobilize the masses for economic development. The political leaders need the enthusiastic cooperation of their people if industrialization is to be quickly and effectively brought about. Frequent appeals are made for sacrifices and the value of hard work emphasized. Of necessity, therefore, the common interest and identity of the nation is emphasized and the concept of separate classes and individuals deprecated. Again, socialism provides the leaders with an ideology with which to rationalize their assumption and use of political power.

Like socialists in other parts of the world, the African socialist leaders are not content with propagating a national form of socialism. Nkrumah's concept of socialism was not just right for Ghana but also for the whole of Africa. 'He [saw] himself', Colin Legum wrote, 'cast in the hero mould: the hero of a free and independent Africa – an Africa built on socialism, the socialism of Consciencism.'[2] His conception of the party too was appropriate for Africa. 'I see before my mind's eye', he said in 1961, 'a great monolithic party growing up ... united and strong, spreading its protective wings over the whole of Africa.' For Nkrumah, Pan-Africanism meant the liberation of Africa from colonial rule and economic exploitation. It meant the creation of a united African state based on socialism. It could not be limited to one nation but had to encompass the continent. Pan-Africanism is, as Tom Mboya wrote in 1963, 'a movement based on our common experience under the yoke of colonialism and is fostered by our sense of common destiny and the presence of traditional brotherhood'. Nyerere, too, sees his concept of socialism extending beyond the confines of Tanzania to embrace the continent. Nor, indeed, must it stop there. 'Our recognition of the family to which we all belong', he has asserted, 'must be extended yet further – beyond the tribe, the community, the nation, or even the continent – to embrace the whole society of mankind. That is the only logical conclusion for true socialism.'

2. Colin Legum, 'Socialism in Ghana: A Political Interpretation', in *African Socialism*, ed. W. H. Friedland and Carl G. Rosenberg, p. 159.

I 5

EUROPEAN COMMUNIST
REVISIONISM IN THE 1960s

Returning to Europe, to the base of socialism in eastern Europe, we find that at the same time as the communist powers in the less developed countries were increasing their state power and adopting militantly revolutionary postures, those in the developed countries of Europe were dismantling some of the props once considered to be essential features of a socialist economy and state. They are to be found dismantling the command economy, the central planning mechanism, and introducing market mechanisms; liberalizing their régimes socially, culturally and politically and, far more important, accepting to some extent the notion that conflicts of interest can and do exist in a socialist society.

Perhaps, after all, communist régimes are no more than temporary phenomena; means of modernizing backward countries. Once modernization has been achieved not only does the communist ideology become obsolete, it also becomes, if rigidly applied, an obstacle to economic growth. The ideology has to be stretched to almost unrecognizable lengths if it is to be reconciled with the economic changes that have to be made if economic growth is to be stimulated and competition with the West engaged in on near-equal terms. And it becomes even more difficult to reconcile it with the new political tendencies that seem inevitably to follow economic reform.

Certainly most of the East European countries were reforming their economies in the 1960s. The reforms were initiated not as a result of a sincere desire to liberalize the régimes but as a result of economic necessity. The highly centralized command economy was not delivering the goods.

It was, as Ota Šik wrote in 1966, 'hampering further economic growth'. The rates of economic growth of the communist states declined and they were unable to meet the changing consumer demands by means of administrative decisions. The system, in short, lacked the necessary flexibility for the new era of consumer-oriented production.

Hence the emphasis of the reforms was upon the decentralization of economic decision-making; it was an experiment, still under way, in market socialism, or what its practitioners preferred to call 'creative Marxism'. The result of economic decentralization led, however, to a transfer of power from the party to industrial managers, to the creation of new economic pressure groups and local élites, and to the development of a form of political pluralism. This put a strain on the political system and threatened the hegemony of the communist party, best expressed by the experience of Czechoslovakia. But then the communist leaders should have foreseen this. It was Marx, after all, who had pointed out that changes in the economic base of society have fundamental repercussions on the political superstructure.

The western communist parties also underwent fundamental change. They became domesticated and to a large extent accepted the political system in which they operated.

(a) Yugoslavia

In spite of the vicissitudes in Soviet policy and the ebb and flow of the reform movement in the eastern bloc, Yugoslavia has consistently remained a more liberal régime. In recent years it has become the leader of a movement, evident in different degrees in the rest of the bloc, towards a more 'open' society.

As a result of a mounting balance of payments deficit Tito introduced new economic reforms in 1965 aimed at making Yugoslav goods more competitive in world markets. Faced with the need to make the economy more flexible if Yugo-slav goods were to be made attractive to the West, the reforms were designed to modernize the economy and make enterprises more responsive to the mechanisms of supply and demand. Wage differentials were allowed to widen, worker–management enterprises were given more freedom in investment decisions, government intervention in the economy was to be ended, the banking system was freed from administrative and political interference and credit was made available to the growing private sector.

This amounted to a move towards a quasi-market system in which capital, goods and services flowed freely. Indeed, profitability 'is assuming a growing precedence over purely political considerations as a basis for measuring successes and allocating resources'.[1] The private sector, especially in the tourist industry where it is particularly important, has been encouraged and still, today, eighty per cent of agri-cultural land is in private hands, though individual hold-ings are limited to twenty-five acres.

The greater autonomy given to enterprises means that there has occurred a decrease in the power of the party over the economy. There have also been critics, like Professor Stefan Vracar, who have suggested the introduction of a two- or multi-party system and others, like Professor Pedrag Vranicki, who have urged a greater degree of intra-party democracy. Although the party has not accepted these sug-gestions many in the party, such as Mijacko Todorović, do accept the need to accommodate the conflicting interests in society to an institutional form. At least there has been an increase in the recognized rights of party members and freer and more open discussions. Similarly there have been demands for the workers to be given the freedom to strike and for the trade unions to become real vehicles for the representation of their interests. This latter suggestion would certainly be a greater danger to the party if it were implemented. At the very least the trade unions would be in

1. Alvin Z. Rubinstein, 'Reforms, Nonalignment and Pluralism', in *Problems of Communism*, March–April 1968, p. 36.

a position to challenge the assertion of the party that it is the custodian of the welfare of the workers.

Few of the proposals for reform listed here are new. They are similar to those put forward in the 1950s and early 1960s. This time, however, the evidence suggests that a real intention exists to make them work.

(b) Hungary

Like Yugoslavia, Hungary does not give its central economic plan the force of law and like Yugoslavia, and excepting the abortive Czechoslovak experiment in liberalization, it has gone further along the road towards economic reform than any other country.

Since becoming First Secretary of the party in 1956 János Kádár has, despite his inauspicious beginning as a lackey of the Soviet Union, followed a policy of controlled and gradual liberalization at home and of improving relations with the West. In 1962 he put forward the rather unorthodox slogan: that 'He who is not against us is with us.'

In the early 1960s Kádár paid lip-service to the idea of the existence of conflicts of group interests within society but he in no way attempted to introduce reforms that would have led to the weakening of the power of the Communist Party. What economic reforms were introduced were done under the auspices of the party, though decision-making was shared with parliament and non-party experts. There was also a campaign in 1966 to enhance the role of the National Assembly as the instrument by which the people controlled the parliament. But whilst the government expressed a desire to include the various interest groups in the decision-making process, no institutional structures were constructed to accomplish this. Economic reforms in the early 1960s were not followed, as they were elsewhere, by political reforms.

In 1968 'new economic mechanisms' were introduced. These were little different from those implemented in the other communist states and were likewise motivated by a desire to increase the economic growth rate and competitiveness. Authority was delegated to enterprises, production related to supply and demand, profit made the measure of efficiency and governmental use made of fiscal and monetary measures to control the economy, rather than detailed central planning. Yet whilst these reforms were similar to those tried elsewhere 'the extent to which the reform has been carried out is more far-reaching in Hungary than anywhere else in eastern Europe except Yugoslavia'.[2]

There has been less financing of investment from the centre, enterprises have been given more freedom to import and export, consumers have been allowed to buy foreign goods and travel to the West, small-scale private enterprise has been encouraged, prices have been allowed to find their own level, trade unions have been consulted on issues of direct concern to the workers and given a veto in certain areas, and profit-sharing has been introduced.

This time the economic reforms have been accompanied by a relaxation of the rigid party control exercised in other areas of life. More freedom exists in the choice of occupation, there is a freer press and more frequent debates about and criticism of the central control of the economy and the new economic policy. And, as in Yugoslavia and Poland, there is now a more tolerant official attitude towards the importation of western culture.

At the same time the communist leadership has been careful to point out that the new reforms have been dictated by economic necessity, that they conform to Marxism–Leninism and do not endanger the position of the party or the loyalty of Hungary to the Soviet Union or the Warsaw Pact. In fact the reforms received official blessing from Moscow in 1969 when Moscow referred to Hungary's 'worthy contribution to the theory and practice of socialist construction'.

Kádár has pursued his reform programme quietly and

2. Harry G. Shaffer, 'Progress in Hungary', in *Problems of Communism*, Vol. XIX, Jan.–Feb. 1970, p. 51.

gradually. Though he appears to have been aggrieved by the invasion of Czechoslovakia and fearful of the consequences for his own programme he is nevertheless thought to have felt that they went too far too quickly. Pragmatism pays, it seems, even in communist states.

(c) Poland

Revisionist opposition to the Polish régime, in spite of the party's attempt to ameliorate the totalitarian rule, continued throughout the 1960s. The best example of the revisionist socialists was the group organized around Jacek Kuroń and Karol Modzelewski, lecturers at Warsaw University. They produced an Open Letter issued to members of the party in 1966. In this they argued that Poland was ruled in an arbitrary and dictatorial manner and that the central party bureaucracy had become a new class which was both ruining the country by economic mismanagement and exploiting the workers. Kuroń and Modzelewski wanted a true proletarian revolution to destroy the existing system, and establish in its place a workers' democracy with a multiparty system, independent trade unions, a workers' militia and full intellectual freedom. After the revolution they anticipated that the factories would be run by workers' councils coordinated by a Central Council of Workers' Delegates. Like Trotsky and Lenin in 1917, Kuroń and Modzelewski hoped that their revolution would stimulate revolution in the rest of the bloc and that this would save Poland from Soviet intervention.

Even the arrest of these naïve and utopian idealists did not stifle further criticism of the régime. Indeed, in 1966 Professor Leszek Kolakowski, a leading Marxist scholar, listed the demands of 1956 that remained unfulfilled. He criticized the absence of democracy and intellectual freedom and the authoritarian manner in which the party oligarchy acted and put the responsibility for the country's economic difficulties on their shoulders. He, however, was only expelled from the party, along with the many others who had defended him. At least the secret visit in the night era, portrayed so vividly by Arthur Koestler in *Darkness at Noon*, had gone.

As a result of economic difficulties in the early 1960s, however, the Party adopted in 1965 new economic guidelines aimed at making the planning process less arbitrary. A calculation of costs and profits was to play a more important note in decision-making at all levels. Even decisions on resource allocation was to be decentralized with some investment decisions delegated to the managers of enterprises, though the state was to continue to fix prices. In fact the reforms remained paper reforms. They were prevented from being implemented by the procrastination and administrative sabotage of Stalinist hardliners. These saw the economic reforms as a threat to the hold of the party over the economy and they were helped in their opposition by the student revolt of 1968.

Further economic difficulties in 1968 led the party to adopt a plan in 1969 for a new economic system. 'From now on', Gomulka said, 'the plan will be built from the bottom upward, from the enterprise, through the associations and ministries, to the Planning Commission.' Though market mechanisms are not to operate, the new policy does at least reduce the role of the central planners. How it will work in practice has yet to be seen. Certainly the arbitrary action of the government in raising prices by nearly thirty per cent in December 1970 led to further 1956-style outbreaks of strikes and riots but which were quickly and quietly smothered, though Gomulka fell in the process. This in itself was extremely important. For the first time a communist leader had been brought down by the workers. It was an indication, to some extent at least, that communist leaders were, if not controlled by, at least responsive to public opinion.

Yet in spite of all the apparently new freedom granted in the 1950s and 1960s the upsurge of debate about Marxism in Poland did not produce either a development of

Marxism or a viable alternative programme for a new form of socialist society. Adam Schaff had asserted in 1959:

We are not afraid to discuss a revision of Marxism, but we are definitely opposed to the liquidation of Marxism. The revisionists failed to carry their point in Poland because their philosophy was based entirely on negation. They had no positive programme to offer the people.

This was not entirely true but there was more than a grain of truth in it.

Moreover, Gomulka and the revisionists have not been without their hard-line Stalinist critics of whom Kazimierz Mijal, the head of the anti-Gomulka Stalinist underground, is the most prominent. He opposed Gomulka in 1957 and has since been actively opposing him with exhortations like this, broadcast in 1967:

We appeal to all Communists in the ranks of the security apparatus to be united in the struggle against revisionism, imperialism and its agents in our country. Put up resistance against the criminal plans of Gomulka-ites and the Zionist agency of traitors.

Nor is he alone. He is supported by many who would like a return to the monolithic party, centralized economy, collectivization, class struggle and police terror of the past.

(d) Czechoslovakia

The Communist Party programme of 1948 spoke of the 'specific' Czechoslovak road to socialism. The Czechs anticipated that, despite the Sovietization of the rest of the bloc in the late 1940s and early 1950s, their country would be allowed to go its own way, particularly as parliamentarianism had brought the communists more success than in most other countries. Indeed, Klement Gottwald, the party leader, followed a policy of national and democratic revolution and explicitly announced that the Czech socialist revolution would not be modelled on that of the Soviet

Union. In fact, of course, the Cominform denounced any but the Soviet model of socialism and this was applied to Czechoslovakia. Yet the imposition of the Soviet model on Czechoslovakia did not appear to arouse the resentment it occasioned in other countries. Nor did the revolts and revisions of the early 1950s, or the Twentieth Congress of the CPSU, engender the same excitement in Czechoslovakia as elsewhere. Of course, the Czechs had a more favourable attitude towards both communism and the Soviet Union, the public was pro-socialist and there was not, as there was in Poland, any counterweight to the power of the communist party in the form of the church or peasantry. Moreover, the accession of Novotný following the death of Klement Gottwald gave rise to the belief that a post-Stalin era was already beginning. Yet the overt Czechoslovak revisionist period did not really arrive until 1968, though there had been a certain amount of critical comment on the system in the 1950s and a more direct and open debate about the state of the economy in the early 1960s. In 1963, for instance, Czechoslovakia experienced a decrease in industrial output, national income and real wages; it was the only industrialized country in the world to have such an experience. As a result Radoslav Selucký launched a major attack on the 'cult of the plan' and there were many, like him and Ota Šik, who argued for the introduction of market mechanisms and a remodelling of the economy.

But the whole period is associated with the name of Alexander Dubček. He had in 1952 made a eulogistic speech at the funeral of the disgraced communist Karol Smidke. Now he criticized Antonin Novotný, President and First Secretary of the party, for 'behaving like a dictator'. He also criticized the methods of the party and its inability to deal with economic and social problems and for meddling in Slovak affairs. As a result of the manifest support for Dubček. Novotný stepped down and was replaced by Dubček. The Central Committee of the party announced that it would embark upon a democratization of the party and society. This was the beginning of the abortive attempt to replace the bureaucratic system of power of the Novotný régime with democratic socialism. The reform movement in Czechoslovakia was not an attempt to dismantle the whole system or abandon socialism, as had been attempted in Hungary, but to provide what the Poles had tried and failed to provide. It was an attempt to synthesize socialism and democracy, to give 'socialism a human face'. As the Action Programme adopted by the Central Committee of the party in April stated:

> In the spirit of our traditions and former decisions, we want to develop to the utmost in this country an advanced socialist society rid of class antagonisms, a society economically, technically, and culturally highly advanced ... offering the opportunities for dignified human life, comradely relations of mutual cooperation among people, and free scope for the development of the human personality.
>
> We want to start building a new, intensely democratic model of a socialist society which will fully correspond to Czechoslovak conditions.

The Programme also emphasized the need for basic changes in the economy and for a decrease in detailed centralized planning.

The need and desire for economic change was the main impetus behind the reform movement. The reformers blamed centralized and bureaucratic planning for the stagnation in the economy, the threatening depression and the paucity of consumer goods. They argued that 'the effective functioning of a socialist economy cannot be assured without the help of a market mechanism', and the reassertion of the sovereignty of the consumer. They advocated the separation of the economy and government administration, the substitution of indicative planning for detailed centralized planning, the use of fiscal and monetary measures to ensure the realization of overall economic objectives and more autonomy to be given to enterprises, even to the extent of them being able to set up new business and conclude contracts with foreign firms. Within the enterprises the reformers urged the setting up of workers' councils responsible for the election of management and the determination of welfare policy and income distribution. Moreover, private enterprise was to be allowed in crafts, retailing and services and more freedom given to private firms.

Similar structural changes were envisaged in order to democratize the political system. Indeed, the power struggle within the party between the revisionists and their opponents over the economic reforms led the former to mobilize the intellectuals and students on their behalf, and these, naturally, made their own demands for increased political and intellectual liberty. First, all civic rights were to be restored, and indeed in June censorship was abolished and the freedoms of speech, association and the press restored. Some reformers advocated a plurality of political parties and many, like Zdeněk Mlynář and Michal Lakatoš, wanted to legitimize pressure groups within the existing system. Moreover, Mlynář advocated that the monopoly of power vested in the Communist Party be handed to a pluralistic National Front. This would be a coalition government elected in free elections and composed of all groups in society.

The party leaders were content to reform the political system under the leadership of the Communist Party. Even the 'Two Thousand Words' manifesto, written by Ludvík Vaculík and signed by many intellectuals, did not challenge the leadership of the Communist Party and both Mlynář and Lakatoš trod carefully on this issue. However, the party itself was to be democratized by the toleration of minority views, the introduction of secret voting, rotation of offices and control of party bureaucrats by the elected party organs. The new President, Ludvik Svoboda, was the first to be elected under the new system of secret voting. In August a draft of a new party statute redefined democratic centralism so as to allow the advocacy of minority views, even after a policy decision had been made, if new evidence could be presented. For the first time in the history of the bloc, a communist party attempted to win the confidence of the people rather than assert its authority. As Richard Lowenthal commented, 'to the rulers of the Soviet bloc, this must have appeared as an outright defiance of Leninist principles'.[3]

It was further planned that the institution of government would not be subject to party control. Parliament was to become the supreme legislative body, a 'change from a mask of dictatorship to an instrument of democracy'.[4]

The experiment in 'humanistic communism' was, however, cut short in August 1968 by the intervention of Soviet tanks. The reformist leaders were arrested, disgraced and purged, as were their supporters in the party, though Svoboda refused to replace the arrested leaders. The Soviet leaders were worried by the possibility of Czechoslovakia accepting West German credits and thus undermining the economic hold of the Soviet Union over the country. They were also apprehensive lest the criticism and reforms in Czechoslovakia infected the rest of the bloc, including the Soviet Union, and that Czechoslovakia might break away from the Warsaw Pact. They intervened, they said, to preserve socialism. As Brezhnev (who had sent a telegram of congratulations to Dubček on his election to First Secretary) formulated the doctrine rationalizing the Soviet invasion:

There is no doubt that the peoples of the socialist countries and the communist parties have and must have freedom to determine their country's path of development. However, any decision of theirs must damage neither socialism in their own country, nor the fundamental interests of the other socialist countries, nor the world-wide workers' movement, which is waging a struggle for socialism. This means that every communist party is responsible not only to its own people but also to all the socialist countries and to the entire communist movement.

Soviet intervention, according to Brezhnev, was to protect

3. Richard Lowenthal, 'The Sparrow in the Cage', *Problems of Communism*, Vol. XVII, No. 6, 1968, p. 20.
4. Radoslav Selucký, *Czechoslovakia: The Plan that Failed*, p. 129.

the communist commonwealth, 'Czechoslovakia's fundamental interests' and its 'independence and sovereignty as a
socialist state'. Whatever else it demonstrated, the Soviet
invasion indicated the desire and ability of the Soviet leaders
to reassert their control over the bloc, to prohibit reforms
that went further than those in the Soviet Union and to
reassert the ideological authority of Moscow in the world
communist movement.

Though the Czechs engaged in passive resistance, they
were urged by their leaders not to provoke the Soviet soldiers. No preparations were made for the defence of the
country; indeed, the invasion seems to have come as much of
a surprise to them as to the rest of the world. They would
have done well to have remembered Chateaubriand's re-
mark that those 'who make revolution by halves are simply
digging their own graves'.

(e) The Western Communist Parties

The legal communist parties of the West have for a long
time been adapting themselves to their respective democratic political systems. They renounced the goal of revolution and instead asserted that they wanted 'structural
reforms' and the preservation of bourgeois liberties. They
repudiated the idea that they wished either to set up a
dictatorship of the proletariat or a totalitarian system on
the Soviet model and talked of things like the 'peaceful road
to socialism' and the 'positive role of Parliament'. So far as
they could, they disassociated their parties from all the un-
popular policies and practice of the Soviet Union. Given
that they had entered the parliamentary arena and wanted
to look respectable, there was little else they could do. The
Czechoslovakia experiment had opened up to them the
possibility that communism, even in eastern Europe, would
seem humane and respectable, with obvious electoral advantages. For a short time it looked as if they could go on
the offensive and point to Czechoslovakia, as the British

Labour Party often invoked Sweden, as the ideal they were working towards instead of constantly being forced on the defensive in acting as apologists for the Soviet régime.

Thus it was not surprising to find the leaders of the communist parties of the West giving their support to the Czech revisionists; the Italian communist Luigi Longo said:

What is happening in Czechoslovakia today [May 1968] is an experiment which will also help certain socialist countries, and in particular the communist parties of the capitalist countries, in the struggle to create a new socialist society – young, open and modern.

The French communist leader Waldeck Rochet pledged support for the reforms and all the western parties, except the insignificant Luxembourg Communist Party, condemned the Soviet use of force.

This was something new, for big and powerful as the French, Italian and Finnish communist parties are, they had rarely explicitly criticized the Soviet Union or repudiated its directives. This is not to say they did not often strike out on their own, as the Italian party did, especially under the leadership of Palmiro Togliatti. Though he had faithfully followed Stalin's twists and turns, he stressed in 1956 the Italian way to socialism: peaceful, parliamentary, multi-party, democratic and with open debate and freedom for art and science. This was a radical departure from the strategy of proletarian revolution which had been advocated by Antonio Gramsci. Yet Togliatti made the change. 'It is impossible,' he once said, 'to conceive realistically of the advance towards socialism outside the fabric of Italian democratic life, outside of the struggle for the objectives that interest the whole society.' Under his leadership the party pursued a strategy of constructively participating in parliamentary and local elections and of making alliances with other parties. Socialism, he believed, would be introduced by the democratic reform of the structure of society.

This was reasserted by the new General Secretary of the party, Luigi Longo, in 1964, when he said the party would continue 'with full respect for constitutional guarantees and for religious and cultural liberties'. In this they would separate themselves from the methods followed in the communist countries.

Of course, Togliatti had asserted the doctrine of separate roads to socialism in his doctrine of polycentralism elaborated in 1956. The whole system, he said, 'becomes polycentric, and even in the communist movement itself we cannot speak of a single guide but rather of a progress which is achieved by following paths which are different'. He argued that socialism could be built in some countries without the communist party being the leading party. Polycentralism implied that the parties in the world would, indeed, be better off if they stopped following the Soviet Union. Their independence would make them more trusted. More than this, he suggested that communists should look for the weaknesses in the Soviet system that had made possible Stalin's excesses.

The Italian Communist Party has, however, always been revisionist and gradualist in the post-war years. 'Modern Italian communism', Kevin Devlin has written, 'may be described, without too much exaggeration, as a compound of Marx, Machiavelli and Madison Avenue.'[5] Its debt to Machiavelli is indicated by the opportunistic way in which it pursues its interests, its sensitivity to social and political events at the expense of dogma and its willingness to make electoral alliances with the socialists which allows it to have a relatively large representation in parliament (roughly one quarter of the seats in the 1960s) and control several local councils. Its debt to, or perhaps even the lessons it could give to, Madison Avenue is shown by the sophisticated way in which it presents its image to the electorate and the world as a progressive, respectable, independent and democratic party. Its criticism of communist régimes is not aimed so much at them as to make the Italian party look respectable by comparison.

5. Kevin Devlin, 'Moscow and the Italian CP', *Problems of Communism*, Vol. XIV, No. 5, 1965, p. 1.

After the war the French Communist Party too became reformist while retaining its class-war rhetoric and the dictatorship of the proletariat. Yet even in the 1920s while denouncing the Third Republic and its social institutions it still, nevertheless, pursued a parliamentary and electoral strategy. After the war it participated in a three-party coalition government which introduced certain measures of nationalization. This period was called one of 'new democracy' by the party, but the name somehow got mislaid when the party left the coalition in 1947. While it still claims and aspires to be the party of the working class, it accepts that socialism in France will be achieved peacefully and that other parties will continue to exist, and it slants its appeal to all classes. It also claims to tolerate disagreements with the party line, but refused to go so far as to accept the violation of the party line by its most eminent philosopher, Roger Garaudy.

Like the Italian party, the French has supported the socialists electorally and supported the governments of Pierre Mendès-France and Guy Mollet, even though under Maurice Thorez it was faithfully, even slavishly, pro-Soviet. Its new leader, Waldeck Rochet, claimed in the 1968 elections that the Communist Party was the 'party of order'. And certainly it was. It refused to take advantage of the revolutionary situation described by Raymond Aron as the 'events of May 1968', the 'psychodrama', and instead adopted a moderating and constitutional role. As Trotsky wrote of Sukhanov, it was 'capable of standing by a revolutionary conception only up to the time when it was necessary to carry it into action'. The Communist Party, for all its professions of proletarian purity, has been integrated into the political system. It accepts the European Economic Community, once described as a 'band of capitalist thieves', and has attempted to become a respectable and accepted party of the Left.

Just as the Italian and French communist parties have been losing their revolutionary élan, so also the Finnish Communist Party has become integrated into Finland's political system. In 1945 it established an electoral front organization with left-wing social democrats and anti-fascists. The Finnish People's Democratic League, as it was called, obtained twenty-five per cent of the vote and the Communist Party entered a coalition government with the Social Democratic and Centre Parties. Whilst a partner in the government, the Communist Party did its utmost to enthuse the workers with the task of rebuilding the war-ravaged economy, and prevent strikes. Ville Pessi argued that whilst it was not possible to build socialism it was possible for good progressive work to be done. It was thrown out of the government in 1948 when it attempted a take-over like that in Czechoslovakia.

In 1966 the party once more joined a coalition government, again with the Social Democrats and the agrarian Centre Party. This was the first time for twenty years that a communist party had held ministerial office in a western government. However, the coalition government did not basically alter the capitalist system. Indeed, it introduced a Stabilization Plan which froze wages more than prices and share dividends. Not all of the party was, however, in favour of communist participation in the coalition or the Stabilization Plan. The opposition condemned the leadership for being revisionist in supporting the Plan, condemning the invasion of Czechoslovakia and indulging in class collaboration. The party had, no doubt, become a defender of the capitalist system, as Marx long ago had warned if the communists attempted to use the capitalist political machine. Yet the opposition was not revolutionary. The most revolutionary slogans it could produce were those advocating more militant collective bargaining.

Outside these countries the communist parties are no more than small sects, irrelevant to political life and the working class. They tend to rely upon the Soviet Union for ideological leadership and certainly for finance. Communist parties did none the less have representatives in the legislature of a number of countries in the 1960s. They had twenty-nine in India, four in Ceylon, Japan and Israel, and a few in Belgium, Holland, Switzerland, Sweden, Luxembourg and Cyprus. Many had lost their more liberal members as a result of the invasion of Hungary in 1956, and lost more as a result of the Czechoslovakian invasion of 1968. Their more radical members departed with the liberalization programme of Khrushchev and joined the even smaller and more sectarian Maoist and Trotskyite organizations.

16

DEMOCRATIC SOCIALISM
IN THE LATE 1950s AND 1960s

The communist parties of Europe were not the only parties to be assailed by revisionism in the 1950s and 1960s. Naturally the results of their revisions of their basic philosophy were more important in that as the parties were in power any changes in their doctrines could and often did have an immediate impact on the way in which the state and economy were managed. But the democratic socialist parties of the West were also engaged in a re-examination of their concept of socialism and, particularly, of the role of nationalization as a means of moving towards the creation of a socialist society. Though the extent of the revision of party doctrine in practice went no further in Britain than in Germany it was accompanied by a greater intellectual debate. What the Germans experienced in the late 1880s and early 1890s with Bernstein the British experienced in the late 1950s. In terms of democratic socialism, Britain became the home of modern revisionism.

In the post-war period much 'of the shift in party posture in Britain and in other nations has been in the form of a continued dilution, now almost liquidation, of traditional socialist doctrine'. This, as Epstein continues, 'is most plain in Britain, West Germany, and other nations where there is a large unified socialist working-class movement'.[1] The socialists were, of course, confronted in the period after the Second World War with a decrease in class consciousness and a general increase in affluence in the western democracies; an affluence, however, that disguised public squalor, as J. K. Galbraith pointed out with reference to the United States

1. Leon D. Epstein, *Political Parties in Western Democracies*, London, 1967, p. 156.

in his *The Affluent Society* (1958). But as the Swedish
social democrat prime minister Per Albin Hansson put it:

We have had so many victories that we are in a difficult
position. A people with political liberty, full employment, and
social security has lost its dreams.

But perhaps they have lost their dreams because the evan-
gelical zeal and revolutionary fervour so characteristic of
the socialists in the first decades of the twentieth century is
now absent. Socialism has been relegated to the seminars of
economists. Even when public squalor has been apparent
and significant minorities of the population have been
shown to be living in poverty the socialist parties have still
found it difficult to inspire the electorate with a desire for
social change, or have not attempted to inspire it. Perhaps
it is not surprising then that in mid 1970 only two social
democratic parties were in power in the world, in Germany
and Sweden; the British party had just unexpectedly lost
an election.

(a) Britain

As we saw in Chapter 10, the British Labour Party had been
de-emphasizing the importance of nationalization to its
socialist objectives. By 1964 nationalization had almost disappeared from official party policy. *The New Britain* (1964)
promised a 'strong and just' government. Nationalization
was replaced by planning. There was a National Plan, soon
dismantled in government, and plans for transport, the
regions, and taxation. Indeed, the major emphasis of the
documents and the speeches of the party leader, Harold
Wilson, was on the need to stimulate economic growth. The
increased rate of economic growth that could be brought
about by a competent government managing a planned
economy would, it was said, allow the party's radical and
egalitarian proposals, like increased national insurance
benefits, wage-related pensions, sickness and unemployment

pay and redundancy payments, to be introduced and paid for. This had, indeed, been the message of *Labour and the New Society*, which had stated that 'major advances in the social services will be possible only if the nation continues to produce more, and produce more, better and more cheaply'.

The party had not lost its idealism, but many argued that it was unsure of its socialism. Certainly there was little doubt that the party was a moderate reformist party and, perhaps more important, an alternative government and not just a party of protest. This was above all the contribution that the revisionists made to party policy and emphasis. They were less concerned about doctrinaire socialism than with the achievement of political power so that their liberal–radical proposals could be implemented. Socialist rhetoric, they seemed to say, could be left to street-corner speakers; in the programmes of the party it caused a loss of votes.

(i) REVISIONISM

The demise of nationalization in programmatic terms was in part due to the success of a 'new' school of thought within the Labour Party labelled 'revisionism'. At the end of the post-war Labour Government the party appeared bereft of new ideas. Its 1918 programme had been virtually implemented and yet little new theory or policy proposals were forthcoming. The party seemed to have little idea of where it was going and still less of where it wanted to go. As Richard Crossman wrote:

The Labour Party has lost its way not only because it lacks a map of the new country it is crossing, but because it thinks maps unnecessary for experienced travellers.[2]

Some members of the party thought in terms of further nationalization, but they had few positive ideas and the right wing of the party was not, to say the least, particularly

2. Quoted in Vernon Bogdanor and Robert Skidelsky, *The Age of Affluence 1951–1964*, London, 1970, p. 92.

in love with the suggestion. Rather, like Herbert Morrison, they favoured a consolidationist policy.

The 'new thinking' came, in fact, from what might be called the moderate intellectual right – what *Tribune* called the 'synthetic radicals of the Movement'. It came from Anthony Crosland, John Strachey, Douglas Jay, Roy Jenkins and Denis Healey, though Evan Durbin's *The Politics of Democratic Socialism* (1940) was an earlier attempt to revise socialism to accord with British conditions. They questioned the appropriateness of proceeding to a collectivized economy by means of further nationalization as they believed it to be a policy no longer relevant to contemporary Britain. Socialist Union was set up in 1951 to 'think out afresh the meaning of socialism in the modern world' and asserted that the approach to socialism should be ethical and humanitarian. The *New Fabian Essays* (1952) edited by Crossman were a further contribution to the search for a new form of socialism and a redefinition of the objects and role of the party. Though little distinctively new emerged from the essays, most of the authors touched upon themes that were later elaborated to become the basis of revisionism. Most, for example, argued that economic society had changed since the 1930s and indicated their awareness of the 'managerial revolution' popularized by James Burnham in *The Managerial Revolution*.

But the most important contribution to the debate was undoubtedly Crosland's *The Future of Socialism* (1956), which is arguably the most outstanding post-war contribution to social democratic theory, followed closely by the contribution of Strachey. Like Bernstein before him, Crosland attempted to show how society had changed from that attacked by earlier socialists and what new policies were necessary if traditional objectives were to be achieved. The basis of his and other revisionists' argument was that a fundamental transfer of economic power had occurred in economic society. He argued that the old-style capitalists had given way to managers, that this process had been accelerated by the development of monopolies and that as a consequence of the division of ownership and control other factors, such as social prestige, motivated managers rather than a single-minded drive for profits. They sought a reputation as progressive employers having good industrial relations and export earnings. He argued that, as a result of full employment, there had been a transfer of power within industry from managers to trade unions and, finally, a transfer of power from capitalism to the state. The state had assumed an increasing responsibility for maintaining full employment, promoting economic growth, managing the balance of payments and redistributing income. It had increasingly intervened (the Conservatives said interfered) in industry and the economy so as to promote social and economic objectives. To Crosland the logic of this was that the ownership of industry was irrelevant to socialist objectives. What was important was control. Indeed, he showed how the maintenance of full employment, the abolition of primary poverty and the structure of the welfare state owed nothing to nationalization and had been preserved by the Conservatives.

What, then, were the socialist ideals that the revisionists subscribed to? Crosland listed five: the abolition of poverty; the maintenance of full employment; the promotion of social welfare; the attempt to achieve solidarity; and the promotion of equality. As Jenkins wrote in the *New Fabian Essays*, 'where there is no egalitarianism there is no socialism'. But the revisionists laid stress not on material equality but upon social equality, the breaking down of social barriers and privileges. Gaitskell summed this up in 1959 when he told the annual conference:

We believe in a classless society – a society without the snobbery, the privilege, the restrictive social barriers which are still far too prevalent in Britain today.

Crosland, too, made an important contribution to the socialist case for greater social equality by his analysis of the role of education in creating social divisions and in conditioning attitudes, and in each case he argued for comprehensive schools, incorporated in the 1964 election manifesto *The New Britain*.

The revisionists were also the stoutest defenders of traditional liberal political values, like liberty, tolerance and freedom – however vaguely these concepts were understood and employed. Yet the Labour Party does not just regard itself as the defender of these political values. Freedom, for example, has also to be widened. As Harold Wilson wrote in *The Relevance of British Socialism* (1964):

> We believe that no man is truly free who is in economic thraldom, who is the slave to unemployment, or economic insecurity, or the crippling cost of medical treatment, who lacks opportunities in both the material and the priceless immaterial scope to a fuller life and the fullest realisation of his talents and abilities.

Given the revisionists' analysis of capitalism, their enumeration of socialist objectives and their contention that nationalization was a means towards the achievement of socialist objectives and not an end in itself, they were led to the conclusion that there was no further need for nationalization. The state could control the economy by other means, and more efficiently. It could do so by fiscal and monetary measures and a social welfare policy. Moreover, they accepted the continued existence of a mixed economy, but one, however, that was planned and managed by the state.

The revisionist theorizing of the 1950s laid the groundwork, along with organizations like Socialist Union and periodicals like *Socialist Commentary*, for Gaitskell's attack in 1959 on Clause Four of the Party Constitution. Although the party had placed little emphasis on nationalization in its election manifesto or policy pronouncements, Gaitskell blamed the 1959 defeat of the party on its doctrinaire image. Clause Four, he said,

> implies that common ownership is an end, whereas in fact, it is a means. It implies that the only precise object we have is nationalization, whereas in fact we have many other Socialist objectives.

He went on to commit himself to an acceptance of a mixed economy for the 'foreseeable future' just as Jenkins had done in his *Pursuit of Progress* (1953) when he had written that a 'mixed economy there will undoubtedly be, certainly for many decades and perhaps permanently'. And 'the reason why a socialist economy requires a private sector', said the Socialist Union pamphlet *Twentieth Century Socialism* (1956), 'is because socialists place a value on individual freedom.' Though the 1959 debate resulted in a defeat for the revisionists with the Party Constitution remaining as it had been in 1918, the party in practice, like the SPD after Bernstein, became increasingly reformist and pragmatic, staking out a claim to the 'middle ground of politics'. Electoral success followed in 1964 and again in 1966.

The revisionists were also united, in the main, on foreign policy, though they became divided in the 1960s on the question of Britain's entry into the European Economic Community. In the 1950s, however, they rejected the idea of the Left that there could be a 'socialist foreign policy' and founded their foreign policy on international power relationships and Britain's national interest. They defended Britain's alliance with the United States, British participation in NATO and SEATO, the rearmament of Germany and increased military expenditure by Britain, as well as its possession of nuclear weapons. Indeed, there were some, like Michael Stewart, who advocated their use by the West first.

The alliance with the USA was defended as a means to stop the spread of communism and also because the USA was seen by them as a country which practised political democracy. To them democracy was more important than any similarities that might exist between the socialism of the Labour Party and that of the Soviet Union. Many had a positive admiration for the political and social system of the United States. As Christopher Mayhew wrote, 'the close alliance with the US was a pleasure; but was also a necessity'. And on the retention of nuclear weapons the revisionists argued that without them Britain would be excessively dependent upon the USA for its defence, that with them we could help to influence US policy.

(ii) THE LEFT

Throughout the period from the defeat of the Labour Government in 1951 to the election of 1964, the revisionists were confronted with a left wing that opposed them on most issues and especially on foreign policy. And just as the revisionists had organizations and periodicals so also did the Left. 'Keep Left' was formed in 1947, led by Richard Crossman, Michael Foot and Ian Mikardo, and had its first major success when it forced the government to reduce the period of military conscription from eighteen months to twelve. The Left, aided by the columns of *Tribune*, denounced US foreign policy, especially the Korean and, later, the Vietnam, war, and Britain's alliance with the USA. Unlike the revisionists the Left had no particular admiration for the social and political system of the United States and many looked more towards the communist states for political inspiration. Led by Aneurin Bevan for a time after 1951, they voted against German rearmament and the increased military expenditure by Britain, became associated with the Campaign for Nuclear Disarmament (formed in 1958) and, in 1960, rejected the leadership's defence policy in supporting a resolution at the Party conference calling for the 'unilateral renunciation of the testing, manufacturing, stockpiling and basing of all nuclear weapons in Great Britain', and another calling for 'a complete rejection of any defence policy based on the threat of the use of strategic or tactical nuclear weapons'. Their victory was, however, short-lived; the policy was reversed the following year.

The Left also opposed the watering down of the commitment to nationalization and argued that further nationalization was needed in order to change economic power relationships. Thus *Keeping Left* (1950) advocated the nationalization of road haulage, steel, insurance, cement, sugar and cotton. The Left regarded the elimination of capitalism to be essential to the achievement of all their other aims. Only 'by means of public ownership could the market be dethroned and public administration established as the central means of control over the economy'.[3] In their eyes the revisionists had either forgotten or did not understand the importance of restructuring the economy if socialist social and welfare objectives were to be successfully introduced. Like the revisionists they also criticized nationalization – but in their case for not being socialist and especially for the absence of workers' participation in management. As *Keeping Left* put it: 'We cannot disguise the fact that the public corporations have not, so far, provided everything which socialists expected from nationalized industries'.

Against Gaitskell and his revisionist supporters they argued that the 1959 election had not been lost because of the existence of Clause Four in the Party Constitution, but because the party had failed to educate the electorate to accept socialism. The party had failed not because it was socialist but because it was not socialist enough and had not been efficient in propagating its socialist message. At the same time, the Left lacked the intellectual apparatus possessed by the revisionists. Whilst they could tune into socialist emotions with their rhetoric, they produced little in the way of coherent alternative policies. Crossman, for example, could do no more than urge the party to admit to the mistakes of nationalization and work out new proposals for decentralizing decision-making and for increased public control. Neither of the proposals materialized in policy form.

Probably the best statement of the Left's position was produced by Emile Burns. In *Right Wing Labour* (1961) Burns described the works of Strachey, Crosland 'and other representatives of right-wing Labour' as 'apologetics for the policies carried out by the Labour Governments, apologetics for British imperialism and monopoly capitalism'. Burns took issue with the revisionists for asserting that the rich

3. Samuel H. Beer, *Modern British Politics*, London, 1965, p. 237.

have disappeared as a result of taxation. He argued that they had ignored share-income and, particularly, the income from the sale of shares, and expenses and he contended that there had not been a substantial redistribution of income. 'The legend of the slaughter of the capitalists under the heavy blows of surtax and death duties', he wrote, 'has no foundation.' As for the alleged divorce between ownership and control, he argued that the directors who still owned shares and still controlled the managers are still motivated by a desire to expand profits, and that the capitalists were now more subtle and had succeeded in seducing labour leaders into the belief that class antagonisms had disappeared. Again, the state, far from controlling monopolies as the revisionists assert, is, he argued, the instrument of monopoly capitalism.

Burns accepted Crosland's statement that surplus value is necessary for economic growth but he argued that there was a difference as to whether this goes to the capitalists for further profit or into a social fund for the general welfare. The former allocation, he asserted, leads, in the classic Marxist formulation, to increased profits, decreased purchasing power, higher unemployment and colonial wars. To advocate a new morality, freedom, equality and fellowship as the revisionists advocate and not economic and social transformation is to put the cart before the horse.

In spite of all the polemics and the often heated exchanges at party conferences the leadership went, particularly under Harold Wilson, its own way. Socialism, it seems, is something the Labour Party turns to in defeat. The Right blame its existence in party programmes, the Left its absence, for poor electoral results. More and more the party has attempted to present itself, if not as the natural governing party, at least as a viable alternative. Hence the motto in 1970, put succinctly, could be said to have been 'Let's carry on with Wilson'. 'Compassionate', 'humane', 'libertarian' the party no doubt is. Whether or not it can be described as socialist depends on how far we are prepared to emasculate the traditional concept of socialism. Perhaps Sam Beer was right after all. Socialism for the Labour Party was an ideology, used to bolster its 'thrust for power'.[4] Given that power is now nearer, socialism is no longer necessary. It still remains, however, to convince those who doubt this and to provide a more durable and sustaining ideology than that of the revisionists.

(b) Germany

After the Second World War the SPD gradually shed its Marxist heritage and concentrated even more than it had done before on obtaining a parliamentary majority. Like the British Labour Party, it concerned itself with immediate reforms and electoral tactics, not socialist theory. It tried, like the Labour Party, to eradicate its class image and hired public relations experts to mould an image for it that would be more attractive to the electorate. And, like the Labour Party, it achieved electoral success in 1965 after a watering down of its socialization programme and a dilution of its policy in a manner considered necessary for increased electoral support. This it received. Its Bundestag representation was increased to 202 in 1965, and in 1966 it entered a coalition with the Christian Social Union, with Brandt as Vice-Chancellor and Foreign Minister. Like the Labour Party, its policies – particularly those for controlling the economy – were virtually indistinguishable from those of its main opponents. To paraphrase C. Wright Mills, with failure horrid things happen to a political philosophy; and with success they happen too.

It has been argued that the moderation, empiricism and welfare socialism of the SPD is a product of the wartime exile of many of the party leaders and officials in Britain and Scandinavia. Yet Kurt Schumacher told the first conference of the SPD after the Second World War that the party was still a Marxist party. On the other hand, Herbert Wehner, vice-chairman of the party, could say in 1958 that

4. ibid., p. 152.

the SPD 'is not and never was a Marxist party'. To show that it never was would require extraordinary semantic acrobatics. That it was not a Marxist party in 1958 cannot be doubted. It had shed its Marxist past, abandoned the Marxist analysis of capitalism and the doctrine of class war, and adopted a more ethical conception of socialism akin to that advocated by Bernstein around the turn of the century. 'The dignity of man, the life of man, and the conscience of man exist prior to the State', its 1959 programme asserted. Now its leaders flirt with the church and it is not uncommon for them to quote from papal encyclicals as, for instance, Brandt did in 1962.

What Bernstein argued and was vilified for in the early 1900s the SPD has adopted today. It accepts the liberal democratic political system and has renounced the final aim of socialism in favour of a movement for immediate reforms. As Willy Brandt wrote in *My Road to Berlin*:

New demands are on the agenda, new reforms will follow. They will usher in neither paradise on earth nor a boring conformity. But they will bring us a more harmonious social order, a constitutional state. This is more than a programme for a day, this is a goal towards which we must continually strive.

The fight now is against class privilege and injustice, and for freedom and dignity. Noble, perhaps even ennobling, objectives but not necessarily socialist. The pluralist society is accepted not only as a means of extending man's freedom but also as something worth defending.

It has been said that as with the British Labour Party, the SPD has gradually moderated its socialization proposals. Given the importance of socialization in the literature of socialism and the similarity of the debate in, and the experiences of, the European social democratic parties, this is worth outlining, if only briefly. In 1946 Viktor Agartz said that the SPD would nationalize all large undertakings, and small ones, too, where it was considered necessary for the national interest. The SPD would, he said, nationalize heavy industry, finance, transport, cement, the building industry, motor car manufacture and monopolies. In addition, cooperatives would become dominant in retail trading. A year later Erik Noelting advocated changing the fundamental basis of the economy by nationalization coupled with central planning and workers' participation in industry. Union leaders, though nominally independent of the party, also favoured increased nationalization. In fact, led by Hans Boeckler, the unions compromised and accepted co-determination, which, in the view of many observers, has not increased the status of the worker and has led to the assumption of managerial functions by the unions, to the detriment of their relationship with their members. Nor has it led to a greater worker share in profits.

In 1949 the SPD was still committed to nationalization. The Duerkheim Sixteen Points included the socialization of the basic and key industries, as well as co-determination. In 1950 a 'shopping list' was produced which included iron and steel, banks, insurance and chemicals. Then the retreat from socialization began. The 1952 list was smaller; the Dortmund Programme of that year mentioned only coal, iron and steel, and power. As in Britain, the emphasis was shifted from nationalization as a means of restructuring the economy to fiscal and monetary measures for controlling it. In 1953 the electoral victory of Adenauer caused the SPD to de-emphasize even this moderate list and praise the efficiency of private enterprise.

In the following years the trend towards an acceptance of the capitalist system was strengthened, in spite of left-wing opposition and resolutions from the more militant members for more nationalization, and their complaints that electoral success had eluded the party not because it was too socialist but because it was not sufficiently socialistic. Party leaders were at pains to present themselves as moderate and responsible, and asked their critics to find a better regulator for the economy than the price mechanism. They also became advocates of a property-owning democracy, forgetting that it was more of an illusion than a fact and that, in any case, the property owned by the 'people' was still insignificant in amount and negligible in terms of the power and privilege it conferred as compared to that possessed by the wealthy few.

Even so, such was the conservatism of the electorate and the opportunism of the SPD that by 1959 the Bad Godesburg Programme could be openly and unashamedly revisionist. It accepted the legitimacy of the profit motive and the party's attachment to Christianity, and announced that 'private ownership of the means of production can claim protection by society as long as it does not hinder the establishment of social justice'. It further asserted that the consumers' freedom of choice and the workers' freedom to choose his job are fundamentals of a socialist economic policy while 'free enterprise and free competition are important features of it'. No mention was made of nationalization. The main objective was to be income redistribution and for this, as the British revisionists had argued, nationalization was irrelevant.

An indication of the shift to the right of the SPD is the announcement made in 1971 by Hans Jochen Vogel, the chief burgomaster of Berlin, that he would not stand for re-election because the executive of his party was 'pursuing a dangerous path' in advocating the socialization of medicine, a nil tariff for public transport and municipalization of development land, insurance and banks. This, he said, was verbal radicalism; they were promoting unrealizable programmes!

If his opinion expresses the state of democratic socialism then it is in a very sorry state. Indeed, the 1971 Bonn conference of the SPD seemed to be obsessed by the proper rate of income tax and Brandt twice intervened to moderate the proposals of the party delegates. 'We are not a party that makes impossible demands,' he said, 'and thus throw doubt on our ability to govern.' Power, not socialism, would appear to be the driving force.

(c) France

In France, on the other hand, the parties of the left are still, theoretically, committed to revolutionary politics. Yet the revolutionary language employed by the leaders of the SFIO was due in part to the existence of a large rival Communist Party and to counter the criticism of the other left groups. This, for example, is the likely explanation of Guy Mollet's use of such language in 1965; an attempt to undermine the appeal of the Federation of the Left led by Gaston Defferre. The party participated in de Gaulle's first government and thereafter adopted a policy of 'constructive opposition' in the Fifth Republic. And yet in spite of the unity of the left for the election of 1968, the democratic left obtained only 20 per cent of the votes. The SFIO prides itself on the purity of its doctrine and yet it is a doctrine that the party has rarely examined and a great deal of freedom is given to its elected representatives. As one of its members put it, 'The party doctrine has become like the Bible. There is the same refusal to change it and to believe in it.'

More extreme in its commitment to Marxism is the PSU. Made up of members of the far left it has denounced the SFIO and the Communist Party for pragmatism and for treason against the working class in compromising with the bourgeoisie when in office. It is, as Stanley Hoffmann has put it, 'a typically intellectual protest movement.'[5] The French, it appears, prefer theory to power.

5. Quoted in Frank L. Wilson, 'The Resistance of Ideology on the French Democratic Left', in Gary C. Bryne and Kenneth S. Pedersen, eds., *Politics in Western European Democracies*, New York, 1971, p. 221.

17

SOCIALISM TODAY

Given the increasing pragmatism of the Western social democratic parties and the ineffectualness of the communist parties it is not surprising that a New Left should emerge in the 1960s and 1970s that eschewed parliamentary politics with its compromises and bargains. In the main it was composed of students who had a vague conception of the 'good society' and a more positive view of militant politics. The 'good society' would be based on a socialist economy, it would be a radical democracy with direct and full democratic participation of its citizens in all decision making. Looking back to the earlier writings of Marx on alienation they denounced what they saw as the sham democracy of the western countries and the bureaucratic élitism of the eastern bloc. Moreover, the 'system', as they called it, was hypocritical and dehumanizing.

What then, was to be done? Some advocated dropping out, others that the system needed to be radically revised and, by far the most numerous and articulate, that it had to be destroyed. This was the position of the Students for a Democratic Society in the United States, the Socialist Students' Federation in Germany, the Provos in Holland and the mass of competing fringe groups in Britain – from the International Socialists to the International Marxist Group.

Thus in the late 1960s the students embarked upon their policy of confrontation with authority so as to show up its basically repressive character. Nearly all the Western industrialized countries witnessed the most articulate and privileged sector of their society occupying their universities and taking up minority causes. Using the 'critical theory' of the 'Frankfurt school of sociology' they opposed the notion of a value-free social science and, instead, supported rational commitment. In particular, the universities were to become the centres of social change, to perform a critical function in society rather than, as they saw it, supporting the *status quo*.

It is not possible here to go into the various strands of thought of the so-called New Left (it was generally anarchistic) or map out the various groups. Indeed, their contours were often changing and many groups disappeared, especially on the graduation of their leaders. However, it will be useful to indicate first the kind of ideology they were combating and then to give some examples of more mature and consistent New Left theories. Indeed, the theory of Herbert Marcuse was one that was often credited with having inspired student protest.

(a) The End of Ideology

In the late 1950s and early 1960s a group of academics started a debate known as the 'end of ideology'. The outstanding figures for the prosecution in this debate were Raymond Aron, Daniel Bell and Seymour Martin Lipset, though they were joined by others like David Aitken and George Lichtheim for the defence. Those arguing that the ideological age had come to an end applauded what they saw as the demise of Marxism and political extremism and the rise of political civility. They argued that there had been a movement towards an integrative political culture in the western democracies, towards the politics of compromise and pragmatism. Yet those arguing that the power of ideologies in politics had declined could not lose. For them ideology meant political fanaticism and political fanaticism had certainly declined. Moreover, Bell and Lipset used the term ideology to mean 'utopian thought' and by the decline of ideology they meant that of Marxist and socialist ideas.

Certainly the evidence supported their contention. Most

of the western socialist and communist parties had become domesticated. As was pointed out in the last two chapters, they had become just one of the teams competing for power, had attempted to become integrated into the political system and were certainly the stoutest defenders of democracy. The passion and the commitment had gone out of left-wing politics. As the editor of a Swedish newspaper, quoted by Lipset, said: 'Politics is now boring. The only issues are whether the metal workers should get a nickel more an hour, the price of milk should be raised or old age pensions extended.'

Nor had the Right escaped this trend. As Lipset wrote, in the western democracies 'serious intellectual conflicts among groups representing different values have declined sharply'.[1] He asserted that it made little difference which political party was in control as the ideological issues dividing Left and Right have been 'reduced to a little more or a little less government ownership and economic planning'. For Bell, too, the old ideologies had lost their truth and their ability to persuade. As he wrote in *The End of Ideology*:

> Few serious minds believe any longer that one can set down 'blue prints' and through 'social engineering' bring about a new utopia of social harmony.[2]

He argued that there had developed in the West a 'rough consensus among intellectuals on political issues: the acceptance of a Welfare State; the desirability of decentralized power; a system of mixed economy and of political pluralism'. All the parties asserted that they were in favour of an increased rate of economic growth and the argument revolved around which party was, or would be, more competent in producing it. But not only the intellectuals had spent their passions. The workers, too, were satisfied with society, mainly because their hopes were not as great as

1. Seymour Martin Lipset, *Political Man: The Social Bases of Politics*, p. 403.
2. Daniel Bell, *The End of Ideology: On the Exhaustion of Political Ideas in the Fifties*, p. 402.

those of the intellectuals. Politics in the West is now represented by the opposition of pragmatic socialists and enlightened conservatives, and it takes a perceptive eye to
discern the difference.

The alleged decline in ideological or utopian politics was
attributed to the increase in general affluence in the western
world. This, it was argued, had resulted in depoliticization,
a growth of apathy and consensus politics, and a decline in
class conflict and class politics. There has been what Bell
called an 'eclipse of distance' in that the poor were closer
to the rich, at least in life styles. The demise of the great
ideologies and ideological conflicts was also attributed by
Bell to the modifications that had been made to the capitalist system and the rise of the welfare state. In this there
were many similarities between what Bell argued was happening and why, and what the revisionists in the British
Labour Party argued should happen. Aron, too, argued that
a compromise had been effected between the rival ideologies
and that as a result faster economic growth, semi-planning
and state intervention had not destroyed existing liberties
or the parliamentary system. Bell also argued that western
disillusionment with communism had occurred as a result
of such things as the Moscow show trials, the Nazi–Soviet
pact, the concentration camps and the suppression of the
Hungarian workers.

Maurice Duverger and others have also propagated another version of the decline of ideology, this time a decline
in the ideological battle between East and West. Duverger
argued that there is a trend towards the convergence
of the socio-economic and political systems of the Soviet
Union and the West. The West, it was said, takes economic
planning more seriously than it previously did, while the
Soviet Union has liberalized the centralized economic system. The result is not only a decline in ideological disputes
but also the likelihood of a future industrial society common
to East and West, one that would be democratic and
socialist.

The protagonists of the notion that there is an end of

ideology did not, however, merely state this as an observable trend. It was also something to be welcomed and applauded. They engaged in what C. Wright Mills called 'an intellectual celebration of apathy'. They eulogized pragmatism and ridiculed intellectual commitment. For them, the basic problems of industrial society had been solved. All that was left was lower-order problems requiring no more than administrative expertise and technical adjustment for their solution. As Raymond Aron wrote in *The Industrial Society*:

Beyond a certain stage in its development industrial society itself seems to me to widen the range of problems referable to scientific examination and calling for the skill of the social engineer. Even forms of ownership and methods of regulation, which were the subject of doctrinal or ideological controversies during the past century seem to ... belong primarily to the realm of technology.[3]

Lipset went further. For him,

democracy is not only or even primarily a means through which different groups can attain their ends or seek the good society; it is the good society itself in operation.[4]

He argued that a democratic society reduces the pressure to increase the 'punitive and discriminating effects of stratification' in that it allows the underprivileged to organize and develop a 'counter power' to that of the establishment within the confines of the political system, an argument not dissimilar to that found in Bernard Crick's *In Defence of Politics*.

Bell has written elsewhere that

each society needs some creed, intellectually coherent and rationally defensible, both to justify itself and to meet the challenge of (or to challenge) other creeds.[5]

3. Raymond Aron, *The Industrial Society*, pp. 164–5.
4. Seymour Martin Lipset, op. cit., p. 403.
5. Daniel Bell, 'The "End of Ideology" in the Soviet Union?', in Milorad M. Drachkovitch (ed.), *Marxist Ideology in the Contemporary World*, London, 1966, p. 80.

And, as for Bell and Lipset, the good society had already arrived then the job of the intellectual was to create the intellectually coherent and rationally defensible creed, not to act as a social critic. His function, admirably performed by these cold pragmatists, is to describe and celebrate the *status quo*. Indeed, there was, as Rousseas and Farganis observe, a 'growing litany' in 'praise of the *status quo*'.[6] Their aim, as the British New Left wrote of the new capitalism, 'is to muffle real conflict, to dissolve it into a false political consensus; to build, not a genuine and radical community of life and interest, but a bogus conviviality between every social group'.[7] So much for Mannheim's notion that the intellectuals were less class-bound than other groups and, therefore, relatively objective.

In the kind of society described and praised by Lipset and Bell 'there is no room for ideologues who, standing on the upper rings of the faith ladder, have become politically de-stabilizing factors. They are, if anything, a direct threat to the continuation of this good society. The modern politician *qua* politician is the man who understands how to manipulate and how to operate in a Machiavellian world which divorces ethics from politics.'[8] Yet, at the same time, Lipset was prepared for – indeed he advocated – the letting loose of the disaffected intellectuals of the West in the underdeveloped world. Their possession of a vision of the future can, in these countries, be a contribution towards progress. And when this progress has been achieved, ideology throughout the world will, it was assumed, be finally dead. In this respect, at least, those who welcomed the 'end of the ideological age' and eschewed visions and commitment had just as much a model of the good society – an equilibrium to which all nations are approaching – and

6. Stephen W. Rousseas and James Farganis, 'American Politics and the End of Ideology', in Irving Louis Horowitz (ed.), *The New Sociology*, London, 1964, p. 268.
7. Raymond Williams (ed.), *May Day Manifesto 1968*, p. 143.
8. Stephen W. Rousseas and James Farganis, 'American Politics and the End of Ideology', in Irving Louis Horowitz (ed.), op. cit., p. 270.

were as optimistic and chiliastic as those they ridiculed.

Moreover, the society they described as the 'good society' has, to a large degree, been created by men who were animated by a passion and motivated by an ideological (utopian) framework; men with specific values and commitments and who tried to construct a society in accordance with their views; men like Bernard Shaw who could say: 'Most men look at things as they are and wonder why. I dream of things that never were and ask why not?

The notion that the end of the ideological age will enable us to view the world unencumbered by value judgements is, as Rousseas and Farganis point out, 'nothing but the delusions of an unsophisticated positivism; which is, in essence, a flight from moral responsibility'.[9] It is also the result of a failure to recognize that facts are what we make and make of them, and that the 'facts' we recognize presuppose a theory of society. Nor, in fact, has poverty been eliminated to the extent that these ideologues of pragmatism suppose, as Michael Harrington has shown for the United States, and Richard Titmus and Peter Townsend and the Child Poverty Action Group, among others, for Britain. Not only does it exist, but indeed the poor are getting poorer in relation to the rich, as Herman Miller has indicated for the United States,[10] and which many studies have demonstrated for Britain. Modern industrial societies have exhibited a steady erosion of the welfare state and a continuous recreation of new forms of poverty. There has also been a weakening of the idea of human rights and dignity on which the conception of the welfare state was based. The welfare state and the values that are inherent in it require strenuous defence if it is not to be treated as just another instrument of social control and economic management.

9. ibid., p. 273.
10. Herman Miller, 'Is the Income Gap Closing?', *New York Times Magazine*, 16 Nov. 1962.

(b) The New Left

The celebration of the end of ideology was premature. Ideology was far from dead. An example of the rise of a new left ideological commitment that rejected consensus politics and was as critical of the socialist parties and the Soviet Union as it was of the Right, is that of the British New Left, associated with the periodical *New Left Review* (NLR). The NLR was formed in 1959 as a result of the amalgamation of the *New Reasoner* (NR) and *Universities and Left Review* (ULR). The NR began as a stencilled sheet circulated in the Communist Party by a small group opposed to the official party who had been shocked and disillusioned by the disclosures of Khrushchev at the Twentieth Congress of the Communist Party of the Soviet Union. Like E. P. Thompson, one of its first two editors, most of the people associated with the group had political experience that went back to the 1930s and were primarily drawn towards and concerned about political developments in the Soviet Union and Eastern Europe. The ULR, on the other hand, was started in Oxford by people of the post-war generation in their late twenties who had been animated by the invasion of Suez by Britain, and Hungary by the Soviet Union. At the same time its first issue, published in 1957, had contributions in it from such old stalwarts of socialism as Isaac Deutscher, G. D. H. Cole and the economist Joan Robinson. When the NR and ULR combined in 1959 to form the NLR its editorial board comprised a strange mixture of ex-communists and traditional left-wing socialists. Although what had brought the two groups together was Suez, Hungary and the Twentieth Congress, amalgamation was aided by the fact that they also adopted a similar attitude towards the 1959 Labour Party election campaign.

Because of the disparate nature of the newly-formed group, the variety of attitudes to be found in the *New Left Review* and the absence of a manifesto, it is difficult to delineate a common analysis and policy without imposing one with all the difficulties of simplification and arbitrary selection that this often entails. Nevertheless, certain common themes and problems can be discerned. On the whole they were neutralist and pacifist, concerned with the problems of nuclear disarmament; racism; supported attempts to strengthen the U N as a peacemaker and donor of aid; opposed to N A T O and in favour of the withdrawal of United States military bases as a first step towards what they saw as an assault on an international political system of bases and client states. As the *May Day Manifesto 1968* put it:

> In Europe we must press for disengagement between East and West in the political sphere (whether in the form of nuclear-free zones and a European Security Pact, or in piecemeal initiatives by individual nations), and for active association in economic, cultural and social spheres.[11]

The New Left also pointed to a new form of economic imperialism, stemming from the growth of multi-national companies which invested, not according to what was in the national interest of the countries in which they operated, but according to considerations of profit. These companies dominated at least the sector of the economy in which they operated, if not the whole economy. Thus there had arisen a new international economic system dominated by the United States. This applied to the developed countries but in the underdeveloped countries, too, the growth that these corporations brought about was without development. Little of the aid went towards the development of indigenous industrialization. It was to serve the economic interests of the aid-donors; it lead to an unbalanced development with a highly industrialized sector side by side with mass poverty.

The New Left, unlike the old, did not accept that capitalism was inevitably doomed. It both could and did serve artificially created needs. What it did not do, however, was to serve rationally determined public needs. It did not, for example, curb the growth of the motor-car industry but it did neglect the needs of public transport. As a result, the

11. Raymond Williams (ed.), op. cit., p. 139.

New Left concluded that economic growth in the West would be slower and less humane than in the East.

Whilst aware of the changes in capitalism, they did not argue like the revisionists in the British Labour Party that the changes were for the better and made capitalism more susceptible to control by the state. Indeed, the changes that had occurred had made it more powerful and more able to control the state, whichever party was in control. Capitalism had, in fact, created new élites. Influenced by C. Wright Mills's *The Power Elite*, they argued:

Despite the recent rise of a certain middle-class meritocracy, there can be little doubt that the Establishment is still drawn from an extraordinarily narrow range of families, schools and colleges.[12]

There still existed a concentration of economic power with the new masters being less, not more, socially responsible than their predecessors. They pointed to the fact that in Britain fifty companies owned nearly half of all company assets and that their investment decisions, crucial to the welfare of many, were made on the basis of profit, not social needs. They went further than this and argued that the likely result would be, in the traditional Marxist fashion, an emphasis on labour-saving machinery, an increase in the wealth of the property-owners, a decreased demand for labour and, hence, decreased wages and increasing impoverishment. This, it should be noted, is the kind of alarmist prophecy that has been made by many during the last hundred years and which has yet to be fulfilled. When the New Left analyses contemporary capitalism it produces many interesting insights. When it turns to a consideration of the future, it becomes either alarmist or utopian.

The New Left is on much stronger ground in its analysis of the economic and social effects of post-war capitalism, in its assertion that it 'creates and ratifies new kinds of poverty' and in challenging the myth that poverty and inequality have been abolished. Indeed, the members of the New Left

12. ibid., p. 118.

and its friends have been particularly instructive in detailing the impact of the new capitalism and consensus politics on housing, education and health and social welfare. Wealth, as they assert, is still grossly unequally distributed and needs to be tackled at its roots, which are in the ownership and control of the economic system.

It is possible, they argue, to change the mechanisms that have created the poverty and inequality in society by a socialist analysis of its causes and a socialist programme to eradicate them. Thus public ownership is put forward as a means of ending the power of the minority which controls society. Besides the nationalization of the economy which they call for, they also advocate the nationalization of British privately-owned foreign shares and securities, intervention in the banking and insurance systems and the creation of new institutions to make national decisions on production and investment. Furthermore, trading agreements should be made with the developing countries and Eastern Europe and a tax on wealth imposed, and its proceeds used to finance new publicly owned science-based industries.

But the demand for public ownership is not just a means of breaking the power of a minority and eliminating poverty and inequality. It is also seen as an essential step towards the creation of a new society: of a society of workers' self-management, the democratic administration of a socialist economy. Hence, Ken Coates and Tony Topham want a society where public accountability is imposed for all private decisions which affect the public, where the market and its instrumental bureaucracies are subjected to rational and public decision, where systems can be fitted to men and not men to systems, where technology is used to liberate labour not reduce its employment and where cooperation is substituted for the warping ethos of competition.

Thus the New Left, and Coates and Topham in particular, advocate workers' control of industry. In the words of the *May Day Manifesto 1968*:

A socialist trade-union policy envisages a step-by-step extension of workers' control to the point where it engages with the policies emerging from the wider democratic process, at which point the power of capital can be isolated and ended.[13]

At which point the capitalist society will give way to a democratically controlled and administered economy. This society will, according to Coates and Topham, allow the full development of the workers' freedom and capacity for self-realization and signal the end to the arbitrary and stunting division of labour. A planned and democratically controlled economy will enable an attempt to be made to secure 'an explosion in the amount of free time, in which men can hunt, fish, make and criticize by turns as the whimsy takes them'.[14] It will, they believe, be a society which results in a 'liberation of all the talents'.[15]

Having accepted that capitalism was not doomed the New Left were forced to outline their new society, to justify it and propagate its values. Many of them, and Perry Anderson in particular, saw this as best accomplished by the conversion of the Labour Party to socialist ideals and objectives, though others placed great emphasis on the education of public opinion. Yet in justifying and propagating the values of their new society, great emphasis was placed upon culture. Indeed, the most original contribution of the New Left to socialist theory has been the linking of a sociology of capitalism with a critique of modern culture. Most argued for what they termed a more democratic culture, for example, as was argued by Raymond Williams in his *The Long Revolution* (1961). In *Culture and Society* (1958) Williams had argued that the level of culture would increase in a socialist society. And, like John Osborne, Kingsley Amis and John Braine (before they became seduced to Toryism), they attacked the contemporary, effete, middle-class culture.

Indeed, the beginning and growth of the New Left went hand in hand with a growing literary revolt against the Establishment. It tied in closely with Osborne's *Look Back*

13. ibid., p. 137.
14. Ken Coates and Anthony Topham, *Industrial Democracy in Great Britain*, London, 1968, p. 409.
15. ibid., p. 410.

in Anger (1956) and the new radical mood exhibited in *Declaration* (1957), *Conviction* (1958) and the writings of Wayland Young and Richard Hoggart. In addition there was a new kind of social realism in films, like *A Taste of Honey, A Kind of Loving, Saturday Night and Sunday Morning, This Sporting Life,* and the radical mood of Doris Lessing's *The Golden Notebook.*

'From this brief enumeration', as Arnold commented, 'it will be seen that the New Left is far from being a uniform phenomenon; indeed where it broadens out into an attack on the *status quo* be it in the universities or in popular entertainment, its existentialist tendencies are more in evidence than the neo-Marxian philosophy of its Socialist adherents.'[16] And yet, unfortunately, the New Left in Britain has been no more than a loose association of intellectuals writing for each other. They have appeared to be content with the dissemination of their ideas through books and journals, and then mainly to the committed, which often meant themselves. If they have often appeared as a self-selecting, self-perpetuating, mutual admiration society cut off from real politics, they have only themselves to blame. In the main they have cut themselves off from potential political influence, have castigated practical politics and cocooned themselves in their own theories and visions. As Bernard Crick has written: 'They brood upon revolution like a fond nightmare and think themselves realists when they repeat, in constantly reinvented forms, Robespierre's aphorism that one cannot make an omelette without breaking eggs.'[17]

(c) Herbert Marcuse

Born in 1898 in Germany, and now a professor at the University of California, Herbert Marcuse has become one of

16. G. L. Arnold, 'The New Reasoners', in Leopold Labedz (ed.), *Revisionism: Essays on the History of Marxist Ideas,* p. 302.
17. Bernard Crick, *In Defence of Politics,* London, 1964, p. 132.

the major prophets of the Left, and especially of the student Left. Why is difficult to understand. He claims to be a Marxist but his Marxism is not that of the Soviet Union, the world communist parties, or even that of Karl Marx. He does not argue his case, he dogmatically asserts it in wild and sweeping generalizations; he does not present evidence for his assertions, he just assumes it – even where it is absent; he does not appear aware of the many difficulties in his case and seems incapable of overcoming them if he were. As Alasdair MacIntyre wrote, 'almost all of Marcuse's key positions are false'.[18]

Marcuse is pessimistic, optimistic, utopian, impatient, intolerant and the upholder of violence as the means of creating a new society and liberating men from the domination of the present. He pretends to be the advocate of freedom and reason, and yet he advocates a revolutionary strategy and a pseudo-philosophy that perverts them.

For Marcuse the essential function of philosophy is to criticize what exists. Philosophy is, he asserts, detached from the concrete world and confronts actuality with potentiality. And Marcuse has become the most far-reaching critic of contemporary industrial society.

Drawing upon the word of Freud, Marcuse argues that civilization is based upon the subjugation of human instincts. Yet whereas Freud argued that repression was to some extent necessary to maintain civilization, Marcuse argues that the extent of repression has been excessive. He distinguishes between what he calls basic repression – the necessary modification of human instincts if civilization is to survive – and surplus repression – the restrictions that are necessary if the existing property and class relations are to be maintained. The bourgeoisie, he asserts, are only able to preserve their own social order by encroaching upon, and harnessing to the maintenance of bourgeois society, that part of a man's personality that strives to express itself. In bourgeois society freedom is restricted to after-work hours, and even then it is severely curtailed.

18. Alasdair MacIntyre, *Marcuse*, p. 7.

M   317

For Marcuse liberalism is, in any case, incipient fascism. It is certainly the ideology of capitalism in its competitive stage, but it also is quickly transformed into fascism when capitalism reaches its monopoly stage. It stands for the principles of freedom and progress but rapidly sheds them when property or the *status quo* is threatened, when it turns into an authoritarian state. It becomes fascist and abandons its liberal principles. Thus he considered Nazism to be the logical outcome of a bourgeois political order. For Marcuse Marxism is now the repository of liberal principles and values and in order to uphold them it has to be, and is, prepared to overthrow the existing society. A theory that was supposed to give hope to the oppressed and alienated proletariat is now conceived of as the vehicle by which liberal political values can return home triumphant.

To what Marcuse describes as the exhausted liberal democratic tradition belongs the ideal of tolerance. In fact, Marcuse argues that liberal society is based on domination but it is a domination so subtle that the majority not only accept it but will it. What is claimed to be tolerance is, in fact, oppression. The human nature of those inhabiting industrial society is moulded by it into conformity; the inhabitants cannot voice their true needs – indeed they do not know them.

Hence the main argument of *One-Dimensional Man* (1964) is that technical progress 'extended to a whole system of domination and coordination, creates forms of life (and of power) which appear to reconcile the forces opposing the system and to defeat or refute all protest in the name of the historical prospects of freedom from toil and domination'. And, as MacIntyre retorted, 'if this thesis were true we should have to ask how the book came to be written and we would certainly have to enquire whether it would find any readers'.[19] The point, however, is that the book was written and read, and MacIntyre wrote another largely devoted to it.

In *One-Dimensional Man* Marcuse attempts to show how misled, indoctrinated, ignorant and corrupted are the

19. ibid., p. 62.

people. The techniques of advanced industrial society have enabled these societies to eradicate conflict by assimilating all dissenting forms into the social order. Like Bell and Lipset, he argues that conflict has disappeared, the working class and the labour movement have been domesticated. Yet whereas they welcome the new situation, Marcuse despises it. For him the consensus is used to repress and dominate. It has achieved this partly by affluence, by satisfying men's needs and so removing the major cause of dissent, protest and revolt. Men, he argues, have become passive instruments of the system. More than this, they have become slaves – slaves by being instruments, things to be dominated and manipulated by vested interests. And they have been manipulated by being told what they want. Here Marcuse makes a distinction between false needs and basic needs. False needs are those superimposed upon the individual by particular social interests in order to repress. Thus the individual's need for material goods is satisfied at the expense of his basic need for liberty. A democratic system is even more pernicious in this than an obviously totalitarian régime. Instead of resting on open force, it rests on the perversion of men's minds. It gives men freedom to choose, but between masters; a system of free competition but with regulated prices; and a free choice of branded goods which maintain man's alienation. The people are, he asserts, dominated by the Establishment, the ruling class and the rich, but are made to believe that their servitude is freedom. In fact, they are indoctrinated by mass advertising and made to assume a false way of life.

For Marcuse, modern industrial society is basically totalitarian because the productive apparatus determines 'not only the socially needed occupations, skills and attitudes, but also individual needs and aspirations'. The masses are kept quiescent by being told what they want and they do, in fact, enjoy a smooth, comfortable 'democratic unfreedom'. All attempts to improve working conditions are but subtle techniques by which the tyranny hides its face. Industrial society has sapped man's will to resist. The

workers have become happy and content. They want to preserve the system, to become part of it and agree on the consensus demand for increased productivity. Man has become
a one-dimensional man in accepting the existing patterns of
thought and behaviour, and in his lack of a critical awareness. Those who refuse to go along with conformism are
categorized as neurotic.

Yet we should not despair. Salvation is at hand. And Marcuse has discovered yet another agency of revolution and
redemption. In spite of all its techniques of repression and
domination, there nevertheless exists an enlightened and
aware minority. The saviours are the 'outcasts and outsiders,
the exploited and the persecuted of other races and other
colours, the unemployed and the unemployable'. They are
the students and the coloured in the advanced countries,
the National Liberation Front in Vietnam, all those, indeed, who are in conflict with the governmental bureaucracies of the advanced industrial societies. These are the
people who exist outside the democratic process and whose
opposition to it is 'revolutionary even if their consciousness
is not'. In particular, Marcuse was impressed (we need to say
was; things have changed, as with all fashions in the last
few years) with the student movement and especially with
its style, its values and language, all of which denied the
validity of those to be found in the conformist liberal
society. These parasites of the industrial system are to save
it. And the people are expected to renounce the élite that
governs and oppresses them at present and put themselves
under an élite of bohemians. Such, as someone once wrote,
is the stuff that dreams are made of.

The role of this enlightened minority is to agitate among
the oppressed and to provoke the system into repressive
measures so that its true nature becomes manifest. Then,
we are led to believe, there will be a spontaneous revolution.
This is what he expects. He also has something to advocate.
The old forms of protest are now of little use because they
are tolerated by the system, and the masses do not know
their true needs. Thus he advocates a new form of tolerance,

what he calls partisan tolerance. Non-partisan or impartial tolerance buttresses and protects the *status quo*. The toleration of the existing society is a toleration of domination and repression. Partisan tolerance, on the other hand, is intolerant to the *status quo*. As the people are indoctrinated and subjected to the repressive tolerance of the system so, he argued, there is a need for counter-indoctrination. Thus he urged the withdrawal of freedom of speech and assembly from those groups, and movements that promote

aggressive policies, armament, chauvinism, discrimination on the grounds of race and religion, or which oppose the extension of public services, social security, medical care, etc.

At the same time, there must be toleration of the Left, of subversion and revolutionary violence. His words, as Maurice Cranston commented, 'are beautifully candid': [20]

As to the scope of this tolerance and intolerance, it would extend to the stage of action as well as of discussion and propaganda, of deed as well as of word ... The whole post-fascist period is one of clear and present danger. Consequently, true pacification requires the withdrawal of tolerance before the deed, at the stage of communication in word, print and picture. Such extreme suspension of the right of free speech and free assembly is indeed justified only if the whole of society is in extreme danger. I maintain that our society is in such an emergency situation, and that it has become the normal state of affairs. [21]

This may require the use of violence but then this for the outsider is acceptable. Indeed, it is used to break an established violent system.

Marcuse believes that a non-repressive civilization is a possibility. He believes that once the surplus repressive elements of modern industrial society are removed, human instincts would be transformed and shed their destructive features, so that even basic repression would be unnecessary.

20. Maurice Cranston, 'Marcuse', in Cranston (ed.), *The New Left*, p. 87.
21. Quoted ibid., pp. 87–8.

Men would live in peace, freedom and sexuality, and labour would at last become pleasurable. Cranston is right to call his politics 'Anarcho-Marxism'.

(d) Frantz Fanon

Frantz Fanon was born in the French Antilles in 1925 and died in a United States hospital in 1961. Though active in the Algerian war, he did not play an important role and he is known mainly through his writings. These, however, only became widely known after his death and then, paradoxically, known best by Europeans and not by the black wretched of the earth he wrote for.

Fanon was obsessed by the problems of racism. At first he believed that his education and personality would enable him to be assimilated into white culture. Indeed, he served in the French army during the war, studied medicine and psychiatry at Lyons and became head of the department at Blida Joinville Hospital in Algeria. As he wrote in *Black Skin, White Masks* (1952):

I am a Frenchman. I am interested in French culture, French civilisation, the French people. We refuse to be considered 'outsiders', we have a full part in the French drama.

Fanon rejected the concept of negritude. The only destiny of the black man was to become white. He refused to advocate the revival of Negro culture and civilization which, he believed, would simply chain the Negro to the past.

Yet in *Black Skin, White Masks* Fanon also shows his awareness that, in spite of his veneer of European education and culture, he was still primarily a Negro. 'When people like me', he wrote, 'they tell me it is in spite of my colour. When they dislike me, they point out that it is not because of my colour. Either way I am locked into the infernal cycle.' In this book Fanon describes the ways in which the blacks were made to feel inferior and guilty because of their colour and culture. As a result they aspired to whiteness, to become, as the TV commercial has it, 'whiter than white' and to take on all its features. They acted like most converts to a new faith and became caricatures of the civilization to which they aspired. It was expressed, too, in their desire, indicated by Eldridge Cleaver, to possess white women: 'When my restless hands caress those white breasts', wrote Fanon, 'they grasp white civilization and dignity and make them mine.' And, in the same way, the black woman searched for a white, or off-white husband. They straightened out their hair, wore bras and make-up.

In fact, the sense of inferiority that has been imposed upon the blacks could not be eliminated by their assimilation into white civilization, for the fact was, as Fanon was aware and as he pointed out in the extract quote above from *Black Skins, White Masks,* they were not accepted by the whites. This sense of black inferiority could only be destroyed by an assertion of the legitimacy of their own blackness and culture. Fanon, therefore, went through a period in which he asserted the validity of blackness. Then, of course, when black became beautiful, the Negroes could not be black enough. The off-whites were inferior and rejected.

Others, notably Aimé Césaire, and particularly in his *Cahier d'un retour au pays natal* and *Discours sur le colonialisme,* had attempted to kindle pride in the black man. Others, too, adopted a defiant attitude towards white culture and praised negritude, like Léopold Senghor of Senegal. But, as David Caute has pointed out, the 'notion of Negritude, for all its outward ferocity, yields a small but vital concession to the prevailing white culture'.[22] The fact that blackness has to be asserted and glorified is itself an indication of the existence of an inferiority complex.

The Algerian war was something of a catalyst in Fanon's thinking. To him it brought the revelation that the world, instead of being divided into black and white, was divided into the colonizers and the colonized. Now he argued that

22. David Caute, *Fanon,* p. 24.

the Negroes' inferiority complex was due mainly to economic causes. The neurotic structure of the individual was a result of his environment and hence, after 1954, Fanon concentrated on the socio-economic causes of mental stress. Colonialism had destroyed the solidarity and culture of the natives by separating and segregating them. Hence in his address to the Congress of Negro Writers and Artists, held in Paris in 1956, he argued that racism was an ideological weapon. It was an inherent element of colonialism. In order to enforce their control, the colonizers destroyed the culture and values of the natives, and black inferiority and guilt at their backwardness followed.

The Algerian war turned Fanon into a revolutionary. 'When I search for Man in the technique and the style of Europe', he wrote in *The Wretched of the Earth* (1965), 'I see only a succession of negations of man, and an avalanche of murders.' In this work Fanon explicitly adopts the mantle of the revolutionary socialist. Alienation, he argued, is caused by the division of the world by the imperialists into rich and poor. The colonized blacks represent social exploitation in its most extreme and advanced form. They are a universal class destined to use violence to overthrow imperialism. Nor are the native bourgeoisie any better than their white masters. They are parasitical, the agents of western capitalism, living in luxury and divorced from the rural population. Whilst formerly the mainstay of the National Liberation Movement, they have become a new élite, the recipients of the power of the former white élite.

Fanon departed from both Lenin and Mao in not believing that the western proletariat was sympathetic to the plight and the cause of the colonial peoples. Indeed, it was the accomplice and beneficiary of the colonial system. That the western proletariat would, eventually, come to the aid of the wretched of the earth was, as Sartre and Senghor came to realize, an illusion. Fanon had, of course, seen the manifest enthusiasm of the French working class for the fight against the Algerian FLN and had witnessed the welcome given to the returning French paratroops in 1957. Moreover he was aware of the vacillation and equivocation of the French Communist Party towards the war.

Thus according to Fanon one should not look to the besotted native bourgeoisie nor to the western proletariat for deliverance from the bondage of colonialism. Instead, the revolutionary class was to be found amongst the poor peasantry. He believed that the revolution would be sparked off in the countryside, move into the towns via the carriers of the revolutionary flame – the *lumpenproletariat* – and be accompanied by violence. For Fanon violence was not only necessary in order to shake off the imperialist yoke, it was also therapeutic. Though repulsed by the violence he had witnessed and seen evidence of during the Algerian war, he eventually came to envisage the use of violence both as a political necessity and, like Bakunin, as a means of social and moral regeneration. Socially, violence on a large scale dissolved tribal rivalries and parochial attitudes; it welded the community together, just as colonialism had divided it. It mutated the family, broke down its hierarchical structure and liberated women as they were now needed to perform military roles. It also enhanced the respect of the natives for medicine and technology; under the impact of necessity it broke down old superstition and distrust. For Fanon, the independence struggle becomes identified with social revolution.

But it was also more than this. It had a pragmatic purpose certainly, but it also was a psychic necessity. It eliminated the long-sustained inferiority complex of the natives, dissolved their despair and apathy. Moreover, as a result of the struggle and the idealism and self-sacrifice that it entails, the revolutionaries were reborn as a class and the *lumpenproletariat*, in particular, were transformed into a productive citizenry. This, of course, is a 'rhetorical excess'. There is no example of such a moral regeneration happening as a result of a revolution being carried out successfully by such a class and Fanon certainly fails to distinguish between the corrupted and other elements of the *lumpenproletariat*. On the other hand, as Fanon pointed out, those countries that had gained independence peacefully were controlled by a black, chauvinistic bourgeoisie. Violence, therefore, was also necessary to prevent this.

Fanon argued that in a revolutionary confrontation the imperialists were doomed. He believed the revolution would be started in the countryside by guerrilla groups. Its success would be dependent upon the ardour of the nation, and would be aided by the fact that the colonies are now markets and that the international trusts would not tolerate a long-drawn-out war. No colonial power, he asserted, could hang on to its colonies indefinitely, given these circumstances. Yet the nations he talks of are hardly such; they are the arbitrary creations of European traders and their governments, and exhibit no identity of interest but instead have different tribes, religions, cultures and languages. Again, colonial countries have shown a marked tenacity of purpose when they have wanted to hold on to their overseas territories, as witness the activities of the Portuguese in Angola, the Americans in Vietnam and the British in Kenya.

Hannah Arendt has argued that Fanon had been influenced by Sorel in equating violence with creativity and other commentators have pointed to his use of myth to sustain revolutionary will. Again, though *The Wretched of the Earth* is supposed to be a survey of the Third World, there is nothing in its pages on Asia. The Algerian revolution is treated as a model for the rest of Africa and yet, as David Caute pointed out, 'Socialist revolutions for which there is neither model nor precedent walk Fanon's pages with as much assurance as instances of degeneration whose actual sources are easy to guess.'[23]

In terms of the post-revolutionary society Fanon advocated the nationalization of production and trading. He also wanted a radically decentralized society, formed mainly out of cooperatives, and in which there would be mass participation. Logically he condemned the one-party states of Africa that had arisen after independence. They were not radical, did not aim at total structural change and were

23. ibid., p. 68.

'violent in words and reformist in action'. To him they represented the dictatorship of the native bourgeoisie intent on its own enrichment; its leaders were no more than 'the director-general of a society of impatient profiteers'. Parties had to be separated from government and decentralized, and had to involve the mass of people in its policy formulations.

CONCLUSION

Over twenty years ago Alexander Gray wrote:

Socialism today is rather like a lost child at the cross-roads, not quite sure where it has come from, and not knowing where exactly it wants to go.[1]

The position is no better today. Indeed, in some respects it is worse. It is worse in the sense that the variety of socialisms has increased, which not only adds to the general confusion as to what socialism is, but also to the dispute as to which is the most legitimate and preferable. Hence, today as always socialists spend as much time disputing with and vilifying each other as they do their opponents on the Right. And the confusion and bitterness within the ranks of self-professed socialists has been exacerbated by all the other interest groups that have arisen claiming to represent the oppressed and the new saviours. For Marcuse it was the enlightened intellectuals and the outsiders, for Fanon it was the damned of the earth, just as it was for Bakunin. Now we have the emergence of a Black Power socialist movement and a revolutionary socialist Women's Liberation Movement. Thus, for Germaine Greer, women are 'the true proletariat, the truly oppressed majority' and the 'revolution can only be drawn nearer by their withdrawal of support for the capitalist system'.[2]

But, most dispiriting of all, the vision and the excitement seems to many to have been distilled from socialist theory and even more from socialist theorists and politicians. If the reformists have not sold out, they have not been conspicuous

1. Alexander Gray, *The Socialist Tradition, from Moses to Lenin*, 1948, p. 458.
2. Germaine Greer, *The Female Eunuch*, London, 1970, p. 22.

by their success in restructuring society. For them the 'system' is not in dispute. They argue about the merits of specific policies in a particular economic and historical context, in relation to short-run ends and never in relation to the system as a whole. They will argue, for example, about the merits of legislating to reform industrial relations, improve housing conditions and provide better social and welfare benefits. Never do they relate these to their fundamental causes in the structure of society and the economy, or consider whether they would bolster or weaken a system they profess to despise. But then we live in a pragmatic age and the electorate, the repository of sovereignty for the democratic reformist socialists, seems to prefer pragmatism to grand designs for radical change. In this situation the onus is on the democratic socialists to engage in a programme of educating the electorate in the realities of power and choice; a responsibility, to be fair, that they have always acknowledged and accepted but one, on the evidence of electoral trends, which they have not adequately discharged. Thus they concentrate on the immediate problems, the solution to which exists in the here and now. But if they are wise, and most are not stupid, they know such solutions can be but temporary palliatives. Perhaps they should recall the words of Herbert Spencer, a reactionary to boot, when he said that 'the ultimate result of shielding men from the effects of folly is to fill the world with fools'. A world of fools will never vote for socialism, however ambiguously it might be defined.

Yet the revolutionary socialists have little with which to inspire us. They have restructured society, they may have created new forms of social wealth, but they have also created vast bureaucratic and dictatorial régimes and many have enriched themselves in the process.

Socialism is not dead, just dormant. It has a future but it is one that it must create for itself. To doubt that it has a future is to cynically accept that men are both irrational and selfish; to believe that they will continue to accept the intellectual defence of a capitalist system that, on the most

impressionistic of evidence, enriches the few at the expense
of the many and stunts their personality into the bargain;
that tolerates conscious waste while millions starve and
which is inevitably inefficient and irrational; to believe that
men are incapable of feeling for others and voting for what
Rousseau called the 'general will'. But above all to have a
future it must create a vision. And visions should not be
disparaged as the property of the mentally deranged and
naïve. As Max Weber put it:

Certainly all historical experience confirms the truth – that
man would not have attained the possible unless time and
again he had reached out for the impossible.

Socialism and poetry are alike. They both combine a
description of the present with an intimation, at least, of its
potential for the future. The last word then, appropriately,
should be Robert Browning's:

... a man's reach should exceed his grasp.

BIBLIOGRAPHY

General and Historical

Cole, G. D. H., *History of Socialist Thought*, 5 vols., London, 1953–60

Dunn, John, *Modern Revolutions*, Cambridge, 1972

Gray, Alexander, *The Socialist Tradition from Moses to Lenin*, London, 1963

Landauer, C., *European Socialism: A History of Ideas and Movements*, 2 vols., California, 1959

Lichtheim, George, *A Short History of Socialism*, London, 1970

Marx

Althusser, Louis, *For Marx*, London, 1970

Avineri, Shlomo, *The Social and Political Thought of Karl Marx*, Cambridge, 1968

Berlin, Isaiah, *Karl Marx: His Life and Environment*, Oxford, 1948–63

Bottomore, T. B. and Rubel, Maximilien (eds.), *Karl Marx: Selected Writings in Sociology and Social Philosophy*, London, 1963

Caute, David (ed.), *Essential Writings of Karl Marx*, London, 1967

Collins, H. and Abramsky, Chimen, *Karl Marx and the British Labour Movement*, London, 1965

Hook, Sidney, *From Hegel to Marx*, 2nd ed., Ann Arbor, Mich., 1962

Lichtheim, George, *Marxism: An Historical and Critical Study*, 2nd ed., London, 1967

McLellan, David, *The Thought of Karl Marx: An Introduction*, London, 1971

Meyer, Alfred G., *Marxism: The Unity of Theory and Practice*, Oxford, 1954–63

Robinson, Joan, *An Essay on Marxian Economics*, 2nd ed., London, 1966

Tucker, Robert C., *Philosophy and Myth in Karl Marx*, Cambridge, 1961
    The Marxian Revolutionary Idea, London, 1970

The Marxist Political Parties

Beer, Max, *Fifty Years of International Socialism*, London, 1935

Bell, Daniel, *Marxian Socialism in the United States*, Oxford, 1968

Cole, G. D. H., *History of Socialist Thought*

Footman, David, *The Primrose Path: A Life of Ferdinand Lassalle*, London, 1946

Gay, Peter, *The Dilemma of Democratic Socialism*, New York, 1962

Joll, James, *The Second International 1889–1914*, London, 1955

Kuhn, Henry and Johnson, Olive M., *The Socialist Labor Party During Four Decades*, New York, 1931

Nettl, J. P., *Rosa Luxemburg*, Oxford, 1967

Plamenatz, John, *German Marxism and Russian Communism*, London, 1954

Roth, G., *The Social Democrats in Imperial Germany*, New York, 1963

Russell, Bertrand, *German Social Democracy*, 2nd ed., London, 1964

Schorske, C. E., *German Social Democracy, 1905–1917*, Cambridge, Mass., 1955

Shannon, David A., *The Socialist Party of America*, London, 1962

Tsuzuki, Chushichi, *H. M. Hyndman and British Socialism*, Oxford, 1961

Lenin and the Bolsheviks

Borkenau, Franz, *The Communist International*, London, 1938

Carr, E. H., *The Bolshevik Revolution 1917–1923*, London, 1963

Deutscher, Isaac, *The Prophet Armed, Trotsky 1879–1921*, London, 1954

    The Prophet Unarmed, Trotsky 1921–29, London, 1959
    The Prophet Outcast, Trotsky 1929–1940, London, 1963

Krupskaya, Nadezhda, *Memories of Lenin*, London, 1970

Lenin, V. I., *Selected Works*, 3 vols., Moscow, 1967

Meyer, Alfred G., *Lenisism*, Cambridge, Mass., 1957

Schapiro, Leonard, *The Origin of the Communist Autocracy 1917–1922*, London, 1955

Schapiro, Leonard and Reddaway, Peter (eds.), *Lenin: The Man, the Theorist, the Leader: A Reappraisal*, London, 1967

Trotsky, L., *Basic Writings*, ed. I. Howe, London, 1964

Ulam, Adam B., *Lenin and the Bolsheviks*, London, 1969

Wolfe, Bertram D., *Three Who Made a Revolution: Lenin, Trotsky and Stalin*, London, 1966

Stalin

Conquest, Robert, *The Great Terror: Stalin's Purges of the Thirties*, London, 1968

Deutscher, Isaac, *Stalin: A Political Biography*, London, 1966
    The Unfinished Revolution: Russia 1917–1967, Oxford, 1967

Djilas, Milovan, *Conversations with Stalin*, London, 1962

Drachkovitch, Milorad M. and B. Lazitch (eds.), *The Comintern: Historical Highlights*, London, 1967

Leites, N., *A Study of Bolshevism*, New York, 1953

Stalin, J., *Problems of Leninism*, Moscow, 1947

East European Revisionism and Western Communism

Aczel, T. and Meray, T., *The Revolt of the Mind*, New York, 1959

Bethell, Nicholas, *Gomulka: His Poland and His Communism*, London, 1969

Brzezinski, Z., *The Soviet Bloc: Unity and Conflict*, Oxford, 1967

Deutscher, Isaac, *Ironies of History. Essays on Contemporary Communism*, London, 1966

Djilas, Milovan, *The New Class, An Analysis of the Communist System*, London, 1966
    The Unperfect Society: Beyond the New Class, London, 1969

Drachkovitch, Milorad M. (ed.), *Marxism in the Modern World*, Oxford, 1967

Fejto, François, *The French Communist Party and the Crisis of International Communism*, London, 1967

Fischer, Ruth, *Stalin and German Communism*, Cambridge, Mass., 1948

M

Socialism Since Marx

Frankland, Mark, *Khrushchev*, London, 1966
Griffith, William E. (ed.), *Communism in Europe: Continuity, Change and the Sino-Soviet Dispute*, 2 vols., Oxford, 1967 and 1968
Kusin, Vladimir V., *The Intellectual Origins of the Prague Spring: The Development of Reformist Ideas in Czechoslovakia*, Cambridge, 1971
Labedz, Leopold (ed.), *Revisionism: Essays on the History of Marxist Ideas*, London, 1962
Lichtheim, George, *Marxism in Modern France*, Cambridge, 1967
Selucký, Radoslav. *Czechoslovakia: The Plan That Failed*. London, 1970
Shawcross, William, *Dubček*, London, 1970
Tornquist, David, *Look East, Look West, The Socialist Adventure in Yugoslavia*, London, 1966
Ulam, Adam B., *Titoism and the Cominform*, Cambridge, Mass., 1952
Whitney, Thomas P., *Khrushchev Speaks*, Ann Arbor, Mich., 1963

China and Asia

Chi, Hoang Van, *From Colonialism to Communism: A Case History of North Vietnam*, London, 1964
Cohen, Arthur A., *The Communism of Mao Tse-tung*, London, 1964
Fall, Bernard B., *The Two Viet-Nams: A Political and Military Analysis*, London, 1963
Fitzgerald, C.P., *The Birth of Communist China*, London, 1964
Giap, Vo Nguyen, *People's War, People's Army*, Hanoi, 1961
Gray, Jack and Cavendish, Patrick, *Chinese Communism in Crisis: Maoism and the Cultural Revolution*, London, 1968
Honey, P. J., *Communism in North Vietnam*, Cambridge, Mass., 1963
Lacouture, Jean, *Ho Chi Minh*, London, 1968
McVey, Ruth T., *The Rise of Indonesian Communism*, London, 1966
Mao Tse-tung, *Selected Reading*, Peking, 1967
Scalapino, Robert A., *The Japanese Communist Movement 1920–1966*, London, 1967

334

Schram, Stuart R., *Mao Tse-tung*, London, 1966
    The Political Thought of Mao Tse-tung, London, 1969
Schwartz, Benjamin I., *Chinese Communism and the Rise of Mao*, London, 1969
Snow, Edgar, *Red Star Over China*, London, 1937
Suh, Dae-soak, *The Korean Communist Movement 1918–1948*, Oxford, 1967
Zagoria, Donald S., *The Sino-Soviet Conflict, 1956–61*, Oxford, 1962

Cuba and Latin America

Castro, Fidel, *History Will Absolve Me*, London, 1968
Debray, Régis, *Revolution in the Revolution*, London, 1968
Draper, Theodore, *Castro's Revolution: Myths and Realities*, New York, 1962
Gerassi, John (ed.), *Venceremos: the speeches and writings of Ernest Che Guevara*, London, 1968
Gott, Richard, *Guerrilla Movements in Latin America*, London, 1970
Horowitz, Irving Louis, et al., *Latin American Radicalism*, London, 1969
Huberman, Leo and Sweezy, Paul M., *Socialism in Cuba*, London, 1969
Matthews, Herbert L., *Castro*, London, 1969
Meneses, Enrique, *Fidel Castro*, London, 1968
Petras, James and Zeithn, Maurice (eds.), *Latin America: Reform or Revolution? A Reader*, New York, 1968
Sinclair, Andrew, *Guevara*, London, 1970
Thomas, Hugh, *Cuba or the Pursuit of Freedom*, London, 1970

Africa

Friedland, W. H., and Rosenberg, Carl G. (eds.), *African Socialism*, Oxford, 1964 Nkrumah, Kwame, *Consciencism*, London, 1964
    Neocolonialism: The Last Stage of Capitalism, London, 1965
Nyerere, Julius, *Freedom and Unity*, Oxford, 1967
Schatten, Fritz, *Communism in Africa*, London, 1966.
Senghor, Leopold-Sedar, *On African Socialism*, New York, 1964

Anarchism, Syndicalism and Guild Socialism

Apter, David E. and Joll, James, *Anarchism Today*, London, 1971
Carr, E. H., *Bakunin*, London, 1937
    The Romantic Exiles, London, 1968
Carter, April, *The Political Theory of Anarchism*, London, 1971
Cole, G. D. H., *History of Socialist Thought*, Vol. I, London, 1954
Glass, S. T., *The Responsible Society: The Ideas of Guild Socialism*, London, 1966
Guérin, D., *Anarchism: From Theory to Practice*, London, 1970
Joll, James, *The Anarchists*, London, 1969
Mann, Tom, *Power Through the General Strike*, London, 1923
Ridley, F. F., *Revolutionary Syndicalism in France: The Direct Action of its Time*, Cambridge, 1970
Rocker, Rudolf, *Anarcho-Syndicalism*, London, 1938
Torr, Dona, *Tom Mann and His Times*, London, 1956
Venturi, Franco, *Roots of Revolution*, London, 1960
Woodcock, George, *Anarchism*, London, 1963
Woodcock, George and Avakumovic, I., *The Anarchist Prince: A Biography of Peter Kropotkin*, London, 1950

Social Democracy

Beatley, Frank (ed.), *The Social and Political Thought of the British Labour Party*, London, 1970
Beer, Max, *History of British Socialism*, London, 1929
Chalmers, David A., *The Social Democratic Party of Germany: from Working Class Movement to Modern Political Party*, New Haven, Conn., 1964
Childs, David, *From Schumacher to Brandt: The Story of German Socialism 1945–65*, London, 1966
Crosland, C. A. R., *The Future of Socialism*, London, 1956
Godfrey, E. D., *The Fate of the French Non-Communist Left*, New York, 1955
Hasler, Stephen, *The Gaitskellites*, London, 1969
Lorwin, V. R., *The French Labour Movement*, London, 1955
McBriar, A. M., *Fabian Socialism and English Politics 1884–1918*, Cambridge, 1962

Miliband, Ralph, *Parliamentary Socialism: A Study in the Politics of Labour*, London, 1964

Pelling, Henry, *Origins of the Labour Party*, 2nd ed., Oxford, 1965
        A short History of the Labour Party, 3rd ed., London, 1968

Poirier, P. P., *The Advent of the Labour Party*, London, 1958

Simmons, Harvey G., *French Socialists in Search of a Role, 1956–67*, London, 1970

Stafford, David, *From Anarchism to Reformism: The Political Activities of Paul Brousse*, London, 1971

The End of Ideology

Aron, Raymond, *The Industrial Society: Three Essays in Ideology and Development*, London, 1967
        The Opium of the Intellectuals, New York, 1962

Bell, Daniel, *The End of Ideology: On the Exhaustion of Political Ideas in the Fifties*, London, 1965

Dahl, Robert A. (ed.), *Political Oppositions in Western Democracies*, London, 1966

Lipset, Seymour Martin, *Political Man: The Social Bases of Politics*, London, 1963

The British New Left

Anderson, Perry and Blackburn, Robin, *Towards Socialism*, London, 1965

Mackenzie, N. (ed.), *Conviction*, London, 1958

Thompson, E. P. (ed.), *Out of Apathy*, London, 1960

Williams, Raymond, *May Day Manifesto 1968*, London, 1968

Marcuse

Cranston, Maurice (ed.), *The New Left*, London, 1970

MacIntyre, Alasdair, *Marcuse,* London, 1970

Marcuse, Herbert, *One-Dimensional Man*, London, 1964
        Eros and Civilization, London, 1969
        Five Lectures, London, 1970

Fanon and Black Power

Barber, Floyd, *The Black Power Revolt*, Boston, 1968

Caute, David, *Fanon*, London, 1970

Cranston, Maurice (ed.), *The New Left*

Socialism Since Marx

Fanon, Frantz, *The Wretched of the Earth*, London, 1965
    A Dying Colonialism, London, 1965
    Towards the African Revolution, London, 1967
Lockwood, Lee, *Conversation with Eldridge Cleaver*, London, 1971
Seale, Bobby, *Seize the Time: The Story of the Black Panther Party*, London, 1970

INDEX

Index

Barker, Ernest, 105

Barncena, Rafael Garcia, 257

Basle Congress (1869), 29

Batista, Fulgencio, 254–8 *passim*, 261; régime in Cuba,254–7 *passim*,264

Bauer, Bruno, 23

Bax, Ernest Belfort, 54, 55

Bazard, Saint Amand, xviii

Bebel, August, 34, 35, 37, 47, 51

Beer, Max, 12, 66, 69, 83, 102, 112

Beer, Samuel H., 193

Behrens, Fritz, 181

Belgium, 57–8, 161, 288

Belgrade, 179

Bell, Daniel, 47, 83, 305–9 *passim*, 319; *The End of Ideology*, 306

Bellamy, Edward, 60, 84; *Looking Backward* (1887), 84

Belloc, Hilaire, 104

Benary, Arne, 181

Benbow, William, 98

Bentham, Jeremy, 66

Berger, Victor, 81

Berlin, 302

Berlin, Sir Isaiah, 4

Berlin Wall, 182

Berne Congress (1919), 204–5

Bernstein, Eduard, 20, 41–6, 46–50 *passim*, 70, 80, 88, 91, 115, 125, 140, 289, 292, 295, 300; articles in *Neue Zeit*, 42; *Evolutionary Socialism*, 42

Bertrand, Louis, 57

Besant, Annie, 66, 107

Bevan, Aneurin, 296

Bible, the, xvi, 71, 191

Birkenhead, Lord, 82

Bismarck, Prinz Otto von, xiv, 34, 37, 40

Black Power, 328

Blanqui, 27, 113; Blanquism, 140; Blanquists, 57, 78

Blatchford, Robert, 71; *Britain for the British* (1902), 71; *Clarion* (newspaper), 71; *Merrie England* (1894), 71

Bloch, Joseph, 11

Blum, Léon, 161, 201

Boeckler, Hans, 301

Bois de Vincennes (Paris), 98

Bolivia, 259, 261

Bologna (1874), 30

Bolsheviks, 118, 120, 123, 140, 147, 148, 151, 169

Bonn Conference (1971), 302

Booth, Charles, 52

Bordeaux Congress of Syndicates (1888), 96

Borkenau, F., 159, 160

Boulangist affair (France), 56, 96

bourgeois and bourgeoisie, 16, 18, 19, 21, 29, 34, 36, 38, 40, 42, 46, 48, 50, 51, 56, 57, 76, 78, 79, 87, 95, 96, 180, 190, 199, 201, 219, 231, 236, 251, 283, 317, 326, 327; Chinese, 211, 218, 219; Russian, 120, 121, 122; dictatorship of, 16, 18; law, 127

Bracke, 36

Bradford, Yorkshire, 71, 72

Bradlaugh, Charles, xiv

Braine, John, 315

Brandt, Willy, 299, 300, 302; *My Road to Berlin*, 300

Braun, Otto, 198

Bray (English socialist), 6

Brazil, 261

Brenan, Gerald, 161–2

Brest-Litovsk delegation, 128

Brezhnev, 282–3

Briand, Aristide, 79, 96

Britain, 134, 161, 162, 163, 175; Marxist political parties in, 52–5; reformist socialism in, 65–75; syndicalism in, 75, 102, 103; guild socialism in, 104–11; General Strike (1926), 110; democratic socialism in, 289, 290–99; 'the home of modern revisionism', 289; poverty in, 310 *See also* Labour Party, British

British Museum, 4, 23

Index

Debray, Régis, 217, 258, 259–61; *Revolution in the Revolution*, 259

Debs, Eugène, 81–4 *passim*, 101

Defferre, Gaston, 303

'democratic centralism', Lenin's, 118

Democratic Federation (British), 52; becomes Social Democratic Federation (SDF), *q.v.*, 53

democratic socialism
in Africa, 265–6; task of, 329
in the late 1950s and 1960s, 289–303; Britain, 290–99 (revisionism, 291–6; the Left, 296–9); France, 303; Germany, 299–302 *See also* Social Democratic Parties in Europe *and* social democrats

Denmark, 84, 161

despotism in socialist states, 20

determinism, 11

Deutscher, Isaac, 146, 153, 168, 170, 311

Devlin, Kevin, 285

Dickens, Charles, 191

dictatorship of the proletariat, 4, 6, 18–19, 22, 29, 61, 65, 95, 117, 121, 124–30 *passim*, 157, 204, 218, 226, 236, 283, 286

dictatorship over the proletariat, 117

Diderot, Denis, 42

Diem, Ngo Dinh, 235

Dien Bien Phu, 235

Disraeli, Benjamin, 52

division of labour, 13, 14, 19, 21

Djakarta, 252

Djilas, Milovan, 95, 129, 188

dock strike (1889), 54

Dortmund Programme (West Germany, 1952), 301

Drachkovitch, Milorad, 146

Draper, Theodore, 254, 258

Dreyfus affair, 56, 78, 96

Dubček, Alexander, 279, 282

Ducroux, Joseph, 234

Duerkheim Sixteen Points (West Germany, 1949), 301

Dumas, the (Russian), 119–20

Durbin, Evan: *The Politics of Democratic Socialism* (1940), 292

Duverger, Maurice, 50, 307

EEC, *see* European Economic Community

East Germany (German Democratic Republic, DDR), 165, 166, 177, 180–83; 'New Course' in, 180, 182

Eastern Europe, xix, 164–6, 176–89, 271–2, 311 *See also* individual countries

Eastman, Max: *The End of Socialism in Russia* (1937), 156

Ebert, Friedrich, 196, 198

economic boom (1871–1914), 45

economism becomes respectable, 137

Egypt, 175

Eisenachers, 34–5

Eisner, Kurt, 46

El Campesino, 162

Enfantin, Prosper, xviii

Engels, Friedrich, 6–7, 9, 12, 16, 17, 28, 39; and Marx, 3, 6, 7, 17; and WES, 23; and 'centralizers', 29; and demise of First International, 32; and Liebknecht, Bebel and Lassalle, 35; and Gotha Programme, 36, 37; and revisionism, 41, 42; and Erfurt Programme, 48; and French socialists, 55; and Guesde, 56; and Keir Hardie, 71; on the working class in Britain (1881), 72; and abolition of the state, 124; and 'labour aristocracy', 132; and intimidation of the masses, 139; and collective farms, 155; and need for compromise and deception, 159–60

Published works: Anti-Duhring (1877), 5; *Class Struggles in France* (Marx, 1895), edited, 39, 41; *Communist Manifesto* (with Marx, 1848), 7; *Conditions of the Working*

Index

Italy, 17, 30, 31, 134, 206, 284–5;
  fascism in, 159
Ivanov of Kursk, 152
Ivory Coast, 265

Janet, xiv
Japan, Japanese, 213, 230, 240
Jaurès, Jean Léon, 57, 77–80 *passim*;
  and war, 80, 87; *L'Armée nouvelle*
  (1910), 80
Java, 248; East, 252
Jay, Douglas, 292
Jenkins, Roy, 292, 293; *Pursuit of*
  Progress (1953), 295
Joint Vigilance Committee (France),
  78
Joll, James, 30, 49, 86
Jones, Ernest, 23
Jones, Jack, 103
July Revolution in Russia (1917), 128
Justice (1884), 53

KANU, *see* Kenya African National
  Union
KPD, *see* Communist Party of East
  Germany
KWP, *see* Korean Workers' Party
Kádár, Jánot, 179, 274, 275
Kamenev, Lev Borisovich, 128
Kant, Immanuel, 43
Kapital, Das (Marx, 1867, 1885, 1894),
  4, 13
Kapp putsch (in Germany), 198
Karelj, Edvard, 188
Karume, Sheikh Abeid, 268
Kautsky, Karl, 40, 41, 42, 47–9
  passim, 87, 88, 114; and Bernstein,
  48, 125; *The Dictatorship of the*
  Proletariat (1918), 125
Keep Left (British left-wing labour
  periodical), 296
Kenya, 266, 326
Kenya African National Union
  (KANU), 267
Kenyatta, Jomo, 266, 267
Keyserling, Count, 83

Khrushchev, Nikita, xix, 145, 168–9,
  171, 173, 174; his revisionism, 145,
  168, 169–76, 288, 311; his secret
  speech to Twentieth Congress
  of Communist Party of Soviet
  Union (1956), 169; and Lenin,
  169, 170; and Stalin, 169–70;
  internal changes, 170–72; his
  successors' policies, 172; and
  international relations, 172–6;
  and war, 173–4; and peaceful
  coexistence, 173; and world communism, 174; and the interests of
  the Soviet Union, 174–5; and
  Eastern Europe, 177–89; and
  Sino-Soviet dispute, 179; and
  'separate roads to socialism', 179;
  –Tito Declaration (1955), 179;
  and Chinese communes, 221,
  228; and nuclear war, 223; and
  'paper tigers', 224; Chinese and,
  228; his flirtation with the West,
  228; and equal leadership (with
  Russia) of world communism,
  228; and a nuclear-free zone in
  Far East, 239
Kienthal (1918), 133
Kim Il-sung, 240–44; personal de-
  tails, 240; his objectives, 240–41;
  and South Korea, 241–2; domes-
  tic policies, 242–3; and inter-
  national affairs, 243–4
Kind of Loving, A (film), 316
Knights of Labor (USA), 60
Koestler, Arthur, 20; *Darkness at*
  Noon, 277
Kolakowski, Professor Leszek, 177,
  276
Korea, 175, 248; divided, 240
  See also North Korea *and* South
  Korea
Korean War (1950–51), 241, 296
Korean Workers' Party (KWP), 240,
  241, 243
Kostor (of Bulgaria), 166
Kremlin, a Pope in the, 146

348

Index

Index

'New Society', New Left's, 314–15
New York (city), 25, 30, 59; Madison
    Avenue, 285; mayoralty of, 60
New Zealand, 203
Niebuhr, Reinhold, 126
Nieuwenhuis, Domela, 139
Nigeria, 265
Nixon, President Richard M., 225
Njono, Lukman, 250
Nkrumah, Kwame, 267–70 *passim*;
    African Personality, 266; *Con-
    sciencism*, 268
Nodong Sin (North Korean news-
    paper), 243
Noelting, Erik, 301
Norris, Frank: *The Octopus* (1901), 84
North Atlantic Treaty Organization
    (NATO), 195, 206, 295, 312
North Korea, 230, 240–44, 247, 248;
    and South Korea, 241–2; indus-
    trialization, 242–3; and inter-
    national affairs, 243–4
    See also Kim Il-sung
North Vietnam, 230, 231–9 *passim*,
    247, 248; Democratic Republic
    of, 234, 235; communism in,
    236–7; People's Army of, 237;
    'Rectification of Errors', 237,
    238; 'Thought Reform', 238;
    'Reform by Manual Labour',
    238; industrialization (1954),
    238; 'between China and the
    Soviet Union', 238–9; and inter-
    national affairs, 238–9; and
    Khrushchev, 239
    See also Ho Chi Minh
Norway, 84, 134, 161
Noska, Sanzo, 246
Nove, Alec, 132
Novotný, Antonin, 279, 280
nuclear test-ban treaty, 175
nuclear war, 172, 223, 224, 225
Nyerere, Julius, 265 267–70 *passim*

Old Age Pensions Act (1908), 74
Oltmares, Andres, 100–101

Orange, A. R., 105
Oriente, 258
Ortodoxo party in Cuba, 256
Osborne, John, 315; *Declaration*
    (1957), 316; *Conviction* (1958),
    316; *Look Back in Anger* (1956),
    315–16
Oslo Declaration (1962), 207
Owen, Robert, xvi–xvii, 7, 8, 53, 66,
    83; Owenite movement in
    Britain, xvi

PKI, *see* Communist Party of Indo-
    nesia
PSU, *see* United Socialist Party of
    France
PZPR (Poland), 184
Paepe, Caesar de, 33, 57
Paine, Thomas (Tom), 14
Pak Hon-yong, 240
Palladino, Carmelo, 30
Pan-Africanism, 270
Pannekeok, Anton, 50
Paris, 3, 90; Bois de Vincennes, 98
Paris Commune, 6, 19, 31, 55, 56, 78,
    123, 124
Park Chung Hee, 242
Parti Ouvrier Belge (1885), 57–8
Parti Ouvrier Français (1882, *formerly*
    Fédération des Ouvriers Social-
    istes de France, *q.v.*), 33, 56, 76
Parti Ouvrier Socialiste Révolution-
    naire (France), 76
Parti Républicain Socialiste (France),
    79
Parti Socialiste Belge (1879), 33
Parti Socialiste de France, 57, 79
Parti Socialiste Français, 79
Parti Socialiste Unifié – Section Fran-
    çaise de l'Internationale Ouv-
    rière (SFIO), 57, 79, 80, 200,
    201–2, 233, 303; declaration of
    principle by, 202
Parvus-Trotsky theory (of permanent
    revolution), 140
Pathet Lao, 239

354

Index

surplus wealth, use of (principle of British Labour Party), 193
Svoboda, President Ludvík, 281, 282
Sweden, 84, 161, 284, 288, 290
Switzerland, 30, 288; Jura, 90
Sylvis, William, 59
syndicalism, syndicalists, 93, 104, 106, 108; in Britain, 75, 102, 103; in France, 83, 89, 93–4, 95–6; revolutionary, 93–103

TUC, *see* Trades Union Congress
Taff Vale decision (1903), 73
Taiwan, *see* Formosa
Tammerfors Conference (December 1905), 119
Tanzania, 265, 267, 268, 270
Taste of Honey, A (film), 316
Tawney, Professor R. H., xiii, 13, 191
Ten Hours Act (1847), 24
Third International (Comintern, *q.v.*, 1919), 112, 133–41 *passim*, 158–63 *passim*, 190, 205, 206, 232, 233; purpose of, 134; small sects in other countries, 134; Stalin and, 148
Third World, 3, 175, 212, 225, 228, 244, 326
See also under-developed countries
This Sporting Life (film), 316
Thomas, Norman, 203
Thompson (English socialist), 6, 7
Thompson, E. P., 311
Thorez, Maurice, 161, 286
Titmus, Richard, 310
Tito, Marshal, 179, 186–9 *passim*, 272; Titoism, 186–9
Todorovic, Mijacko, 273
Togliatti, Palmiro, 284, 285; his polycentralism, 188, 285
Topham, Anthony, 314
Tours Congress (1920), 200, 233
Townsend, Peter, 310
Toynbee, Arnold J., 225

Trade Disputes Act (1906), 74
Trade Union Act (1913), 74
trade unions, 6, 7, 24, 31, 45, 50, 52, 54–61 *passim*, 64, 68, 70–76 *passim*, 82, 83, 85, 99–103 *passim*, 107, 108–9, 114, 273, 275, 276, 301; and the International, 31, 85; and syndicalism, 94; in the Soviet Union, 158
Trade Unions, General Federation of (proposed by Tom Mann), 103
Trades and Labor Alliance (USA, 1895), 60
Trades Union Congress (TUC), 71, 72–3, 75, 107, 110
Tran Quyuh, 238
Tranamael (Norwegian communist leader), 138, 161
Tribune, 292, 296
Trieste, 186
'Triple A' (revolutionary movement in Cuba), 257
Trotsky, Leon, 116–17, 120, 121–2, 128, 150–51, 153, 158, 245, 286; and Lenin, 116–17, 119; and 'permanent (world) revolution', 122, 123, 124, 150, 151; and revolution in Russia, 121–3; on Stalin, 147, 157; and Stalin, 149, 150, 151; and Stalin's Constitution for the Soviet Union, 157–8
    Published works: Autobiography, 117; *Our Political Tasks* (1904), 116, 139; *Period up to the Ninth of January, The* (1905), 122; *Results and Prospects* (1906), 122; *Revolution Betrayed, The* (1936), 151
Trotskyism, 150; Trotskyites, 169
Truman doctrine, 167
Truong Chinh, 231, 238
Tsiranana, President, 267
Tsuzuki, Chushichi, 54
Tucker, Benjamin, 89
Tucker, Robert, 17, 18, 20
Tunisia, 265
Turkey, 28

Index

U2 'spy' aircraft (of USA), 182
UAR, see United Arab Republic
ULR, see Universities and Left Review
UN, see United Nations
USSR, see Soviet Union
Ulam, Adam, 69, 133, 136, 211; The Unfinished Revolution, 211
Ulbricht, Walter, 180, 182
under-developed countries (colonial, semi-colonial and ex-colonial, 131, 145, 153, 211, 224, 225, 226, 309, 312
    See also Third World
Union of Democratic Control, 75
Union of Post Office Workers, 111
United Arab Republic (UAR), 265
United British Congress (1891), 86
United Nations (UN), 207, 241, 312
United Socialist Party: of East Germany (SED), 165, 180, 181, 182; of France (PSU), 202, 303
United States of America (USA), 30, 31, 33, 101; miners' strike (1873), 30; Marxist political parties in, 59–62; German immigrants (1871–95), 59; reformist socialism in, 81–5; Socialist Party in, 81–4, 203–4 (see also Socialist Labor Party); and Soviet Union, 159, 174, 175; and Poland, 186; and Yugoslavia, 187; socialism in, see Socialist Party in, also Socialist Party in USA and Socialist Labor Party; and Formosa, 224; and China, 224, 225, 227; and revolutionary movements, 225, 226; and Viet Cong, 226; and Vietnam, 232, 236, 239; and South Korea, 240, 241; and Communist Party of Japan, 246–7; and Cuba, 257; and Castro, 261; and Guevara, 261; Negroes of, 266; affluence and public squalor in, 289; and Britain, 295–6; poverty in, 310; overseas military bases of, 312;

economic domination by, 312
Universal German Workingmen's Association, 34
Universal German Workmen's Association (Chicago, 1869), 59
Universities and Left Review (ULR), 311
unskilled workers exploited by skilled workers, 102
Utopians criticized, 8, 19

Vaculík, Ludvík, 281
Vaillant, Édouard, 79, 80, 86, 87
Vandervelde, Émile, 58
Vargo, Eugene, 167
Veblen, Thorstein: Theory of the Leisure Class (1899), 84
Venezuela, 261
Venturi, Professor Franco, 25
Vienna International (1921), 205
Viet Cong, 226
Viet Minh, 234, 236
Vietnam, 163, 207, 226, 230, 231–9, 248, 326; divided, 235; war in, 236, 296
    See also North Vietnam and South Vietnam
Vietnamese revolution, 212, 231–9
    See also Ho Chi Minh
Vietnamese Workers' Party, 231
Vieweg, Kurt, 181
Viviani, René, 77, 79, 96
Vo Nguyen, 238
Vogel, Hans Jochen, 302
Vogt, Hugo, 60
Vollmar, George von, 40, 41–2, 42
Voroshilov, K. E., 128
Vracar, Professor Stefan, 273
Vranicki, Professor Pedrag, 273

WES, see Workers' Educational Society
wages, iron law of (Lassalle's), 36
Wallas, Graham, 66
Warsaw, 137; Pact, 179, 275, 282; University, 276

361

Index